D0758230

Bloom's Modern Critical Views

African-American
  Poets: Volume I
African-American
  Poets: Volume II
Aldous Huxley
Alfred, Lord Tennyson
Alice Walker
American Women
  Poets: 1650–1950
Amy Tan
Arthur Miller
Asian-American
  Writers
August Wilson
The Bible
The Brontës
Carson McCullers
Charles Dickens
Christopher Marlowe
Cormac McCarthy
C.S. Lewis
Dante Alighieri
David Mamet
Derek Walcott
Don DeLillo
Doris Lessing
Edgar Allan Poe
Émile Zola
Emily Dickinson
Ernest Hemingway
Eudora Welty
Eugene O'Neill
F. Scott Fitzgerald
Flannery O'Connor
Franz Kafka
Gabriel García
  Márquez

Geoffrey Chaucer
George Orwell
G.K. Chesterton
Gwendolyn Brooks
Hans Christian
  Andersen
Henry David Thoreau
Herman Melville
Hermann Hesse
H.G. Wells
Hispanic-American
  Writers
Homer
Honoré de Balzac
Jamaica Kincaid
James Joyce
Jane Austen
Jay Wright
J.D. Salinger
Jean-Paul Sartre
John Irving
John Keats
John Milton
John Steinbeck
José Saramago
J.R.R. Tolkien
Julio Cortázar
Kate Chopin
Kurt Vonnegut
Langston Hughes
Leo Tolstoy
Marcel Proust
Margaret Atwood
Mark Twain
Mary Wollstonecraft
  Shelley
Maya Angelou

Miguel de Cervantes
Milan Kundera
Nathaniel Hawthorne
Norman Mailer
Octavio Paz
Paul Auster
Philip Roth
Ralph Waldo Emerson
Ray Bradbury
Richard Wright
Robert Browning
Robert Frost
Robert Hayden
Robert Louis Stevenson
Salman Rushdie
Stephen Crane
Stephen King
Sylvia Plath
Tennessee Williams
Thomas Hardy
Thomas Pynchon
Tom Wolfe
Toni Morrison
Tony Kushner
Truman Capote
Walt Whitman
W.E.B. Du Bois
William Blake
William Faulkner
William Gaddis
William Shakespeare
William Wordsworth
Zora Neale Hurston

Bloom's Modern Critical Views

CARSON McCULLERS
New Edition

Edited and with an introduction by
Harold Bloom
Sterling Professor of the Humanities
Yale University

BLOOM'S
LITERARY CRITICISM
An imprint of Infobase Publishing

Bloom's Modern Critical Views: Carson McCullers, New Edition

Bloom's Literary Criticism
An imprint of Infobase Publishing
132 West 31st Street
New York NY 10001

Library of Congress Cataloging-in-Publication Data

Carson McCullers / edited and with an introduction by Harold Bloom. — New ed.
    p. cm.   (Bloom's modern critical views)
  Includes bibliographical references and index.
  ISBN 978-1-60413-394-3 (hardcover)
  1. McCullers, Carson, 1917–1967—Criticism and interpretation. 2. Women and literature—Southern States—History—20th century. I. Bloom, Harold.
  PS3525.A1772Z584 2009
  813'.52—dc22

                                        2008038918

Bloom's Literary Criticism books are available at special discounts when purchased in bulk quantities for businesses, associations, institutions, or sales promotions. Please call our Special Sales Department in New York at (212) 967-8800 or (800) 322-8755.

You can find Bloom's Literary Criticism on the World Wide Web at
http://www.chelseahouse.com

Contributing Editor: Pamela Loos
Cover designed by Takeshi Takahashi
Printed in the United States of America
Bang EJB 10 9 8 7 6 5 4 3 2 1

This book is printed on acid-free paper.

All links and Web addresses were checked and verified to be correct at the time of publication. Because of the dynamic nature of the Web, some addresses and links may have changed since publication and may no longer be valid.

Contents

Editor's Note

My introduction stresses that the salient character trait of McCullers's protagonists is their tragic capacity to love impossible recipients of their erotic desires.

Tony J. Stafford comments on the anguish of addressing an absent God in *The Member of the Wedding*, while Rachel Adams very sensitively analyzes McCullers's more-than-bisexual stance.

For Cynthia Wu, the short stories of McCullers provide a more nuanced perspective on southern "whiteness," after which Sarah Gleeson-White opens a Bakhtinian window on notes of the grotesque without which Carson McCullers could not have existed.

Loneliness in *The Ballad of the Sad Café* is established by Doreen Fowler as the motivation for that work's return of the repressed, while for Betty E. McKinnie and Carlos L. Dews southern ambivalence brutally triumphs over the tense ambiguities of *The Member of the Wedding*.

Harper Lee is contrasted with McCullers by Jeff Abernathy, who implicitly finds more strength in the exploration of race by McCullers, which seems to me right.

The Heart Is a Lonely Hunter, my own favorite McCullers, receives an appreciation by Jennifer Murray, who sees that empathy is the book's strong element.

Naomi Morgenstern analyzes the dialectic of erotic contract and erotic gift in *The Ballad of the Sad Café*, after which this volume concludes with Ellen Matlock-Ziemann's shrewd argument for McCullers's drive to expand gender boundaries as a way of redemption from patriarchal authority.

HAROLD BLOOM

Introduction

"I become the characters I write about and I bless the Latin poet Terence who said, 'Nothing human is alien to me.'" That was the aesthetic credo of Carson McCullers, and was her program for a limited yet astonishingly intense art of fiction. Rereading her after nearly twenty years away from her novels and stories, I discover that time has enhanced *The Heart Is a Lonely Hunter* and *The Ballad of the Sad Café* and perhaps rendered less problematic *Reflections in a Golden Eye*. What time cannot do is alter the burden for critics that McCullers represents. Her fiction, like her person, risked that perpetual crisis of Eros of which D.H. Lawrence was the poet and Freud the theoretician. Call it the tendency to make false connections, as set forth by Freud with mordant accuracy in the second paragraph of his crucial paper of 1912, "The Dynamics of the Transference":

> Let us bear clearly in mind that every human being has acquired, by the combined operation of inherent disposition and of external influences in childhood, a special individuality in the exercise of his capacity to love—that is, in the conditions which he sets up for loving, in the impulses he gratifies by it, and in the aims he sets out to achieve in it. This forms a *cliché* or stereotype in him, so to speak (or even several), which perpetually repeats and reproduces itself as life goes on, in so far as external circumstances and the nature of the accessible love-objects permit, and is indeed itself to some extent modifiable by later impressions. Now our experience has shown that of these feelings which determine

the capacity to love only a part has undergone full psychical development; this part is directed towards reality, and can be made use of by the conscious personality, of which it forms part. The other part of these libidinal impulses has been held up in development, withheld from the conscious personality and from reality, and may either expend itself only in phantasy, or may remain completely buried in the unconscious so that the conscious personality is unaware of its existence. Expectant libidinal impulses will inevitably be roused, in anyone whose need for love is not being satisfactorily gratified in reality, by each new person coming upon the scene, and it is more than probable that both parts of the libido, the conscious and the unconscious, will participate in this attitude.

All of McCullers's characters share a particular quirk in the exercise of their capacity to love—they exist, and eventually expire, by falling in love with a hopeless hope. Their authentic literary ancestor is Wordsworth's poignant Margaret, in *The Ruined Cottage*, and like his Margaret they are destroyed, not by despair, but by the extravagance of erotic hope. It is no accident that McCullers's first and best book should bear, as title, her most impressive, indeed unforgettable metaphor: *The Heart Is a Lonely Hunter*.

McCullers's few ventures into literary criticism, whether of Gogol, Faulkner, or herself, were not very illuminating, except in their obsession with loneliness. Her notes on writing, "The Flowering Dream," record her violent, physical response to reading Anne Frank's diary, which caused a rash to break out on her hands and feet. The fear of insulation clearly was the enabling power of McCullers's imagination. When she cited Faulkner and Eugene O'Neill as her major influences, she surprisingly added the Flaubert of *Madame Bovary*, where we might have expected the Lawrence of *The Rainbow* and "The Prussian Officer." But it was Emma's *situation* rather than Flaubert's stance or style that engrossed her.

Mick Kelly, McCullers's surrogate in *The Heart Is a Lonely Hunter*, remains her absolute achievement at representing a personality, presumably a vision of her own personality at the age of twelve. Vivid as the other lonely hunters are—the deaf mute John Singer; Biff Brannon, the café proprietor; Jake Blount, alcoholic revolutionary; Dr. Benedict Mady Copeland, black liberal and reformer—the book still lives in the tormented intensity of Mick Kelly, who knows early to be "grieved to think how power and will / In opposition rule our mortal day, / And why God made irreconcilable / Good and the means of Good." That is the dark wisdom of Shelley in "The Triumph of Life," but it is also a wisdom realized perfectly and independently by Mick Kelly, who rightly fears the triumph of life over her own integrity, her own hope, her own sense of potential for achievement or for love. The Shelleyan passage becomes pure McCullers if we transpose it to: "And why God made irreconcilable / Love and the means of Love."

The Heart Is a Lonely Hunter would not maintain its force if its only final vision were to be the triumph of life, in Shelley's ironic sense. McCullers gives us a tough-grained, last sense of Mick Kelly, bereaved, thrown back into an absolute loneliness, but ongoing nevertheless:

> But now no music was in her mind. That was a funny thing. It was like she was shut out from the inside room. Sometimes a quick little tune would come and go—but she never went into the inside room with music like she used to do. It was like she was too tense. Or maybe because it was like the store took all her energy and time. Woolworth's wasn't the same as school. When she used to come home from school she felt good and was ready to start working on the music. But now she was always tired. At home she just ate supper and slept and then ate breakfast and went off to the store again. A song she had started in her private notebook two months before was still not finished. And she wanted to stay in the inside room but she didn't know how. It was like the inside room was locked somewhere away from her. A very hard thing to understand.
>
> Mick pushed her broken front tooth with her thumb. But she did have Mister Singer's radio. All the installments hadn't been paid and she took on the responsibility. It was good to have something that had belonged to him. And maybe one of these days she might be able to set aside a little for a second-hand piano. Say two bucks a week. And she wouldn't let anybody touch this private piano but her—only she might teach George little pieces. She would keep it in the back room and play on it every night. And all day Sunday. But then suppose some week she couldn't make a payment. So then would they come to take it away like the little red bicycle? And suppose like she wouldn't let them. Suppose she hid the piano under the house. Or else she would meet them at the front door. And fight. She would knock down both the two men so they would have shiners and broke noses and would be passed out on the hall floor.
>
> Mick frowned and rubbed her fist hard across her forehead. That was the way things were. It was like she was mad all the time. Not how a kid gets mad quick so that soon it is all over—but in another way. Only there was nothing to be mad at. Unless

the store. But the store hadn't asked her to take the job. So there was nothing to be mad at. It was like she was cheated. Only nobody had cheated her. So there was nobody to take it out on. However, just the same she had that feeling. Cheated.

But maybe it would be true about the piano and turn out O.K. Maybe she would get a chance soon. Else what the hell good had it all been—the way she felt about music and the plans she had made in the inside room? It had to be some good if anything made sense. And it was too and it was too and it was too and it was too. It was some good.

All right!

O.K.!

Some good.

One can call this "Portrait of the Artist as a Young Girl" and see Mick as a visionary of "the way things were." She has the strength of McCullers's endings that are not wholly negations:

Biff wet his handkerchief beneath the water tap and patted his drawn, tense face. Somehow he remembered that the awning had not yet been raised. As he went to the door his walk gained steadiness. And when at last he was inside again he composed himself.

(*The Heart Is a Lonely Hunter*)

Even in death the body of the soldier still had the look of warm, animal comfort. His grave face was unchanged, and his sunbrowned hands lay palm upwards on the carpet as though in sleep.

(*Reflections in a Golden Eye*)

The most remarkable of these conclusions is the vignette called "The Twelve Mortal Men" that serves as epilogue or coda to *The Ballad of the Sad Café*:

The Forks Falls highway is three miles from the town, and it is here the chain gang has been working. The road is of macadam, and the county decided to patch up the rough places and widen it at a certain dangerous place. The gang is made up of twelve men, all wearing black and white striped prison suits, and chained at the ankles. There is a guard, with a gun, his eyes drawn to red slits by the glare. The gang works all the day long, arriving huddled in the prison cart soon after daybreak, and being driven off again in the gray August twilight. All day there is the sound of the picks striking into the clay earth, hard sunlight, the smell of sweat. And every day there is music. One dark voice will start a phrase, halfsung, and like a question. And after a moment another voice will join in, soon the whole gang will be singing. The voices are dark in the golden glare, the music intricately blended, both somber and joyful. The music will swell until at last it seems that the sound does not come from the twelve men on the gang, but from the earth itself, or the wide sky. It is music that causes the heart to broaden and the listener to grow cold with ecstasy and fright. Then slowly the music will sink down until at last there remains one lonely voice, then a great hoarse breath, the sun, the sound of the picks in the silence.

And what kind of gang is this that can make such music? Just twelve mortal men, seven of them black and five of them white boys from this county. Just twelve mortal men who are together.

The rhetorical stance or tone of this is wholly McCullers's and is rather difficult to characterize. In context, its reverberation is extraordinary, working as it does against our incapacity to judge or even comprehend the grotesque tragedy of the doomed love between Miss Amelia Evans and Cousin Lymon, with its consequence in the curious flowering and subsequent demise of the sad café. We, as readers, also would rather love than be loved, a preference that, in the aesthetic register, becomes the defense of reading more intensely lest we ourselves be read, whether by ourselves or by others. The emotion released by the juxtaposition between the music and its origin in the chain gang is precisely akin to the affect arising from McCullers's vision of the tragic dignity of the death of love arising so incongruously from the story of Miss Amelia, Cousin Lymon, and the hideous Marvin Macy.

TONY J. STAFFORD

"Gray Eyes Is Glass": Image and Theme in The Member of the Wedding

In *The Lonely Hunter*, Virginia Carr's biography of Carson McCullers, the author notes that McCullers, in her desire for warmth and tenderness from those around her, habitually used her eyes as a way of "communicating a closeness that denied actual physical touching, yet mirrored in one's pupils the exchange of souls" (296). Carr also observes that McCullers "always looked intently at a person she loved" and especially at the eyes, which she "gazed fixedly into" (296). Interestingly enough, this same personal habit of gazing fixedly at someone appears in the autobiographical character of Frankie Addams in McCullers' *The Member of the Wedding*, and McCullers uses Frankie's pattern of behavior, along with other vision motifs, as a way of leading the reader/viewer into a better understanding of the play's more elusive concerns.

The opening stage directions of the play describe Frankie Addams as "standing in the arbor gazing adoringly at her brother Jarvis and his fiancée Janice" (1). Casual and trivial though the action may seem, the stage picture of Frankie staring intently at someone becomes, through numerous repetitions, an action fraught with meaning. It is, among other things, a ploy on Frankie's behalf to be noticed and thus included not only in this couple's relationship but in the relationships of others as well. Moreover, this opening tableau establishes through the action of the eyes a visual motif that

From *American Drama* (Fall 1993): pp. 54–66. © 1993 by American Drama Institute.

functions as an integral part of the play's language and provides a context for a deeper insight into the play's philosophical import.

A close study of the opening scene reveals that Frankie's chief action throughout the scene is gazing silently at the couple. Frankie, after the opening tableau, apparently is to hold her position until the time for her to help Berenice serve drinks; when she has finished serving, she then, according to McCullers' stage directions, "perches on the ground before Janice and Jarvis and stares adoringly at them" (3), which she continues to do during the ensuing conversation. Yet again, just before the scene closes, Frankie lets "her look linger on Janice and Jarvis" and, linking the deed with the feeling, languidly announces that "I never believed in love until now" (8–9). Soon afterwards, Jarvis stands up and "gazes fondly around the yard and arbor" and then "pulls [Janice] up and stands with his arm around her, gazing around him" (10). As the scene ends, a telling stage picture is presented: Frankie gazes fondly upon the couple but is not included, while Janice and Jarvis together gaze at the arbor and exclude Frankie from their embrace. It is a foreshadowing of the painful experience that lies ahead.

While visual imagery occurs in a limited way in McCullers' novel, she has in translating her narrative to the dramatic form responded to the stage's need for physical action by expanding the act of staring into a recurring deed, accompanying that behavior with a number of allusions to eyes, sight, and related matters. Moreover, eyes and sight are the subject of more than a few conversations, including discussions of physical sight and eyes, the use of "seeing" words as a metaphor for various mental activities, talk of superstitions and folklore about seeing and eyes, and stories of things seen and unseen.

Ultimately, the visual motif leads into a deeper sense of the play's themes, which are, as McCullers herself has said, about "moral isolation" (Carr, *Hunter*, 335) and "the will to belong" (Carr, *Hunter*, 341). Everything from the title itself to the last scene concerns Frankie's desire to belong to somebody or some group, especially to Janice and Jarvis, as a way of overcoming her feelings of isolation and loneliness. Frankie, it appears, is close to the philosophical position of Bishop Berkeley, who holds that "existence is identical with perception: *esse = percipi*"; he adds, "to say that things exist when no mind perceives them is perfectly unintelligible. Hence, to exist means to be perceived" (Thilly 360–61). Frankie seems to modify Berkeley's view to fit her own situation: to be included one must first be seen, and if one is not seen, one cannot possibly be included. While she may be sure that as long as a person is not seen one is definitely not included, she also presumes the opposite—that therefore to be seen is to be included. Her supposition is of course false, and the drive of the play is toward exposing its invalidity. On yet another level, the play is about the isolation and solitude of the human condition in general, and the song, "His Eye Is On The Sparrow," draws upon sight imagery in order to articulate this larger concern.

In addition to the presence of the sight motif in Frankie's efforts with Janice and Jarvis, seeing, and sometimes not seeing, are important in her interchange with others as well—the club members next door, her own father, John Henry, and, most significantly, Berenice.

Frankie hopes to be admitted to the club of girls her own age, and her method appears to be the same, for she tells Janice that "I watch them here from the yard" (6). When the girls come into the yard, she says, "I'm mighty glad to see you," thinking that they have come to announce her selection into the club, but when they inform her that the new member is Mary Littlejohn, Frankie's response is, "why she's not even cute" (20). Thus another aspect of Frankie's strategy is revealed: not only must one be seen, but one must also look acceptable in order to be accepted, an attitude which accounts for her numerous trips to the mirror.

In another scene involving the neighborhood club, McCullers utilizes powerful stage techniques in order to bracket and give emphasis to Frankie's desperate effort to stare her way into inclusion. After an outburst of high energy, "punching things with her fist and shadow boxing" (62), Frankie suddenly stops. The room becomes quiet. She crosses to the window, where she is joined by John Henry, the piano next door becomes still, and Berenice "turns her head to see what has happened." A moment has been created in which the slightest action becomes magnified. Three girls in clean dresses pass through the yard, and "Frankie *watches* them silently at the window" (62, emphasis added). Then, the tense moment is broken by means of humorous incongruity when Frankie, realizing that her tactic has failed, gives vent to her sense of being excluded, screaming out, "what do you sons-of-bitches mean crossing my yard?" (62) and commanding them off her "Papa's property." Berenice gives Frankie advice that is applicable beyond the present situation by telling her, "make like you don't see them" (62).

Another dimension is added when she stares at a different peer group. As a pre-pubescent girl, Frankie does not yet understand what transpires in physical intimacy. When Barney MacKean and Helen Fletcher cross her yard, she "watch[es] them from the window," but her ignorance is underscored when she says that they go behind the West's garage to "do something bad," but "I don't know what it is" (59). Perhaps if Frankie understood just what it is the young couple does "back there," she would then know why gazing is powerless as a means of being included in any couple's alliance.

The association in Frankie's mind between being looked at and being "looked after" may well find its basis in her attitude toward her father, who is, as the stage directions indicate, "absent-minded," "set in his habits," and "old-fashioned." He is not, in other words, a highly aware, gregarious, or demonstrative human being, and meeting the emotional demands of a thirteen-year-old girl may be beyond his reach. But in Frankie's mind, two facts come together: he does not look at her and he does not care about her. In his presence, she feels lonely and isolated. To Berenice, she complains that he does not "listen to any of my plans," that he just sits there "with his nose to the grindstone" and responds to her questions with "kind of grunts," and that he "never listens to what I say." Based on this kind of evidence, she "wonders if Papa loves me or not" (54). In a confrontation with her father, she pleads with him to "look!" at her and then laments that "sometimes I think you have turned stone blind." When he appears uncertain as to what he is to look at, she vents her frustration: "Papa, why is it you don't ever notice what I have on or pay any serious mind to me? You just walk around like a mule with blinders on, *not seeing or caring*" (67, emphasis added).

Frankie is, of course, mistaken. Berenice explains to her that "he loves you," but "he is just a busy widowman—set in his ways" (55). When he realizes the degree of her suffering over having been excluded from the wedding party, he awkwardly reaches out to her by asking, "what makes you want to leave your old papa like this?" (99). Then, in his own inarticulate way, he tries to include her in his life by inviting her down to the store and offering to let her "play with those old watch springs" (103), sharing with her those things that he values. Self-absorbed though he may be and "blind as a mule" to her needs, he loves her, and his fatherly love belies his daughter's inverted logic that not seeing equals not caring.

In one scene involving her cousin John Henry, whose "gold rimmed spectacles . . . give him an oddly judicious look" (2), Frankie spends valuable stage time giving him a seeing test and concludes that "if I were you I'd just throw those glasses away. You can see good as anybody" (24). While it may at first seem difficult to justify the scene in terms of length of action, on the other hand, it does contribute to the development of the vision motif and builds on other action related to seeing and looking. When Berenice reprimands her, Frankie explains that she was only doing it for John Henry's "own good" because the glasses "don't look becoming" (24), a fact which, in Frankie's mind, could endanger his acceptability. The subject of John Henry's vision closes with Frankie saying, "I bet Janice and Jarvis are members of a lot of clubs" (24). While it may sound like a non sequitur, in Frankie's mind it is logical that the subject of eyes and seeing brings thoughts of belonging.

Other kinds of sight references are linked with John Henry. Immediately following the scene above, John Henry initiates a discussion of Berenice's "new glass eye" by searching in her purse for it. When he wearies of that conversation, he turns to "pickin at the doll's eyes," which Frankie tells him to take "somewhere out of my sight" (27), acting upon her belief that not to see is to reject. She rejects the doll, even though it is a gift from Jarvis, because she believes it is a child's toy. Finally, it is John Henry who asks the pregnant question, "is the glass eye your mind's eye?" (91) and creates the telling refrain, "grey eyes is glass" (79).

Frankie's conversations with Berenice are replete with allusions to sight, including discussions of Berenice's glass eye, each's claim to be able to "see" into the mind of the other, Berenice's stories of how vision experiences initiated each of her troubled affairs with men, and Frankie's matching tales of her own sight experiences.

Although Berenice sometimes wears a glass eye, at the beginning of the play she is wearing a black patch over the empty eye socket, a circumstance which, in addition to drawing attention to the eyes at the beginning of the play, immediately communicates the fact that her physical sight is impaired by at least fifty per cent and that to Berenice, as to anyone visually impaired, eyes and sight are matters of importance. But Berenice, it soon becomes apparent, compensates with other kinds of vision. Moreover, the glass eye itself figures prominently in several discussions, as, for example, when John Henry initiates a discussion by digging it out of Berenice's purse. While Berenice is inserting the eye, John Henry remarks that "the blue glass eye looks very cute," but Frankie opines that "I don't see why you had to get that eye. It has a wrong expression—let alone being blue" (25). When John Henry asks which of Berenice's eyes has better vision, Berenice explains that her glass eye, her right eye, "don't do me no seeing good at all" (25). Still, "I like the glass eye better," John Henry insists, "it is so bright and shiny—a real pretty eye" (25). Suddenly, with all this talk of eyes, Frankie inevitably makes the association: "Janice and Jarvis. It gives me this pain just to think about them" (25). Berenice then closes the subject by again alluding to eyes: "It is a known truth that gray-eyed people, are jealous" (25).

The image of the glass eye begins to be applied in other ways and thus to acquire broader significance. Berenice claims, for example, that "I can see right through them two gray eyes of yours like they was glass" (79), to which John Henry responds by chanting the refrain, "gray eyes is glass" (79). Frankie in turn "tenses her brows and looks steadily at Berenice" while Berenice continues, "I see what you have in mind . . . I see through them eyes" (80). John Henry repeats his refrain twice more, "gray eyes is glass," "gray eyes is glass" (81). And a syllogism is created: gray eyes are glass, Frankie's eyes are gray, ergo, Frankie's eyes are glass, metaphorically speaking; glass eyes, as Berenice has already established, "don't do . . . no seeing good at all." More specifically, glass eyes, i.e., Frankie's gray eyes, are ineffective in their looking, and this fact precludes Frankie's staring her way into Janice's and Jarvis' union, even though Frankie's "glass eyes" do allow Berenice to see through them, figuratively speaking, and know what Frankie is thinking.

Berenice concurs with Frankie that eyes are important in one's relations with others and holds other beliefs about them. She relates several tales about her involvement with men which began with a "sight" experience. Frankie opens the discussion by telling Berenice about something "queer" that happened to her earlier in the day when she passed "this alley" and "caught a glimpse of something in the corner of my left eye . . . And this glimpse brought to my mind . . . my brother and the bride that I just stood there and couldn't hardly bear to look and see what it was." But, disappointingly, it turned out to be just "two colored boys," "but it gave me such a queer feeling" (73).

Berenice stares at Frankie and asks, "can you see through these bones in my forehead?" When Frankie attempts to elaborate, Berenice says she has shared the same disappointment:

> I know what you mean. You mean right here in the corner of your eye . . . you suddenly catch something there. And this cold shiver run all the way down you. And you stand there facing Jesus knows what. *But not . . . who you wanted it to be.* And for a minute you feel like you been dropped down a well. (73, emphasis added)

"Yes, that's it," says Frankie, without realizing that she has acknowledged that sight can be unreliable and a betrayal.

Berenice, who believes that "everything I seen come to me as a kind of sign" (75), continues the conversation. First came the time when in church she put her head down on the pew and "my eyes were open . . . when suddenly this shiver ran all the way through me. I had caught sight of something from the corner of my eye" (76). It was the first time she "ever laid eyes on [that] big old no-good Jamie Beale" (77) and his smashed thumb, which reminded her of Ludie's thumb. Second came the time when "I seen this shape appear before me . . . I almost dropped dead there on the sidewalk . . . [because] from the back view it looked like he was Ludie's ghost or Ludie's twin" (78). This turned out to be Henry Johnson, who "went crazy" on her (78). Apparently intended as cautionary tales about relying on sight experiences, these stories, so says Berenice, "apply to everybody" and are a "warning" to Frankie "about that wedding tomorrow" (79).

Ultimately, the real emphasis of the looking motif is on Frankie. After her attempt in the opening scene to gaze her way into Janice's and Jarvis' union, the couple departs for Summerhill, and Frankie is left to analyze her feelings, reflect on what happened, and make plans for their return, all of which discussions make reference to eyesight.

In reminiscing about their initial visit, Frankie declares that they were "the two prettiest people I ever saw" (15), that "I just never saw any two people like them" (13), and that, look as hard as she might, "I couldn't see all of them I wanted to see. My brains couldn't gather together quick enough to take it all in" (15). She tells Berenice that "I see them just as plain as I see you. Plainer" (48). She "swear[s] to Jesus by my two eyes" (42) that she will get herself included, and then, according to McCullers' unusual stage directions, she "gazes around the walls of the room" (42), as though practicing her skill. When she queries, "how did I act[,] what did I do," Berenice confirms that "you just watched the pair of them like they was ghosts" (39).

Throughout the rest of the play, sight allusions appear randomly in support of the eye motif. The stage directions on some dozen occasions use words such as "stare," "gaze," "watch," "look," "glance," and "glimpse" to describe Frankie's behavior, and the object of her sight is either Berenice, people passing through her yard, the room, or, most often, the mirror, in which she either practices her staring or regards her "looks." She dreams of her life with the couple and the time when they will be called upon to give "an eye witness account about something" (61). Finally, she muses over the phenomenon of passing a stranger in the street when "the eyes make a connection" and then "you never see each other again . . . not in your whole life" (86). Without realizing it, she has admitted once again the inefficacy of eyes in establishing connections.

After the wedding and after her father has "hauled her off the wedding car," which she had forced her way into, Frankie is escorted by her father into the kitchen where she "flings herself on the kitchen chair and sobs with her head in her arms on the kitchen table" (99). When Janice and Jarvis return to console her, she refuses to look at them and "keeps her face buried in her arms and does not look up," in which position she stubbornly remains while they plead with her. This tableau is the reverse of the opening one in which Frankie stared "adoringly" into the faces of these same people, but the logic is the same, although conversely applied: I cannot be looked at because "I am not included." Janice begs Frankie not to "hide your sweet face from us" and to "sit up." When Frankie eventually "raises her head slowly," she "stares with a look of wonder and misery," and as Janice and Jarvis exit, she "still stares at them as they go down the hall" (100). The only use for eyes now is to watch them leave, thus confirming that she is excluded and that staring has failed to gain her admission into the relationship.

Frankie, on the verge of puberty, can be seen in the course of the play as developing an expanding awareness not only of mating and sexual union but of a larger world beyond the familiar kitchen and the intimacy of Berenice and John Henry. She is given to adolescent philosophizing and seeks to make abstractions based on her limited experiences with life: she wonders about identity—"doesn't it strike you as strange that you are you and I am I?" (85); about time "while we're talking right now, this minute is passing.

And ... no power on earth can bring it back again" (91); and about the ultimate isolation of human beings—"there are all these people I will never know" (86). Moreover, the world of which Frankie is becoming aware is a "sudden place." She is beginning to see that it is a society in which there is bigotry, violence, and injustice (e.g., Honey Camden's encounters with the legal system), that it is a world in which the atomic bomb has been exploded, and that life is haunted by the spectre of death (Berenice enlightens Frankie and John Henry with a simple fact of life, "everybody has to die" [71]).

Significantly, all these benumbing thoughts occur in the scene near the end of Act II, descending on the trio as they sit around the kitchen table. To ward off the scary thoughts, John Henry begins to sing the reassuring words,

> I sing because I'm happy
> I sing because I'm free,
> For His eye is on the sparrow,
> And I know He watches me. (91)

He is immediately joined by Berenice and Frankie. Oliver Evans asks the question, "What ... is one to make of this song?" He asserts that the words seem appropriate in Berenice's mouth, that a grim irony exists in John Henry's singing it, and that for Frankie the song is totally inappropriate and that she "feels no such sense of security" (151). Indeed, it may be that the song's real significance lies in the fact that it utilizes eye and sight imagery, with attendant implications, which would suggest that the reassuring thought that God is watching them is undercut by the inference that gazing and watching do not guarantee that one is cared for.

This invocation of divine gazing deepens the sight motif. The loneliness, isolation, and terror that fill the three characters as they huddle around the kitchen table may be seen as an analogue for the human condition in general. To this extent, *The Member of the Wedding* echoes the personal angst of Carson McCullers; apparently, McCullers often felt a sense of alienation from an indifferent God. Carr points out that McCullers suffered from "a sense of abandonment, a loss of God and godliness which haunted her, intermittently, much of her life" (*Hunter* 194). Carr cites several incidents that give testimony to McCullers' theological views, but one of the most dramatic occurred one evening when McCullers was sitting around with a group of other writers at the Yaddo Colony and, apropos of nothing, suddenly cried out, "I've lost the presence of God!" (195). Such deep feelings of despair seem to be behind the metaphysical statement of the play and to underscore the irony of the comfort found in the song by the three characters, all of which is brought out through an examination of eye and sight imagery.

Works Cited

Carr, Virginia Spencer. *The Lonely Hunter: A Biography of Carson McCullers*. New York: Carroll and Graf Publishers, Inc., 1985.

————. *Understanding Carson McCullers*. Columbia: University of South Carolina Press, 1990.

Evans, Oliver. *The Ballad of Carson McCullers: A Biography*. New York: Coward-McCann, Inc., 1966.

McBride, Mary. "Loneliness and Longing in Selected Plays of Carson McCullers and Tennessee Williams." *Modern American Drama: The Female Canon*. Rutherford, NJ: Fairleigh Dickinson University Press, 1990.

McCullers, Carson. *The Member of the Wedding: A Play*. New York: New Directions Books, 1951.

Thilly, Frank. *A History of Philosophy*. New York: Henry Holt and Company, 1952.

Weales, Gerald. *American Drama Since World War II*. New York: Harcourt, Brace, and World, 1962.

RACHEL ADAMS

"A Mixture of Delicious and Freak": The Queer Fiction of Carson McCullers

In April 1963 an aging Carson McCullers made a final visit to the deep South, where she met twenty-six-year-old Gordon Langley Hall at a party in Charleston. At the end of the evening, she pulled him aside as the other guests began to go home and studied him intently for a moment without speaking, then remarked gently, "You're really a little girl."[1] Years later, physicians concurred that Hall, who had been sexed male at birth, was biologically female and capable of bearing children. Classified as a transsexual, Gordon Langley Hall underwent gender reassignment surgery to become Dawn Pepita Hall. She subsequently married her black butler, John-Paul Simmons, and gave birth to a daughter.[2] In a 1971 interview, Hall-Simmons credited McCullers with giving her the courage to acknowledge what were at that time highly unconventional desires: "Carson, her senses sharpened by her own affliction, saw me for what I was in a moment of truth and her heart went out to me. I was a freak, yes, a freak, like one of her own characters."[3] Hall-Simmons attributes McCullers's uncommon insight to her "affliction," undoubtedly a reference to the author's chronic illness but also—in the context of an account concerned with the precise correspondence of sex and gender—possibly to her erotic interest in women as well as men and her preference for triangulated rather than coupled love affairs.[4] However, it was not only McCullers's experiences but her position as an author, a

From *American Literature* 71, no. 3 (September 1999): pp. 551–583. © 1999 by Duke University Press.

creator of freaks, that enabled her to recognize Hall-Simmons's difference. McCullers's ability to author deviant bodies has, for Hall-Simmons, a direct relationship to her capacity to recognize the pain experienced by real persons designated as "freaks." Likewise, Hall-Simmons's loneliness and marginality become meaningful through the equation of her freakish condition with that of McCullers's characters.

Indeed, as Hall-Simmons's analogy indicates, McCullers's fiction is populated by freaks, characters constrained by corporeal anomalies that defy the imposition of normative categories of identity. These freaks suffer an alienation from their bodies that parallels their experiences of estrangement within and isolation from the society of others. Repeatedly, critics of McCullers's work have attributed her characters' suffering to an existential anguish inherent in the human condition. Even those who recognize particular forms of race- or gender-based oppression tend to connect them to "the variety and complexity of human isolation and . . . the destructive repercussions of that alienation.[5] This perspective ignores the historical specificity of McCullers's writing, in which freakish characters point to the untenability of normative concepts of gender and race at a moment when these categories were defined with particular rigidity.

This essay seeks to recontextualize two of McCullers's post–World War II novels—*Member of the Wedding* (1946) and *Clock without Hands* (1961)— by exploring the significance of two interlocking concepts that occupy a privileged position in her writing: the freak and the queer. As McCullers uses these terms, their function depends not upon their correspondence to any fixed identity but upon their opposition to normative behaviors and social distinctions. The queer refers loosely to acts and desires that confound the notion of a normative heterosexuality as well as to the homosexuality that is its abject byproduct. Freaks are beings who make those queer tendencies visible on the body's surfaces. Freaks and queers suffer because they cannot be assimilated into the dominant social order, yet their presence highlights the excesses, contradictions, and incoherences at the very heart of that order. Sometimes, as in the case of Gordon Langley Hall, they inhabit its most intimate and selective social circles. Far from the archetypal portraits of human alienation that so many have detected in McCullers's work, this interplay of personal suffering and social critique is situated firmly within the context of historical events: the end of World War II, the paranoia and conformity that characterized the onset of the Cold War, and the brewing dissatisfaction of racial and sexual minorities.[6] Moreover, the discomfort freaks and queers experience does not take place solely at the level of existential abstraction but is concretized in their uneasy relationships to material things. In the postwar United States, consumer spending was linked to an increased emphasis on domesticity and the family. The purchase of homes and durable goods such as cars, appliances, and furniture seemed to herald an unprecedented national affluence that promised to neutralize economic differences among American citizens.[7] McCullers's characters participate in this consumer economy, but the material possessions they covet are always inappropriate, luxury items that indicate a desire in excess of respectable, family-oriented modes of mass consumption.[8] Rather than guaranteeing entry into the comfortable anonymity of consumer culture, the ownership of frivolous things instead draws attention to the irreconcilable differences of the freak's body, which provide the visible evidence of queer desires that cannot be domesticated.

The deviant body is thus a site of extreme constraint in which any attempt to conceal its differences only makes its abnormality more apparent. At the same time, McCullers's freaks are figures of possibility whose queer transgressions of sexed, gendered, and racial boundaries enable a productive reconsideration of normative social relations. While resistance often remains at the level of imagined potential for her characters, the reader open to the queer suggestions of McCullers's fiction is left to consider the possibilities of a world free from the tyranny of the normal. In her most famous and critically acclaimed novel, *Member of the Wedding*, the awkward relationship between bodies and things highlights the limitations of an idealized femininity and facilitates the imagination of a new social order, one that would reject the normal in favor of the queer possibilities of the freak's extraordinary corporeal form. These notions resurface in McCullers's final work, *Clock without Hands*, where the borders of normative masculine identity are threatened by freakish permutations of race, age, and sexual difference. In these novels, the freak and the queer emerge as contradictory figures that haunt the innermost recesses of the normal, where deviant bodies suffer alienation and violence but also where fantasies of remaking the world are germinated, nurtured, and articulated. McCullers thus engages in a project of social criticism that, at its most penetrating, reveals the links between sexual intolerance and racial bigotry, and, at its most hopeful, recognizes—in the gaps between characters' longings and the suffering they endure—the queer inconsistencies and excesses at the center of the social order that contain the possibility for its refashioning.

QUEERS, FREAKS, AND RACIAL DIFFERENCE

Before turning to McCullers's fiction, it is necessary to elaborate the relationship between her insistent use of the queer and its current redeployments, the link between the queer and the freak, and finally, the way that each of these categories is inextricably bound to problems of racial difference. What McCullers means by the queer is vague but suggestive. Her invocation of the term *queer* is frequently associated with her characters' receptiveness to otherwise unthinkable permutations of sex and gender, which are defined in opposition to normative categories of identification and desire. Such a veiled deployment of the queer is unsurprising at a historical moment when it regularly functioned as a shaming mechanism to legitimate discrimination and physical violence against homosexuals.[9] McCullers's depiction of nonnormative gender and sexual identities may be illuminated by reading her fiction through the lens of recent work on queer theory. My point is not that McCullers, writing during an era when the dominant culture was intensely homophobic, anticipated the present revolutionary politics of queer theory and activism but, rather, that contemporary articulations of the queer offer an ideal vocabulary for understanding previously closeted aspects of her fiction. At the same time, her understanding of the conjoined histories of race and sexuality is important to queer theory's interest in exploring interlocking forms of difference. In both *Member of the Wedding* and *Clock without Hands*, sexual difference always functions in relation to the hierarchical relationship between black and white that structures Southern culture. In these texts, the histories of racial and sexual difference cannot be separated from the ownership of material possessions that enable some forms of deviance to be closeted while bringing others clearly into view.

The *queer* of queer theory and social activism is a self-conscious redeployment of the pejorative connotations that accompanied the term during McCullers's lifetime.[10] Her use of the queer manifests an acute awareness of these connotations as well as the presence of readers who might construe the term differently. The multiple valences of the queer in her fiction derive from her own encounters with the homophobia of the dominant culture as well as with communities that encouraged a more diverse array of sex and gender identification. Much of *Member of the Wedding* was written during World War II, a period of increased sexual freedom in the United States brought about by the separation of families, the growth and diversification of urban populations, and the disturbance of established social and economic configurations.[11] Moreover, in 1940 McCullers and her husband, Reeves McCullers, moved to New York, one of the primary centers for a flourishing sexual subculture. There her penchant for dressing in men's clothing was well received, she fell in love with a series of women, and she lived for a time with a "queer aggregate of artists"[12] that included gay poet W. H. Auden and stripper Gypsy Rose Lee. Yet outside her own heterogeneous circle of acquaintances, *queer* was a shaming appellation used as an accusation of sexual deviance and an excuse for violence.[13] *Member of the Wedding* and *Clock without Hands* are narratives that understand the dangers of a publicly visible sexual difference while depicting alternative spaces where those differences might be welcomed and explored.

Love ya
have a good
day

Although McCullers is frequently described as an author who writes sensitively about same-sex desire, the term *homosexuality* does not adequately capture the wide array of erotic identifications and groupings that appear among her characters, and it is a word that rarely appears in her work. Despite the fact that one of her queer characters, Jester Clane, has read about "homosexuals," he resists the association with sexual pathology and is determined to kill himself "if it turned out he was homosexual like the men in the *Kinsey Report*."[14] Unlike the word *homosexual*, *queer* does not suggest an identity-based category, and it more accurately describes the heterogeneity of intimate erotically charged relationships and currents of desire in McCullers's fiction. Mirroring the diffuse proclivities of her characters, McCullers in her own life rejected attempts to link the unpredictable flows of human desire to the type of categorical definitions suggested by homo- or heterosexuality. Like the transsexual Gordon Langley Hall, the author experienced a discrepancy between normative gender roles and her own sexual preferences that led her to declare to her friend Newton Arvin, "Newton, I was born a man."[15] Although this definitive proclamation suggests the popular belief shared by many of her contemporaries that the lesbian was an invert—a woman possessed by male desires—McCullers was attracted to both men and women. She was involved in at least one intense, triangulated erotic relationship that included her husband and composer David Diamond.[16] In addition to sharing her husband's love for Diamond, Carson was also drawn to women such as Greta Garbo, Katherine Anne Porter, and the Countess Annamarie Clarac-Schwarzenbach, with whom she had a passionate affair. Similarly intimate and complex erotically charged relations surface throughout her oeuvre to suggest that, far from being the norm, heterosexuality and its institutions are always threatened by the polymorphous nature of desire itself.

Current deployments of queer theory not only allow for a more supple understanding of intimacy but also help to explain how McCullers's fiction resists the regimes of the normal that dominated American culture in her time. Writing of queer activism in the 1990s, Michael Warner has argued that "the insistence on 'queer'—a term initially generated in the context of terror—has the effect of pointing out a wide field of normalization, rather than simple intolerance, as the site of violence."[17] In other words, the *queer* of contemporary queer politics is conceived not in opposition to heterosexuality per se but as a broader defiance of all kinds of oppressive social norms. If *homosexuality*, and corresponding terms such as *gay* and *lesbian*, describe a same-sex desire grounded in a politics of identity, *queer* counters a range of normalizing regimes and calls into question the knowledge/power system from which identity-based categories are derived. Queer, as McCullers employs it, poses a persistently messy obstacle to any systematic codification of behavior or desire.

McCullers's recognition of the tyranny of the normal produces the link between queer and freak that surfaces repeatedly in her fiction. The freak is defined as such precisely by her visible inability to fit into recognizable social and bodily categories. The freak is associated historically with the sideshow, where, throughout the nineteenth and early twentieth centuries, women, people of color, and those with developmental and physical disabilities were exhibited as "human curiosities" for entertainment and profit. The spectacle of the deviant body, heightened by props and the barker's hyperbolic pitch, was intended to reinforce, by contrast, the normality of the onlooker, who enjoyed the comfortable anonymity of her position as a member of the audience.[18] The difference between the paying spectators and the freak was spatially reinforced by the fairgoers' distance from the display platform. However, in McCullers's fiction, freak shows fail to cement the distinction between deviance and normality, instead calling the viewers' own normality into question through their identification with the bodies onstage, which remind them of their own lonely, uncomfortable experiences of embodiment. Rather than depicting the sideshow as the exclusive domain of freaks, McCullers suggests that each of her characters is, in some sense, a freak who cannot conform to normative standards of comportment and physical appearance.[19] Thus the sensation of being "caught" that so many of her characters experience is derived not from their status as outsiders but from the fact that they inhabit a repressive social order unable to recognize the queerness at its center.

Finally, questions of visibility and closeting figure prominently in McCullers's fiction in relation to racial, as well as sexual, difference. McCullers's use of the queer is nuanced by an understanding of the way that racial differences have unevenly affected the history of sexual difference within various communities. Delineating the important future projects for queer studies, Judith Butler writes that "queering" must entail a history that considers "the differential formation of homosexuality across racial boundaries, including the question of how racial and reproductive relations become articulated through one another."[20] McCullers's fiction offers important insights about the ways in which sex, gender, and racial relations are interconnected without collapsing the distinctions among them. In both *Member of the Wedding* and *Clock without Hands*, the struggle for queer forms of intimacy cannot be understood apart from the racial hierarchies that structure Southern culture in the postwar period.

THE GAZE OF THE HERMAPHRODITE

Although the adult McCullers frequently dressed in men's clothing and took pleasure in flaunting unconventional sexual preferences much like those of her freakish characters, as a teenager her odd clothing and awkward body drew the contempt of her more feminine classmates, who threw rocks at her because she was "freakish-looking" and "queer."[21] The author's own experiences thus attuned her to clothing's dual capacity to normalize and, when worn inappropriately, to transform normality into freakishness. McCullers recognized that in this atmosphere the intentional abuse of fashion could be used to protest rigid social codes, but she was also aware that others whose differences could not be neutralized by clothing or accessories were unable to engage in such playful experimentation. Instead, they experienced a fearful relationship to their bodies, which subjected them to exclusion and violence. In *Member of the Wedding* and *Clock without Hands*, clothing holds the powerful allure of normalization—the ability to cover over the body's irregularities—but at the same time it threatens to unveil the characters' queer tendencies through their inability to wear it appropriately.

Many of McCullers's female characters, in particular, are characterized by a bodily excess that obstructs their ability to perform the roles expected of them or to successfully don the required accoutrements of femininity.[22] Frankie Addams, the boyish twelve-year-old protagonist of *Member of the Wedding*, worries that her excessive height will eventually render her suitable only for display as a sideshow exhibit, because a summer growth spurt has made her feel that she is "almost a big freak."[23] Barefoot, wearing "a pair of blue black shorts [and] a B.V.D. undervest," "her hair . . . cut like a boy's" (*MW*, 2), Frankie awkwardly attempts to conceal her body's development beneath the childish androgyny of boys' clothing. Inspecting herself in the mirror she determines that "according to mathematics and unless she could somehow stop herself, she would grow to be over nine feet tall. And what would be a lady who is over nine feet high? She would be a Freak" (*MW*, 16–17). Associating femininity with diminutive stature, Frankie anxiously predicts that once a woman reaches a certain height her gendered identity is effectively negated, for she ceases to be "a lady" and becomes instead "a Freak." Fearful that she will be unable to "stop herself," Frankie equates bodily size with self-control and excessive growth with moral inadequacy. If bodily shape is indicative of personal worth, a female giant is grotesquely inappropriate simply by virtue of her immensity, which signals desires and aspirations inappropriate to typical codes of feminine behavior. From Frankie's perspective, the body is a visual signpost indicating perverse desires that could otherwise remain hidden. It is no accident that the imagined outcome of her unprecedented growth spurt will be her transformation into a freak, for at the sideshow, where deviance is represented as a visible quality, the bodies of freaks promise to tell all there is to know about the value of the persons who inhabit them. Throughout the narrative, the adolescent Frankie remains torn between a queer eroticism that attracts her to the fantastic possibilities of all that is freakish and the social codes that define the appearance and behavior of a "normal" young woman in contrast to the abnormality of the freaks at the sideshow. The novel ends without resolving this tension; however, its conclusion implies that she may be able to transform her experiences of gender confusion into more productive energies, rather than repressing them in favor of a socially acceptable heterosexual femininity.

Frankie's more conservative fears about her own bodily excess are closely associated with the Freak Pavilion she visits faithfully at the annual Chattahoochee Exposition, where Giants, Midgets, Fat Ladies, and Wild Men are displayed before an audience of astonished onlookers. A particularly heavy crowd surrounds the booth exhibiting the "Half-Man Half-Woman, a morphidite and a miracle of science" (*MW*, 18) whose divided body poses a fascinating challenge to the universality of the binary opposition between the sexes. The Hermaphrodite has the potential to unravel the entire system of sexual categorization based on the distinction between male and female. This disruptive ambiguity necessitates her/his classification as a freak, a designation that places a safe distance between the spectacle of bodily deviance and the normally gendered onlookers in the audience. The threat of hermaphroditism is further distilled by the absolute and visible division between genders, each of which is indicated by costuming that covers one half of the body: "[T]he left side was a man and the right side a woman. The costume on the left was a leopard skin and on the right side a brassiere and a spangled skirt" (*MW*, 18). The Half-Man Half-Woman's clothing thus creates the appearance of freakishness, while warding off the more dangerous indeterminacy of a third sex in which the difference between "man" and "woman" would be blurred and hybridized. In contrast, the true Hermaphrodite embodies the bisexuality that McCullers saw as inherent in most human eroticism.[24] This more indeterminately gendered body surfaces throughout her fiction in characters such as Cousin Lymon and Miss Amelia in *Ballad of the Sad Café*; Singer, Antonapoulos, and Biff Brannon in *The Heart Is a Lonely Hunter*; and Captain Penderton and Anacleto in *Reflections in a Golden Eye*, all of whom combine qualities of masculine and feminine to suggest a model of sexuality based on a continuum rather than strict binary oppositions.[25]

For the adolescent Frankie at the beginning of the novel, terrified by the maturation of her own body and hurt by the cruel rejection of her peers, the Hermaphrodite signals an unwelcome sexual indeterminacy. Instead of exploring the possibilities of multiple sexualities and genders, she attempts unsuccessfully to assert her own femininity through the forced imposition of new behavior and clothing. Replacing the undershirt and shorts of the previous day, which on a more mature woman could be the costume of a butch lesbian rather than that of a tomboy, Frankie dresses "in her most grown and best, the pink organdy, and put[s] on lipstick and Sweet Serenade" (*MW*, 46).

This change in clothing is accompanied by a new name, F. Jasmine, intended to herald her metamorphosis into a young woman whose grace and maturity will replace the old Frankie's tomboy lifestyle. The femininity she so desires is encapsulated in the orange satin gown she buys for her brother's upcoming nuptials, a garment that holds the promise of adulthood and inclusion, the possibility of becoming a "member of the wedding." The new dress is an important component in her imagined transformation from gangly teenager to attractive woman, and Frankie repeatedly insists on the beauty of the garment rather than her appearance in it, as if the dress alone had the power to alter or erase the identity of the wearer. Her illusions are challenged by the black housekeeper Berenice, who reflects critically on the juxtaposition of the bargain-basement evening gown with her charge's boyish appearance: "Here you got on this grown woman's evening dress. Orange satin. And that brown crust on your elbows. The two things just don't mix" (*MW*, 84). The excesses of the gown foreshadow Frankie's subsequent exclusion from the heterosexual bliss of her brother's honeymoon: its lurid color is inappropriate to the occasion, and it is too large, signaling her unreadiness to assume the part of the mature woman intended to fill out its contours. Instead of transforming Frankie into a woman, the gown highlights the discrepancy between the body's awkward suspension between youth and adulthood, and the garment's unfulfilled promise of glamour and sophistication.

Although the misfit between dress and body proclaims Frankie's failure to acquire a more conventional femininity, other characters in *Member of the Wedding* purposefully manipulate the trappings of one gender or the other to signal a queer identity that resists the normative logic of heterosexual categorization. Unlike the orange satin gown, which cannot enable Frankie's transformation into a mature woman, the pink satin blouse is instrumental in Lily Mae's ability to accomplish a similar metamorphosis. Berenice entertains her incredulous charges with the tale of the effeminate male Lily Mae Jenkins, who "fell in love with a man named Juney Jones. A man, mind you. And Lily Mae turned into a girl. He changed his nature and his sex and turned into a girl" (*MW*, 76). Lily Mae, who "prisses around with a pink satin blouse and one arm akimbo," wears the cues of an intentionally performative homosexuality. Berenice criticizes Frankie's attempt to become a woman simply by putting on more mature feminine clothing, but her account of Lily Mae reinforces the idea of sexuality as a continuum by suggesting that a man who desires another man can voluntarily change from one sex to the other, a change that is heralded by the exaggerated assumption of feminine performance and clothing. In Berenice's queer story gender is a matter of preference, and sexual identification is defined through one's choice of erotic attachments; the body literally evolves in conformity with the desires of its inhabitant and the garments that clothe it. "Nature," as Berenice uses the term, refers to one's erotic tendencies rather than, as in the word's more conventional usage, to those aspects of self that are static and unalterable.

Berenice's story is one example of the instructive range of positions on the relationship between sexuality and gender articulated by the three central characters in *Member of the Wedding*. The improbably frequent repetition of the word "queer" throughout this text leaves traces for a reader open to its suggestion that, rather than occupying any singular or normative position, sexuality is composed of multiple identifications and erotic possibilities. Although it would be difficult to argue that *Member of the Wedding* is a novel about homosexuality, the repeated use of the queer functions as an open secret. For those who wish to explore its possibilities, the queer reinvests unconventional erotic relations, both real and imagined, with positive valences.[26] Lori Kenschaft has described as lesbian the imagined community of readers the novel creates; however, as I have argued, *queer* seems a more accurate term because it is generated by the vocabulary of the novel itself. Moreover, it accounts for the wide array of erotic groupings that appear in McCullers's work, many of which do not involve the same-sex desire or intimacy between women that the term *lesbian* connotes.[27]

For Frankie, the queer is often associated with unpleasant, tentative forays into the world of heterosexual romance, such as the "queer sin" she commits with Barney MacKean, a neighborhood boy, and the attentions she receives from a drunken sailor in a smelly hotel that make her "feel a little queer" (*MW*, 68). Such uses of the term work to queer heterosexuality by revealing that it is neither natural nor universally pleasurable. At more affirmative moments, the queer accompanies various characters' attempts to reimagine the world as a space more accommodating to sexual difference. The kitchen, where the novel's primary action takes place, is "hot and bright and queer" and decorated with "queer drawings of Christmas trees, airplanes, freak soldiers, flowers" (*MW*, 7); there, Berenice entertains Frankie and John Henry with stories of "many a queer thing" (*MW*, 75).[28] Perhaps it is the tale of Lily Mae and the pink satin blouse that inspires Frankie's fantasy of remaking the world to allow for a better correspondence between gendered identification and biological sex, which then leads to a heated, unresolved debate between the kitchen's three occupants:

> [Frankie] planned it so that people could instantly change back and forth from boys to girls, whichever way they felt like and wanted. But Berenice would argue with her about this, insisting that the law of human sex was exactly right just as it was and could in no way be improved. And then John Henry West would very likely add his two cents' worth about this time, and think that people ought to be half boy and half girl, and when

the old Frankie threatened to take him to the Fair and sell him to the Freak Pavilion, he would only close his eyes and smile. (*MW*, 92)

In contrast with the tenor of her previous story, Berenice responds negatively to Frankie's proposal by arguing for a fixed and impermeable "law of human sex." While Frankie holds out for a world where erotic desire would remain open to reconfiguration "whichever way they felt like and wanted," her plan affirms the necessity of a correspondence between sex and gender when she makes the conservative assertion that a body must occupy only one side of the binary divide at a time: "boys" or "girls." John Henry offers yet another alternative, in which individuals would be a strange mix of tendencies—"half boy and half girl"—precluding the polarized opposition between male and female. Frankie's threat to take him to the Freak Pavilion reflects her conviction that one cannot be at once male and female without being a freak, suitable only for display before an astonished audience of normally sexed people. Her classification of the Half-Man Half-Woman as a freak, based on her own anxious experiences at the carnival, confirms the official message of the Freak Pavilion by asserting the Hermaphrodite's difference from the viewer. Instead of the embodiment of sexual possibilities, the Hermaphrodite's queer mix of male and female is transformed into a spectacle at the freak show, affirming the normality of the audience and the clear discernability of sexual differentiation, as evidenced by stereotypically gendered clothing. Although Frankie's anxieties about her own queer desires force her to repudiate John Henry's vision, by the end of the novel she is more receptive to the possibility of sexual indeterminacy. Her assumption of the adult name Frances may signal her acceptance of a typical adolescent femininity, but it may also indicate her openness to a more unconventional identity, for, as Kenschaft has argued, "'Frances' may be less aggressively boyish than 'Frankie,' but it is nevertheless androgynous when spoken."[29]

Frankie is thus torn between the excitement of awakening sexual possibilities and her desire to pass from the queer sexual indeterminacy of "that green and crazy summer" into a more typical relationship between her body and the things that surround it. Her experiences are echoed in the story of Jester Clane, the teenage protagonist of *Clock without Hands* who is tormented by anxiety over his developing erotic attraction to other men. While both feel alienated by rigid codes of gendered comportment and imperative heterosexuality, as a male, Jester enjoys a larger degree of freedom and social mobility than Frankie. But as a gay male he also occupies a more dangerous position because of the threat he poses to the rabidly homophobic patriarchal order of his small Southern town.[30] As Gayatri Spivak has written of *The Heart Is a Lonely Hunter*, "although women and male homosexuals are both marginal as 'non-serious' versions of the male norm, the woman has a recognized use in the male economy of reproduction, genealogy and the passage of property. The male homosexual, on the other hand, has only the unrecognized use of sustaining as criminal or monstrous the tremendous force of the repressed homoeroticism of the patriarchy."[31] Because McCullers names homosexuality more directly in *Clock without Hands*, the queer secret that cannot be articulated in the earlier novel can be mobilized for more direct criticism of the particular social and historical circumstances that generated such an atmosphere of terror. However, the invocation of such a clinical term also has the opposite effect of diffusing the capacious possibilities of the open secret posited by the queer.

Jester, like Frankie, is a teenager plagued with doubts about his sexuality. More conventionally attractive than his female counterpart, Jester's body still bears an awkward relationship to the clothing that covers it. Initially he is described as "a slight limber boy of seventeen . . . [who] wore blue jeans and a striped jersey, the sleeves of which were pushed back to his delicate elbows" (*CWH*, 24). Dressed in the typical costume of a teenage boy of the 1950s, Jester's queer difference is implied by his effeminate slenderness and delicacy, a suggestion that is furthered by his grandfather's affectionate references to him as "Lambones" and "darling." In the company of Jester and his overly solicitous grandfather, the town pharmacist Malone observes that something about Jester makes him seem "a 'stranger'—he had never been like a Milan boy. He was arrogant and at the same time over-polite. There was something hidden about the boy and his softness, his brightness seemed somehow dangerous—it was as though he resembled a silk-sheathed knife" (*CWH*, 25). What Jester's conventionally boyish clothing and respectful behavior conceal is the intense shame of his unrequited and deeply queer love for his classmate Ted Hopkins, "the best all-around athlete in the school" (*CWH*, 42), and his mannish English teacher, Miss Pafford. In a small Southern town that adheres to strict codes of racial, gender, and class distinction, the affluent white Jester is indeed a "stranger" who will ultimately transgress all of these boundaries in his secretive passion for a black man. Rather than being dangerous to others, the softness of his body, the visible evidence of sexual perversion, in fact puts him in danger of the violence that will inevitably accompany the detection of his secret.

If the freak-loving public in *Member of the Wedding* is fascinated by the Half-Man Half-Woman's challenge to strict gender divisions, sexual panic in the predominantly male world of *Clock without Hands* crystallizes around arguments over the *Kinsey Report*, which documented the sexual practices of postwar Americans in unprecedented scientific detail. Assuming the unbiased tone and methodology of science, Kinsey was able to discuss America's sex life with explicit candor, shocking the reading public by revealing the pervasiveness of same-sex desire and practices among men.[32] While the Freak Pavilion in *Member of the Wedding* makes the difference between deviance and normality visible, the *Kinsey Report* in *Clock without Hands* suggests that freaks have infiltrated the normal world. Kinsey's study comforts Jester by assuring him that he is not alone in his desire for other men but disturbs him by classifying his desire as "homosexual," an appellation laden with connotations of medicalized deviance. In an argument with his grandfather, the reactionary Judge Fox Clane, Jester defends the *Report* as "a scientific survey of the sexual activities in the human male," while the hypocritical Judge, who "had read the book with salacious pleasure, first substituting for the jacket the dust cover of *The Decline and Fall of the Roman Empire*" (*CWH*, 83), declares it "pornographic filth" (*CWH*, 84).

Significantly, the debate over whether the *Kinsey Report* is science (derived from empirical evidence) or pornography (the product of deviant fantasies) hinges on the question of whether the offenses in question are visibly apparent. When Judge Clane objects, "Science my foot. I have been an observer of human sin for close on to ninety years, and I never saw anything like that," Jester's impudent retort questions the accuracy of his vision: "Maybe you ought to put on your glasses." Like the audience at the Freak Pavilion, the Judge assumes the position of an impartial observer, a distancing strategy that affirms his normality in contrast to the spectacle of deviance he views before him. In a society conditioned by such spectacles, the Hermaphrodite displayed in the House of Freaks is a "miracle of science," an object that can be observed and classified according to its qualitative difference from the viewer. Participating in the logic of the freak show by insisting that deviance must be visible, Judge Clane shrugs off the threatening possibility of covert homosexual activity as the fantasy of "an impotent, dirty old man" (*CWH*, 83). Ironically, this hidden desire is precisely the strangeness that Malone perceives in the youthful Jester at the beginning of the novel. It is a secret that is repeatedly intimated in the dialogue between Jester and his grandfather, a conversation that flirts with the possibility of disclosure but is rendered ineffectual by the Judge's panicked inability to listen to what his grandson is saying and Jester's lack of a vocabulary that would enable him to reveal his concerns with honesty and purpose.

For Jester, the *Kinsey Report*'s scientific validity is crucial to the affirmation of his normality, for he "was afraid, so terribly afraid, that he was not normal ... [because] he had never felt the normal sexual urge and his heart quaked with fear for himself, as more than anything else he yearned to be exactly like everyone else" (*CWH*, 84). Jester's desire "to be exactly like everyone else" reflects a typically adolescent self-loathing; at the same time, it participates in a larger cultural obsession with conformity that is characteristic of the Cold War United States, with its insistence on a definitive opposition between queer desires and the normal sexual urge indicative of authentic masculinity. For a public particularly concerned with normality, the queer signifies a dangerous refusal to foreclose one's options by accepting a monolithic understanding of sexuality and identification.[33] However, the irony of Jester's longing "to be exactly like everyone else" is that nearly "everyone else" in McCullers's fiction is plagued by queer tendencies that cannot be classified within a system of normative heterosexuality. Despite the fact that the story of Jester's failed love for the mulatto Sherman Pew ends with the promise of closure—"his odyssey of passion, friendship, love, and revenge was now finished"—his future remains as unfinished as that of the androgynous Frances. For a mainstream audience, this conclusion may imply that Jester has moved from a childish homoeroticism to mature heterosexuality; for the queer reader, however, it suggests that he has begun to accept desire and identification as "crazy and complex" (*CWH*, 202) rather than conforming to predetermined social norms.

The possibilities of this more diffuse sexuality are multiplied by a profound connection in McCullers's work between sexual and racial oppression, both of which operate by turning some persons into freaks in order to confirm the normative (white) heterosexuality of others. As Thadious M. Davis has argued, "Without collapsing the difference of race and gender, McCullers attends in her literary production, with varying degrees of intensity, to race in the representation of women in the South. She assumes the intricate connections of race and gender, particularly in conjoining the two categories and inscribing race in gender."[34] Despite her awareness of this connection, McCullers also is sensitive to important distinctions between racial and sexual discrimination, for often the empathetic attraction of queer white characters like Frankie and Jester to black characters results in misunderstanding and further alienation. The crucial distinction between racial and sexual difference is that queer sexuality has the potential to remain dangerously undetected, whereas race in McCullers's fiction is the visible signifier of difference in spite of her characters' attempts to alter or conceal bodily attributes that make them the targets of discrimination and abuse.

WHY BERENICE WANTED A BLUE EYE

Besides the Half-Man Half-Woman, another Freak Pavilion exhibit described in some detail in *Member of the Wedding* is the "Wild Nigger . . . from a savage island . . . [who] squatted in his booth among the dusty bones and palm leaves and ate raw living rats." Unlike the other freaks, the black man's exoticism is undermined by the rumor that "he was not a genuine Wild Nigger, but a crazy colored man from Selma" (*MW*, 17). This speculation implies that "freak" is not an inherent quality, but an identity imposed on certain bodies to justify their exclusion from the privileges of an anonymous normality. The grotesque spectacle of the wild man is made possible by drawing on the familiar equation of blackness with savagery, deviance, and exoticism.[35] His prominent presence in the account of the Freak Pavilion, where the audience's anxieties about sexual normality are provoked and assuaged by the spectacle of the Half-Man Half-Woman, draws attention to the intimate relationship between racial and sexual difference in McCullers's fiction. In *Member of the Wedding* and *Clock without Hands*, black characters must negotiate, with varying degrees of success, the complex diversity of their own communities and a society that views them as one-dimensional types like the "Wild Nigger" at the Freak Pavilion.

The connection between racial and sexual otherness is reinforced by Frankie and Jester who, in their struggle to come to terms with unconventional erotic urges, are drawn to black characters who have extensive experience with discrimination and bigotry. Frankie, who is attracted to the "stir of company" (*MW*, 124) in Berenice's crowded home, identifies particularly with the homosexual Honey Brown, "a sick-loose person" (*MW*, 35) who "feel like he just can't breathe no more" (*MW*, 114). Initially Frankie "did not understand the hidden meaning" in his family's description of him as "a boy God has not finished. Such a remark put her in mind of a peculiar half-boy—one arm, one leg, half a face" (*MW*, 122). The image of a freakish half person gives way to sympathetic identification as she becomes aware of Honey's plight as a black, homosexual man. Imagining a world where race, like gender, is fluid and shifting, Frankie replaces her fantasy of deviant corporeality with one of racial transgression, in which the light-skinned Honey leaves the South and "change[s] into a Cuban" (*MW*, 125). While this is a moment of enlightenment for Frankie, her suggestion is untenable for obvious reasons, and the end of the novel finds Honey incarcerated after a drug-induced crime spree. Likewise, Jester falls passionately in love with Sherman Pew, his grandfather's young mulatto secretary. Although Sherman showers the white boy with physical and verbal abuse, Jester feels a "creepy thrill" (*CWH*, 67) when he listens to Sherman's singing. He responds to Sherman's fabricated tales of collective black protest with envious admiration. If Jester's sexual shame comes from his inability to experience "passion," his feelings for Sherman assure him of his capacity for desire, and fantasizing about the black boy allows him "to become a man" by having sex with a female prostitute. As we will see, while Jester derives personal satisfaction from his love for Sherman, the white boy's affections cannot counteract the pervasive discrimination that thwarts Sherman's attempts to improve his social and economic situation.

Part of Berenice and Sherman's appeal to white teenagers confused about their sexual identities is that their bodies, like that of the Hermaphrodite, resist classification into neatly opposed categories. Berenice's tales of "many a queer thing" involve the transgression of racial as well as sexual boundaries, suggesting that the queer in McCullers's fiction encompasses multiple and intersecting forms of difference. With one blue glass eye that "stared fixed and wild from her quiet, colored face" (*MW*, 3), Berenice herself is a freakish mix of the natural and artificial.[36] Although the narrative voice proclaims the eye as the "only . . . thing wrong about Berenice" and professes bemused ignorance—"why she had wanted a blue eye nobody human would ever know" (*MW*, 3)—as the story unfolds it becomes clear that Berenice's body mirrors her rejection of white notions of beauty and her delight in situations of racial and gender transgression. While the appeal of the prosthetic eye itself is aesthetic rather than functional, its color is treated as an excessive luxury much like the lurid orange material of Frankie's bargain-basement gown or Lily Mae's pink satin blouse. For Berenice, "who always spoke of herself as though she was somebody very beautiful" (*MW*, 79), the blue glass eye raises the possibility of moving beyond normative standards of appearance and the damaging racial hierarchies that accompany them.

In *Clock without Hands* a similar hybridity characterizes Sherman Pew, whose startling blue eyes subject him to repeated analysis by the white men he encounters. The visible evidence of miscegenation, Sherman's body is perceived differently by various characters whose responses to him delineate their own fantasies and anxieties about racial mixing. Jester, who is trying to come to terms with his sexuality, fixates on Sherman as the object of his desire. Jester's grandfather, the racist Judge who hires Sherman as his secretary and harbors the "queer" fantasy of reinstating segregation (*CWH*, 155), sees the black boy as a "veritable jewel" (*CWH*, 113) and uses their relationship as the reassuring evidence of his own benevolent paternalism. Malone, who has just discovered that he is dying of leukemia, encounters Sherman as he cuts through an alley and notices the boy's "unnatural appearance": "Once those eyes were seen, the rest of the body seemed also unusual and out of proportion. The arms were too long, the chest too broad—and the expression alternated from emotional sensitivity to deliberate sullenness" (*CWH*, 15). The blue eyes, which appear "unnatural" juxtaposed with dark skin, cause Malone to perceive Sherman as a freak whose entire body is grotesquely disproportionate. Although the boy does nothing more than look at Malone, the pharmacist "automatically" uses Sherman's unusual appearance to classify him as a delinquent. As in his encounter with Jester, whom he classifies as "dangerous" and "strange," Malone, in his treatment of Sherman, arrogantly assumes the power to make moral determinations based on an initial visual perception. As they stare at one another, "it seemed to Malone that the blaze [in Sherman's eyes] flickered and steadied to a look of eerie understanding.

He felt that those strange eyes knew that he was soon to die" (*CWH*, 16). While Sherman couldn't possibly know of Malone's diagnosis, the pharmacist reads his own fears about death into the exchange, imbuing Sherman's alien gaze with an "eerie understanding."

Malone's reaction to Sherman's gaze parallels Frankie's experience in the Freak Pavilion, where the exhibits frighten her because they look back at her "as though to say: we know you" (*MW*, 18). Both Frankie and Malone, accustomed to experiencing the Other as a distant spectacle, are disturbed by having their stare returned. They respond by imparting a mysterious and improbable knowledge to the freaks' impassive look. The momentary discomfort occasioned by the realization that the freakish Other is able to look back has the potential to productively destabilize the familiar hierarchies through which these characters navigate the world. Frankie will eventually embrace this instability, while Malone will die having learned nothing and asserting that "nothing mattered to him" (*CWH*, 207). The near-collision of Malone and Sherman, in which Sherman's mere presence fills Malone with dread of "something momentous and terrible," serves as a paradigm for race relations throughout *Clock without Hands*, in which white men's fears and desires come to pose as attributes of Sherman's person, regardless of his actions.

While Sherman, like Jester, longs for normality, the crucial difference between them is that Jester can conceal his queer tendencies while Sherman's body makes him a target of discrimination and abuse. Unlike Berenice, Sherman's hostility bars him from satisfying personal relationships in the black community, and he feels each act of violence against people of color in his own body, the visible marker of difference that turns him into a freak who is neither black nor white. Sherman's somatic response to news of racial violence is coupled with his desire for a normative respectability that would insulate him from personally experiencing such violence. Respectability, for Sherman, is signified by a large vocabulary, which he consistently misuses in attempts to impress Jester, and the acquisition of luxury items such as expensive whiskey, caviar, and silk bedspreads. If Jester is attracted to other men, Sherman bears a similar erotic relation to material things: as Sherman strokes his bedspread admiringly, Jester feels "an inexplicable creepy thrill" (*CWH*, 67) from observing Sherman's pleasure. Despite boasting of affairs with women, both black and white, Sherman's true passion is for his possessions, which promise the security and fulfillment he is unable to attain through intimacy with others. Sherman is an obedient subject of the Cold War era, when the ownership of things was a form of patriotism that distinguished U.S. citizens from Communist sympathizers. However, his desires also threaten more traditional social divisions in which access to education and material possessions is racially determined.

Like Frankie and her ill-fitting dress, Sherman's inability to use material things successfully to conceal his difference highlights the undeniable visibility of his black body and the commodity's untenable guarantee of privilege and inclusion. As in *Member of the Wedding*, frivolous clothing is an important signifier of Sherman's distance from his inappropriate social aspirations: "He had two Hathaway shirts and wore a black patch on his eye, but it only made him look pathetic instead of distinguished and he bumped into things" (*CWH*, 63). The Hathaway shirts advertisement that attracts Sherman's attention features a series of successful white men wearing eye patches. A blank silhouette in the final slot accompanied by the slogan, "to be announced soon," suggests that the man to flesh out the space might be the consumer himself, transformed by purchasing a Hathaway shirt. In his acquisition of shirt and eye patch, what Sherman fails to notice is that the silhouette is white, that instead of indicating unlimited possibilities the space is reserved for someone already marked for wealth and social privilege. Unable to secure social legitimacy through the ownership of such status symbols yet disdainful of the community inhabited by other black characters in the novel, Sherman is a freak who occupies a dangerous liminal space between black and white.

Finally, Sherman's fetishization of material things as compensation for racial inequality, the death of his parents, his lack of education, and the absence of erotically satisfying relationships bring about his violent death. Having secretly fantasized that the blue-eyed Judge who patronizingly calls him "son" is his father, Sherman is enraged to discover that the Judge was involved in the death of his parents, whose racial identities do not conform to his fantasies about them. Instead of the stereotypical scenario of a black woman brutally raped by a white man, Sherman unveils a queer reversal in which his white mother engaged in consensual sex with a black man, "like Othello, that cuckoo Moor!" (*CWH*, 184). He responds to this unsettling knowledge by seeking out a dangerous and excessive visibility, using white water fountains, bathrooms, churches, and restaurant counters, where he becomes frustrated when his transgressions fail to attract attention. Ultimately Sherman's shattered fantasy of political enfranchisement gives way to demands for another kind of equality—the right to be a consumer. In contrast to his earlier desire for luxury items, Sherman at the end of the novel attempts to become a properly domesticated consumer by renting a house in a white neighborhood and going on a deadly shopping spree to furnish it.[37] If he can vote only in fantasy, his actions insist that the right to purchase on credit is truly color-blind. In the 1950s advertisements and television shows equated the possession of commodities with being a normal American; thus, purchasing things becomes a way for Sherman to proclaim his citizenship. A black man who has always felt violence to his race in his own body, who has lived in constant awareness that black was once the possession of white, Sherman is literally consumed by an "ecstasy of ownership" (*CWH*, 196), by the possibility of owning himself and his possessions.

However, in McCullers's fiction freaks cannot easily reconcile their inappropriate bodies with the orderly world of Cold War consumer culture. When Jester rushes to warn Sherman that an angry mob is gathering, Sherman responds by showing off his new purchases, refusing to leave the things that will ensure his death at the hands of resentful white citizens. The house that becomes "all of Sherman's world" (*CWH*, 197), a space where he can briefly enjoy the pleasures of ownership, distracts him from the dangers of his black body. Nonetheless, a black man who can own rather than be property poses a threat to the white citizens who bomb Sherman's house as a means of violently reasserting his difference from them, for their normality can only be secured by transforming him into a dangerous freak. As Robyn Wiegman has argued, in a lynching "differences among men are so violently foregrounded that one can no longer cling to the rhetorical homogeneity attached to the masculine."[38] Sherman's death makes all too clear the profound gulf that separates him not only from Jester but also from the resentful working-class men who see their whiteness as their only claim to superiority. Dramatically demonstrating divisions among men, lynching thus gives the lie to the false leveling of differences promised by the consumption of commodities. While *Clock without Hands* challenges the existence of normative masculinity by suggesting that all of its male characters—Malone, dying of leukemia; Judge Clane, disabled by obesity and a stroke; Jester, a closeted queer; Sherman, a mulatto—are freaks, it nonetheless asserts that some forms of freakishness are more dangerous than others, and racial difference remains the most damaging and divisive of all social categories. The most important scenarios in McCullers's fiction are thus those in which characters of various races imagine a world that does not rely on hierarchical distinctions among persons for its social organization.

"A MIXTURE OF DELICIOUS AND FREAK"

Fantasies in McCullers's fiction are the most significant way of envisioning alternatives to corporeal inequalities that create an atmosphere of alienation and claustrophobia. In this respect, the scene in *Member of the Wedding* discussed earlier, in which Frankie, Berenice, and John Henry "judge the work of God, and mention the ways how they would improve the world" (*MW*, 91), is crucial.[39] If the world around them is torn by conflicts audible in the persistent buzz of wartime news on the radio, these three characters compensate for inadequacies in their own lives by generating utopian fantasies of remaking the world. Each occupant of the kitchen takes a turn weaving a fantasy that reflects individual longings while, at times, interweaving with the fantasies of the other two, so that "their voices crossed and the three worlds twisted" (*MW*, 92). This model of collective imagining that can momentarily bridge differences in age, race, and gender among its collaborators is especially important in the work of remaking.

Frankie's fantasy, in which persons would be able to change from one sex to another at will, responds to anxieties about her developing sexual identity. Louise Westling has argued that these progressive fantasies are undone by the novel's movement towards "Frankie's ultimate submission to the inexorable demand that she accept her sex as female."[40] This reading places an undue emphasis on the novel's ending and forecloses the possibilities of its more radically affirmative moments.[41] Moreover, a negative understanding of Frankie's acceptance of female sexuality ignores the lesbian implications of "the wonder of her love" (*MW*, 151) for her new friend Mary Littlejohn at the close of the narrative. Frankie's obsession with becoming "a member of the wedding"—the narrative's eponymous organizing concept—might be interpreted as evidence of a conservative socialization process that conditions young girls to desire a conventional femininity that culminates in marriage and motherhood. But instead of longing to replace the bride, Frankie's ultimate fantasy is to become a part of the community formed by Janice and Jarvis. The queer desire to be not a "bride" but a "member" challenges the normative heterosexuality of the marriage couple by imagining a social organization based on triadic relations, much like those the author sought in her own life. In both novels, alienated characters long for membership, a mode of identity that is relational, inclusive, and nonhierarchical.

The models of sexuality and race generated by the three inhabitants of the kitchen are fluid and open to many different permutations. In Berenice's imagination, "there would be no separate colored people in the world, but all human beings would be light brown color with blue eyes and black hair. There would be no colored people and no white people to make the colored people feel cheap and sorry all through their lives" (*MW*, 91). In this new world free of racial bigotry, both Berenice, with her blue glass eye, and Sherman Pew, born with dark skin and blue eyes, are model citizens: freakish mixtures of black and white, nature and artifice, that defy normative hierarchies of difference. Berenice's proposal entails a radical reconfiguration of race that would not simply reverse white domination of black but obliterate the entire system of differentiation based on bodily appearance by making each person a racial hybrid. The hybridity that causes Berenice and Sherman to be figures of ridicule—and in Sherman's case, violence—would instead become the norm.

But six-year-old John Henry's fantasy is the queerest of all. In contrast with Frankie's fearful experience of the Freak Pavilion, John Henry is enamored of the Pin Head, who "skipped and giggled and sassed around, with a shrunken head no larger than an orange, which was shaved except for one lock tied with a pink bow at the top" (*MW*, 18). Unafraid of the freaks, John Henry declares, "[S]he was the cutest little girl I ever saw," indicating an acceptance of the Pin Head as a part of his world, and even raising the possibility of a growing erotic attraction. In fact, John Henry's delight at dressing in women's clothing brings out his own freakishness by making him look "like a little old woman dwarf, wearing the pink hat with the plume, and the high-heel shoes" (*MW*, 117). A character whose ill-suited clothes make him appear both young and old, male and female, John Henry most completely embodies the potential of the freak to provide alternatives to the exclusionary norms that structure his culture. Instead of a shameful inability to fit a proscribed role, wearing someone else's clothing generates the potential of new and varied possibilities. John Henry's model of remaking the world is one that, in its disorder and particularity, can incorporate "a mixture of delicious and freak":

> [H]e did not think in global terms: the sudden long arm that could stretch from here to California, chocolate dirt and rains of lemonade, the extra eye seeing a thousand miles, a hinged tail that could be let down as a kind of prop to sit on when you wished to rest, the candy flowers. (*MW*, 91)

Unable to "think in global terms," John Henry imagines a world that values specificity over totalizing models of identity. Like recent articulations of the queer, John Henry's proposed heterotopia is not organized around a consistent, determining logic of identification, but, rather, it revels in quirky opposition to all that is normal. The long arm and extra eye that allow for a more expansive community outside the South's stifling regionalism, the excremental appreciation of "chocolate dirt and rains of lemonade," the hinged tail that recalls our inextricable connection with the animal world, all suggest a sympathetic appreciation of the body and its many variations. The best that a freak can be, John Henry contracts meningitis and suffers a gruesome death, "screaming for three days [with] his eyeballs walled up in a corner stuck and blind" (*MW*, 152), for in McCullers's fiction, bodily difference often must be hidden, normalized, or punished, leaving hope for change in the utopian imaginings of a better world. However, as the more mature Frances embarks on an exciting new relationship with Mary, she holds onto the queer possibilities suggested by John Henry, whom she remembers "at twilight time or when the special hush would come into the room" (*MW*, 153).

At the end of *Member of the Wedding*, Frances and Mary return to the fair but not to the Freak Pavilion, "as Mrs. Littlejohn said it was morbid to gaze at freaks" (*MW*, 152). This explanation for their avoidance might indicate Frankie's submission to the older woman's authority, thus serving as evidence of her ultimate normalization. But such a reading remains unconvincing in a narrative so saturated with references to the queer. Rather than a sign of their obedience to Mrs. Littlejohn's prohibition, the young women's abstinence more plausibly indicates their recognition that the world is composed of freaks, that they no longer need to secure their own normality by exploiting a less fortunate Other. The logic of the freak show, which insists on cordoning off the differences of some to proclaim the sameness of everyone else, is precisely the logic that led to Sherman's death and to Honey and Berenice's feeling that "we all caught" (*MW*, 114).

A queer reading can move beyond this conclusion because it draws attention to forms of membership that are not based on being caught within the confines of identity-based categories. This is not a move that McCullers's characters are often able to make, but it is something that they consistently imagine and towards which they struggle. The queer and the freak are terms that counter the binary logic of sexual and racial division and, by seeing themselves in this way, her characters are both able to identify the "caughtness" that they feel and the possibility of imagining it otherwise. This is the corrective lesson that queer theory brings to the identity politics that caused disillusionment in the wake of the women's, civil rights, and gay rights movements. Rereading McCullers's work from this perspective does not provide a coherent plan of action but rather a place to begin thinking about what it would be like to inhabit a community rooted in heterogeneity rather than sameness, desire rather than prescription, where each member can find in herself "a mixture of delicious and freak."

NOTES

I wish to thank Maurizia Boscagli, Giles Gunn, Carl Gutierrez-Jones, and Chris Newfield for their comments on earlier versions of my work on McCullers. I am also grateful to my colleague Gina Dent for her insightful reading of this article, to my colleague David Eng for sharing his work on race and queer theory, and to my able research assistant, Marisa Parham. Particular thanks are due Jon Connolly for his generosity and patience at every stage of the writing process.

1. Virginia Spencer Carr, *The Lonely Hunter: A Biography of Carson McCullers* (Garden City, N.Y.: Doubleday, 1975), 519.

2. For a more complete account of Hall's life in Charleston, see James T. Sears, *Lonely Hunters: An Oral History of Lesbian and Gay Southern Life, 1948–1968* (Boulder, Colo.: Westview Press, 1997), chap. 5.

3. Carr, *Lonely Hunter*, 519.

4. Eve Sedgwick has discussed the eroticism of triangulated relationships in *Between Men: English Literature and Male Homosocial Desire* (New York: Columbia Univ. Press, 1985), where she argues that the heroine in the Western literary tradition often functions

as the conduit for an intimate erotically charged struggle between two male competitors. McCullers's own complex erotic life more than once placed her at the apex of such a triangulated affair, and in what follows I will propose that there may be pleasure not only in the homosocial bond between men, but in the woman's position as intermediary.

5. Pamela Bigelow, "Carson McCullers," in *Gay and Lesbian Literature*, ed. Sharon Malinowski (Detroit, Mich.: St. James Press, 1994), 257. Critics who have argued that McCullers's characters symbolize universal human alienation include Virginia Spencer Carr, *Understanding Carson McCullers* (Columbia: Univ. of South Carolina Press, 1990); Ihab Hassan, *Contemporary American Literature, 1945–1972* (New York: Frederick Ungar, 1973); Klaus Lubbers, "The Necessary Order," in *Carson McCullers*, ed. Harold Bloom (New York: Chelsea House, 1986), 33–52; Frances Freeman Paden, "Autistic Gestures in *The Heart Is a Lonely Hunter*," *Modern Fiction Studies* 28 (autumn 1982): 453–63; Louis D. Rubin, "Carson McCullers: The Aesthetic of Pain," in *Critical Essays on Carson McCullers*, ed. Beverly Lyon Clark and Melvin J. Friedman (New York: G. K. Hall, 1996), 111–23; and Lynn Veach Sadler, "'Fixed in an Inlay of Mystery': Language and Reconciliation in Carson McCullers's *Clock without Hands*," *Pembroke Magazine* 20 (1988): 49–53. Among those who acknowledge the depiction of homosexuality in McCullers's work but make similar claims for universality are Stephen D. Adams, *The Homosexual as Hero in Contemporary Fiction* (New York: Barnes & Noble Books, 1980); Pamela Bigelow and Clare Whatling, "Carson McCullers," in *The Gay and Lesbian Literary Heritage*, ed. Claude J. Summers (New York: Henry Holt, 1995), 470–71. For a useful overview of McCullers criticism, see Lisa Logan, introduction to *Critical Essays on Carson McCullers*, ed. Clark and Friedman, 1–16.

6. For discussion of McCullers's postwar drama as social criticism, see Lisa Logan and Brook Horvath, "Nobody Knows Best: Carson McCullers's Plays as Social Criticism," *Southern Quarterly* 33 (winter–spring 1995): 23–33.

7. On the relationship between consumption, domesticity, and the postwar economy, see Stephanie Coontz, *The Way We Never Were: American Families and the Nostalgia Trap* (New York: Basic Books, 1992); Jackson Lears, "A Matter of Taste: Corporate Cultural Hegemony in a Mass-Consumption Society," in *Recasting America: Culture and Politics in the Age of Cold War*, ed. Larry May (Chicago: Univ. of Chicago Press, 1989), 38–60; and Elaine Tyler May, *Homeward Bound: American Families in the Cold War Era* (New York: Basic Books, 1998). This perceived homogeneity is, of course, countered by the particularity of many Americans' lives. Recent analyses of urban life, youth culture, and sexual and racial minorities indicate a previously unrecognized complexity and conflict during the postwar years. See, for example, the essays in *The Other Fifties: Interrogating Midcentury Icons*, ed. Joel Foreman (Urbana: Univ. of Illinois Press, 1997) and in *Not June Cleaver: Women and Gender in Postwar America, 1945–1960*, ed. Joanne Meyerowitz (Philadelphia: Temple Univ. Press, 1994).

8. For an analysis of how the desire for luxury items poses a queer resistance to the socially sanctioned consumerism of the Cold War economy, see Robert Corber, "Resisting the Lure of the Commodity: *Laura* and the Spectacle of the Gay Male Body," in Corber, *Homosexuality in Cold War America: Resistance and the Crisis of Masculinity* (Durham: Duke Univ. Press, 1997), 55–78.

9. On homosexuality during the postwar period, see Robert Corber, *In the Name of National Security: Hitchcock, Homophobia, and the Construction of Gender in Postwar America* (Durham, N.C.: Duke Univ. Press, 1993), and *Homosexuality in Cold War America*; John D'Emilio, *Sexual Politics, Sexual Communities: The Making of a Homosexual Minority in the United States, 1940–1970* (Chicago: Univ. of Chicago Press, 1983); John D'Emilio and Estelle Freeman, *Intimate Matters: A History of Sexuality in America* (New York: Harper &

Row, 1988); Kenneth Lewes, *The Psychoanalytic Theory of Male Homosexuality* (New York: Simon and Schuster, 1988); and Colin Spencer, *Homosexuality: A History* (London: Fourth Estate, 1996).

10. As Judith Butler describes the earlier significance of the term, "'queer' has operated as one linguistic practice whose purpose has been the shaming of the subject it names or, rather, the producing of a subject through that shaming interpolation" (*Bodies That Matter: On the Discursive Limits of "Sex"* [New York: Routledge, 1993], 226).

11. According to D'Emilio and Freeman, the social circumstances of World War II contributed to the development of homosexual subcultures in major cities such as New York and San Francisco. Despite the repressive atmosphere of the Cold War, these subcultures continued to expand, flourishing in the 1960s (*Intimate Matters*, part 4). See also Corber, *Homosexuality in Cold War America*; and D'Emilio, *Sexual Politics*, part 1. On the rise of queer urban spaces in the modernist period, see Joseph Boone, "Queer Sites in Modernism: Harlem/The Left Bank/Greenwich Village," in *The Geography of Identity*, ed. Patricia Yaeger (Ann Arbor: Univ. of Michigan Press, 1996), 242–72.

12. So named by poet Louis Untermeyer, who recalled attending "a gay (in both senses of the word) occasion at which Auden and Gypsy Rose Lee were present" at the home McCullers shared with Auden and George Davis (quoted in Carr, *Lonely Hunter*, 199).

13. Indeed this violence has been so pervasive that "queer bashing" is one of the compound words listed under "queer" in the *OED*. While it is difficult to trace a precise genealogy of the term, it is clear that *queer* was used almost entirely as a negative label during McCullers's lifetime. For brief reference to previous pejorative uses of the term, see Lauren Berlant (with Elizabeth Freeman), "Queer Nationality," *The Queen of America Goes to Washington City: Essays on Sex and Citizenship* (Durham, N.C.: Duke Univ. Press, 1997), 145–74; Butler, *Bodies That Matter*; Lisa Duggan, "Making It Perfectly Queer," in *Sex Wars: Sexual Dissent and Political Culture*, ed. Lisa Duggan and Nan D. Hunter (New York: Routlege, 1995), 155–72; Spencer, *Homosexuality*; and Michael Warner, introduction to *Fear of a Queer Planet: Queer Politics and Social Theory*, ed. Michael Warner (Minneapolis: Univ. of Minnesota Press, 1994). George Chauncey details the significance of *queer* between 1890 and 1940, when it was used by male homosexuals to differentiate themselves from the more effeminate *fairies*. According to Chauncey, *queer* did not become a derogatory term until the mid-twentieth century. See Chauncey, *Gay New York: Gender, Urban Culture, and the Making of the Gay Male World, 1890–1940* (New York: Basic Books, 1994).

Lori Kenschaft argues that "[i]n 1946, when *Wedding* was published, 'queer' (like 'gay') was a code word known to many 'in the life' but few outside; it was frequently used to identify oneself to another discretely, under the public eye but without public knowledge" ("Homoerotics and Human Connections: Reading Carson McCullers 'As a Lesbian,'" in *Critical Essays on Carson McCullers*, ed. Clark and Friedman, 221). Despite Kenschaft's assertion that *queer* functions as a code among insiders, historical evidence indicates that it was also widely used during this period to condemn the innate abnormality of the homosexual. Just three years later, an article on homosexuality as deviant perversity entitled "Queer People" would appear in the mainstream magazine *Newsweek* (10 October 1949, 52+).

14. Carson McCullers, *Clock without Hands* (Boston: Houghton Mifflin, 1961; reprint, New York: Penguin, 1979), 86. Subsequent references, cited parenthetically as *CWH*, will be to the Penguin edition.

15. Quoted in Carr, *Lonely Hunter*, 159.

16. Carr's biography chronicles the numerous queer erotic arrangements in which McCullers and her husband engaged throughout their relationship. Unfortunately, Carr's descriptions are frequently tinged with condescension or homophobia. She offers this

summary, for example: "Having sexual problems himself which he could not resolve, Reeves was incapable of coping with his wife's sexual inclinations or of *helping her to become more heterosexually oriented.* Carson was completely open to her friends about her tremendous enjoyment in being physically close to attractive women. She was as frank and open about this aspect of her nature *as a child would be in choosing which toy he most wanted to play with*" (*Lonely Hunter*, 295, italics mine).

17. Warner, introduction to *Fear of a Queer Planet*, xxvi.

18. Freak shows were most popular in the United States between 1840 and 1940, when audiences from all walks of life paid to stare at the spectacle of human bodies on display at low-budget traveling shows, World's Fairs, and dime museums. The best historical accounts of freak shows are offered by Robert Bogdan, *Freak Show: Presenting Human Oddities for Amusement and Profit* (Chicago: Univ. of Chicago Press, 1988); the contributors to *Freakery: Cultural Spectacles of the Extraordinary Body*, ed. Rosemarie Garland Thomson (New York: New York Univ. Press, 1996); and Leslie Fiedler, *Freaks: Myths and Images of the Secret Self* (Simon and Schuster, 1978; reprint, New York: Anchor Books, 1993). For more theoretical interpretations of the freak, see Elizabeth Grosz, "Intolerable Ambiguity: Freaks as/at the Limit," in *Freakery*, ed. Thomson, 55–68; Mary Russo, *The Female Grotesque: Risk, Excess, and Modernity* (New York: Routledge, 1994); Rosemarie Garland Thomson, *Extraordinary Bodies: Figuring Physical Disability in American Culture* (New York: Columbia Univ. Press, 1997); and Susan Stewart, *On Longing: Narratives of the Miniature, the Gigantic, the Souvenir, the Collection* (Baltimore: Johns Hopkins Univ. Press, 1984). While Grosz and Russo read the freak within the context of feminist theory, Thomson also links freak shows to the history of disability in the United States. On freaks in the context of the dime museum and World's Fairs, see Andrea Stulman Dennett, *Weird and Wonderful: The Dime Museum in America* (New York: New York Univ. Press, 1997), and Robert Rydell, *All the World's a Fair: Visions of Excess at American International Expositions, 1876–1916* (Chicago: Univ. of Chicago Press, 1984). For a dazzling reading of the freak show as the "material unconscious" of Stephen Crane's *The Monster*, see Bill Brown, *The Material Unconscious: American Amusement, Stephen Crane, and the Economies of Play* (Cambridge: Harvard Univ. Press, 1996), 199–245.

19. Using a somewhat different vocabulary, Rubin wrote of McCullers's fiction, "[I]t isn't that freaks are commentaries or criticisms on normality; they *are* normality" ("Carson McCullers," 118).

20. Butler, *Bodies That Matter*, 229. Likewise, articulating the possibilities of a queer Asian American studies, David Eng remarks that "in its consistent elision of race as a conceptual category for analysis, mainstream gay and lesbian scholarship fails … to embrace queerness as a critical methodology for the understanding of sexual identity as it is dynamically formed through racial epistemes" ("Out Here and Over There: Queerness and Diaspora in Asian American Studies," *Social Text* 52/53 [fall–winter 1997]: 41–42). On the necessity of a more complex analysis of racial difference within queer theory, see Eve Kosofsky Sedgwick, "Queer and Now," *Tendencies* (Durham, N.C.: Duke Univ. Press, 1993), 1–20; Steven Seidman, "Deconstructing Queer Theory or the Under-Theorization of the Social and the Ethical," in *Social Postmodernism: Beyond Identity Politics*, ed. Linda Nicholson and Steven Seidman (New York: Cambridge Univ. Press, 1995), 116–41; and Warner, introduction to *Fear of a Queer Planet*). Rosemary Hennessey has noted the neglect of class-based analysis among queer critics ("Queer Visibility in Commodity Culture," in *Social Postmodernism*, ed. Nicholson and Seidman, 142–83).

21. This is the standard argument of feminist scholarship on McCullers, which concentrates on her female characters' resistance to feminine behaviors and expectations.

See, for example, Ellen Moers, *Literary Women* (New York: Doubleday, 1976); Louise Westling, *Sacred Groves and Ravaged Gardens: The Fiction of Eudora Welty, Carson McCullers, and Flannery O'Connor* (Athens: Univ. of Georgia Press, 1985); and Barbara A. White, "Loss of Self in *The Member of the Wedding*," in *Carson McCullers*, ed. Bloom, 125–42. The limitation of this argument is that by focusing exclusively on female characters it neglects the relations among men and between men and women in McCullers's fiction that put pressure on traditional gender categories in more radical ways.

22. This anxiety is shared by Frankie's counterpart Mick Kelly in McCullers's first novel, *The Heart Is a Lonely Hunter* (Boston: Houghton Mifflin, 1940; reprint, New York: Bantam, 1953). Page references are to the Bantam edition. Anticipating Frankie's tortured relationship to the freak show, Mick's friend Harry Minowitz attempts to quiet her doubts about her excessive growth with a less-than-comforting reassurance: "Once I saw a lady at the fair who was eight and a half feet tall. But you probably won't grow that big" (94).

23. Carson McCullers, *The Member of the Wedding* (Boston: Houghton Mifflin, 1946; reprint, New York: Bantam, 1969), 2. Subsequent references, cited parenthetically as *MW*, will be to the 1969 edition.

24. See Carr, *Lonely Hunter*, 169, 171, and 296 for examples of McCullers's theory of bisexuality as it was manifest in her own life.

25. This characteristic of McCullers's fiction prefigures recent theories that posit the transsexual body as a site where rigid distinctions between sexes and genders break down. See Judith Butler, *Gender Trouble: Feminism and the Subversion of Identity* (New York: Routledge, 1990); Marjorie Garber, *Vested Interests: Cross Dressing and Cultural Anxiety* (New York: Routlege, 1992); Grosz, *Intolerable Ambiguity*; and Sandy Stone, "The *Empire* Strikes Back: A Posttranssexual Manifesto," *Camera Obscura* 29 (May 1992): 151–78. These critics see the transsexual/transgendered body not as a freakish anomaly but as evidence that the sex-gender system is more open to variation and multiplicity than the polarized categories of male and female allow.

26. See D. A. Miller, *The Novel and the Police* (Berkeley and Los Angeles: Univ. of California Press, 1988), on the relationship between the "open secret" and the novelistic form. As Kenschaft rightly points out, "a reader who was unfamiliar with gay slang circa 1940 would miss certain implications of McCullers's texts, even though those texts could reasonably be read and interpreted without that knowledge" ("Homoerotics and Human Connections," 222).

27. Kenschaft acknowledges that "few of McCullers's characters are adequately described as homosexual: They are an adolescent girl falling in love with an engaged couple, an Amazonian woman infatuated with a bird-like man, a married man who never consummates the marriage but is entranced by his wife's desire for other men" ("Homoerotics and Human Connections," 226–27). As these examples attest, *lesbian* may be too specific a category to describe either the polymorphous desires of McCullers's characters or the unpredictable identifications of her readers.

28. In addition to these references to the "queer," see *MW* 2, 4, 22, 23, 27, 34, 85, 94, 116, 141.

29. Kenschaft, "Homoerotics and Human Connections," 228.

30. For oral histories documenting the experiences of gay men in the South during the Cold War/pre-Stonewall era, see Sears, *Lonely Hunters*.

31. Gayatri Spivak, "A Feminist Reading of Carson McCullers's *Heart Is a Lonely Hunter*," in *Critical Essays on Carson McCullers*, ed. Clark and Friedman, 136.

32. For analyses of the social function and reception of the *Kinsey Report* in postwar America see Chauncey, *Gay New York*; D'Emilio and Freeman, *Intimate Matters*; Lewes,

Psychoanalytic Theory of Male Homosexuality; Elaine Tyler May, *Homeward Bound*; and Barbara Ehrenreich, *The Hearts of Men: American Dreams and the Flight from Commitment* (New York: Anchor, 1983).

33. Recent studies of homosexuality during the Cold War period demonstrate a conflation of the demonized identities of the homosexual, the Communist, and the alien. See, for example, John D'Emilio, *Making Trouble: Essays on Gay History, Politics, and the University* (New York: Routledge, 1992); Robert Corber, *In the Name of National Security* and *Homosexuality in Cold War America*; Lee Edelman, "Tearooms and Sympathy; or, Epistemology of the Water Closet," *Homographesis: Essays in Gay Literary and Cultural Theory* (New York: Routledge, 1994).

34. Thadious M. Davis, "Erasing the 'We of Me' and Rewriting the Racial Script: Carson McCullers's Two *Member(s) of the Wedding*," in *Critical Essays on Carson McCullers*, ed. Clark and Friedman, 207.

35. On the representation of racial difference in freak shows, see Bogdan, *Freak Show*, and Thomson, *Freakery*.

36. Thadious M. Davis argues that Berenice's differently colored eyes offer "a sense of the unexpected in human nature" ("Erasing the 'We of Me,'" 208); however, the prosthetic eye also calls into question the very notion of "human nature," suggesting a more radical incentive to expand or explode the category.

37. Sherman's failed political protest must be contrasted with that of the Judge's savvy black housekeeper, Verily. Having endured the Judge's racism for years, she eventually demands that he make social security payments. When the Judge refuses, she quits her job to take a more legitimate and better-paying position, demonstrating an agency and political knowledge that Sherman does not possess. Sherman's rejection of his white acquaintances, as well as the black community of which Verily is an active part, makes him a freak who refuses all social categories. Verily's presence in the narrative indicates McCullers's awareness of important differences within racial communities as well as between them.

38. Robyn Wiegman, *American Anatomies: Theorizing Race and Gender* (Durham, N.C.: Duke Univ. Press, 1995), 82.

39. For a similarly affirmative reading of community in the café scenes in *The Heart Is a Lonely Hunter* and *Ballad of the Sad Café*, see Kenschaft, "Homoerotics and Human Connections," 230–31.

40. Westling, *Sacred Groves and Ravaged Gardens*, 127.

41. See also Horvath and Logan, who read the stage version of *Member of the Wedding* as a story of Frankie's normalization, which, they argue, is an allegory for the conformity of postwar American culture ("Nobody Knows Best").

CYNTHIA WU

Expanding Southern Whiteness:
Reconceptualizing Ethnic Difference
in the Short Fiction of Carson McCullers

In Carson McCullers' 1936 collection of short stories, *The Ballad of the Sad Café and Other Stories*, issues of ethnic difference, white racialization, and the negotiation of identities play a central role. This is not surprising, considering that the loosely imagined body of texts known as "the Southern Renaissance" has a strong preoccupation with these themes. Southern writers, both Anglo- and African American, have long foregrounded the "race question" in representing and imagining the New South following the Civil War, and McCullers is no exception. Her characters grapple with what it means to be white in the South, what it means *not* to be white, and what it means to challenge or comply with the standards of whiteness. However, what differentiates *The Ballad of the Sad Café and Other Stories* from most other pieces of southern literature is the relative absence of African American characters. If, as many theorists of race in the United States have pointed out, notions of "black" and notions of "white" are mutually constitutive and exist in a hierarchical binary, can whiteness ever be reconceptualized in a way that does not define it against and above blackness? In other words, can "white" exist apart from "black"?

I argue that McCullers attempts to answer "yes" to such questions by introducing European immigrant characters into southern fiction. This gesture interrogates white southern identity through means other than

From *The Southern Literary Journal* 34, no. 1 (Fall 2001): pp. 44–55. © 2001 by the Department of English of the University of North Carolina at Chapel Hill.

comparisons to black southern identity. It is important to note that the absence of African American characters in this collection of stories is not an oversight that resulted from presenting some new form of ethnic difference. Rather, this absence is functional. It serves to isolate and explore in some depth a new valance of race emerging in the New South without having to revert to the well-trodden path of imagining racialization within the black–white binary.

McCullers' conceptual replacement of the African American with the European immigrant in her examination of racial and ethnic difference has its counterpart in southern labor history. During the late-nineteenth and early-twentieth centuries, many southern states launched campaigns to attract European immigrants in response to the labor shortages caused by black migration to the West and Southwest immediately after the Civil War and to the North during the Great Migration. For a South struggling to rebuild itself both economically and ideologically, European immigrant labor seemed a viable and even more favorable replacement for black labor.

An avid recruiter of European immigrant labor in the years immediately following the Civil War, Richard Hathaway Edmonds founded a white-supremacist newsletter called the *Manufacturers' Record* to provide coverage on southern industry and capitalism. Edmonds launched the aggressive campaign to recruit laborers from Europe as a way to compensate for the declining black laborer population in the South. However, he intended for only immigrants of Anglo- and northern European stock to fulfill his goals. By the 1880s, the wave of immigrants from these areas gave way to those from eastern and southern Europe. This new influx of immigrants, Edmonds believed, did not assimilate properly and threatened the Anglo-European racial integrity of the South. By the 1920s, the *Manufacturers' Record* reversed its stance toward immigration, embracing nativist sentiments along with the rest of the United States and becoming one of the most vocal anti-immigrant publications.

Even if the South's desire for white immigrant labor had not been conflicted from the start, the region's attractiveness to European newcomers paled in comparison to that of the North. Southern historian Martha G. Synott argues that the South's attempt to lure and retain immigrants was doomed from the beginning because it lacked the high wages and inexpensive land that could be found in the North. And from the point of view of the employers, southern landowners were more willing to exploit black labor because of their impression that Jim Crow laws regulated the autonomy of blacks, making them more docile and reliable than immigrants. Moreover, the European immigrants were seen as being both lax about racial segregation and racially different in themselves. This impression only caused more problems for a South that still held on to ideals of maintaining Anglo-American supremacy.

This contentious dynamic between black labor and European immigrant labor was not isolated to the South nor was it new to the post–Civil War period. The northern economies and the southern economies were interdependent; labor and economic developments in the North had a bearing on the South and vice versa. The already sizable European immigrant presence in the northern states by the end of the nineteenth century affected the demographics of the laborer population in the southern states. Two separate articles by historian Jay R. Mandle, who takes a qualitative approach, and economist William J. Collins, who relies on empirical data, assert that European immigration to the North discouraged the entry of southern blacks and delayed the Great Migration. Historian Noel Ignatiev claims that during the nineteenth century, capitalism pitted the economic interests of Irish immigrants against those of slaves and free blacks. This maneuver, which met the North's labor demands, prolonged slavery in the South and the economic exploitation of free blacks on a national scale.

Both the conceptual and actual replacement of the black southerner with the European immigrant in the economy of the South finds its literary analog in McCullers' short fiction. Just as the one could not easily be replaced by the other in the southern economy without reaping certain ideological repercussions, this substitution in McCullers' literature creates a similar shockwave in the fabric of southern whiteness. Whereas African American characters had traditionally performed the function—or, the labor—of signifying ethno-racial difference in white southern literature, McCullers replaces them with European immigrants who perform the same task, albeit with different results. As I mentioned earlier, the absence of African American characters in this collection of McCullers' short fiction does not result from neglect: as she demonstrates in other texts, McCullers creates complex African American characters and interrogates the black–white racial divide in intricate ways. *The Member of the Wedding* (1946) is one example, and *The Heart Is a Lonely Hunter* (1940) contains both African American and European immigrant characters. However, at this stage of the Southern Renaissance, the absence of African Americans characters in *The Ballad of the Sad Café and Other Stories* is an enabling device. It becomes a strategic way of isolating white ethnic difference in reconceptualizing white identities in the New South.

In Andre Schwarz-Bart's novel, *The Last of the Just*, Ernie Levy, who dies in a concentration camp at the novel's end, is one of thirty-six "just men." The just men are martyrs in Jewish mythology who are chosen to shoulder one thirty-sixth of the world's suffering each. Whenever a just man dies, another receives a calling to take his place; this paralineal descent continues, according to Schwarz-Bart, until the cataclysmic event of the Holocaust. The calling to become a just man is always received with ambivalence: it is at the same time both good and bad news, burden and honor.

I use this legend of the thirty-six just men as a metaphor for the ambivalence with which Jews occupy the category "white."[1] In the two stories that I consider below, "The Ballad of the Sad Café" and "Wunderkind," Jewish men waver from effeminate caricature to wielder of white patriarchy, both burdened and honored by discursive whiteness. Their inability to be pinned down and fully inscribed challenges whiteness from within and reconceptualizes racialization apart from the black–white template.

McCullers makes an oblique suggestion to the possibility of a racially integrated black–white community at the end of "The Ballad of the Sad Café." The "twelve mortal men," the singing chain gang consisting of seven black men and five white men, appear in the final scene of the novella as a somewhat utopian community against which the fractured semblance of community in the small, all-white town is unfavorably compared. This gesture towards "settling" the problem of black–white racial discord, however contrived or unrealistic, opens up uncluttered space for the exploration of ethnic differences among whites. Indeed, it is at the beginning of "The Ballad of the Sad Café" that the European immigrant makes his tentative entrance, not as an actual character but as a reference in a minor character's speech.

In an early scene, a hunchbacked stranger who later becomes known as Cousin Lymon has just arrived at the Café that Miss Amelia owns. In his attempt to verify a distant kinship with Miss Amelia, he becomes frustrated and begins to cry. One of the observers notes of his behavior, "I'll be damned if he ain't a regular Morris Finestein" (9). The narrative goes on to explain, "Morris Finestein was a person who had lived in the town years before. He was only a quick, skipping little Jew who cried if you called him a Christ-killer, and ate light bread and canned salmon every day. A calamity had come over him and he moved away to Society City. But since then, if a man were prissy in any way, or if a man ever wept, he was known as a Morris Finestein" (9). Another observer agrees about the condition of the hunchback and his similarity to the former Jewish resident of the town: "Well, he is afflicted . . . There is some cause" (9). In this description of Cousin Lymon comparing him to Morris Finestein, there is the understanding that the town regarded Finestein as an outsider. Similar to Cousin Lymon's past, Finestein's origins are mysterious. Finestein's initial arrival in the small town had been most likely regarded with some curiosity, given the way the town had received Cousin Lymon, and his departure to a more urbanized area to escape the taunting of his provincial neighbors was probably noted with equal, if not more, excitement. The outsider status that Finestein carries makes him susceptible to an intense scrutiny of his actions and mannerisms.

For example, Finestein's tendency to cry becomes associated with his personhood. What might be a perfectly reasonable response to being ostracized by his neighbors becomes an "affliction" by which he is defined. In addition, this affliction, his crying, is feminized by the townspeople. This welding of effeminacy with what is Jewish—or, in other words, "foreign"—becomes clear when the narrator states that if any other man exhibited this "prissy" behavior, he would then be labeled a "Morris Finestein." The feminization of the Jew has its roots in Nazi-related anti-Semitism which believed that, among other things, Jewish men could menstruate, and it stems from the Jewish body's subjugation under various patriarchal medical and scientific treatises that labeled it deviant and inferior. As Sander Gilman notes, "the very analysis of the nature of the Jewish body, in the broader culture or within the culture of medicine has always been linked to establishing the difference (and dangerousness) of the Jew" (39). Furthermore, "it seems to be impossible to speak of the idea of difference, such as the difference of the Jew, without evoking this sense of the constructed difference of the body" (242). The reductions of the Jew to his body—its feminization—functions in the same way women have been relegated to their corporeality.

Given these factors, the name "Morris Finestein" bestowed on Cousin Lymon is especially apt, since science and medicine have similarly created and inscribed people with disabilities, reducing them to their bodies. Defined as genetically inferior by the totalizing discourses of medicine, the feminization of the disabled based on physiognomic difference can even be discerned in the rhetoric of the ancient Greeks. In his *Generation of Animals*, Aristotle describes the female body as a deformed or mutilated male body, conflating femininity with physical aberrance. These similarly constructed categories of deviance that inscribe the Jew and the disabled become a way of marking difference, ethnic or otherwise, through means that do not take into account the black–white racial binary that, at least in this story, has been dissolved in a harmonious chorus of song.

Departing from this description of a meek and feminized—or even debilitated—Jewish man, McCullers develops Jewish masculinity in another direction in "Wunderkind," the story following "The Ballad of the Sad Café" in the collection. In this narrative about the relationship between a fifteen-year-old pianist and her music instructors, Frances is a former child prodigy who begins to question her flagging talents at the piano. Her instructor, Mr. Bilderbach, and his associate, Mr. Lafkowitz, seem benign and patient with her, but it becomes increasingly clear that they are, at least in part, responsible for Frances's musical frustration. Alice Hall Petry argues that Frances is plagued by the undercurrent of sexual energy running between her and her music instructors, and that her ambivalence about continuing to be a musician stems not from her conception of herself as a failed pianist but from the subtly threatening, erotically-tinged relationship that her instructors have encouraged. Mr. Bilderbach is a loving, generous father figure to Frances; however, the relationship that both he and Mr. Lafkowitz have developed with Frances is questionably intimate. As a budding adolescent unable to confront the power differential between herself and the older men who are her teachers, Frances becomes flustered and disillusioned with music, eventually giving it up at the end of the story.

Petry's claims, however, gloss over the fact that Frances's instructors are German-speaking immigrants. She does acknowledge Frances's fascination with the aura of foreignness surrounding her teachers when she writes that Frances "long[s] to deny the American name and identity derived from her biological father (who is given the American generic name of 'dad')" and that she "would much prefer a background like that of her surrogate father, the Dutch-Czech, German-bred Bilderbach" (32), but she drops the implications of this dynamic in her discussion of the erotic overtures that play in the background. I am convinced, however, that Frances's perception of her instructors' cosmopolitanism is an integral part of the sexually charged relationship she finds herself maintaining with them. Although I realize that this is not part of Petry's project, the importance of what it means for a U.S.-born white woman to be fascinated by European foreignness and cowed by the erotic overtures initiated by immigrant men is lost in her article. Had Frances's instructors been Anglo-Americans, "Wunderkind" would be a very different story.

Compared to Bilderbach's cosmopolitanism, Frances's own Cincinnati upbringing seems disappointingly banal.[2] Then there is Frances's envy of the violinist with the Germanic name, Heime Israelsky, who is three years her junior. Looking at his picture in a music journal, Frances notes with some disdain that the knickers-clad Heime still has his child-like looks, an asset for young classical musicians. Unlike Frances, he has moved beyond the status of local talent, having performed in Carnegie Hall. For a brief moment, Frances allows herself to consider the possibility that his reception and his success have something to do with his being Jewish before dismissing the idea, but not altogether.

This somewhat petty and immature jealousy that Frances feels for the child Heime gives way to her feelings of intimidation by Mr. Bilderbach and Mr. Lafkowitz. McCullers' decision to place these two characters in a position of authority over the native-born white woman complicates the fact that had Mr. Bliderbach and Mr. Lafkowitz appeared in the previous story, "The Ballad of the Sad Café," they would have been the recipients of abuse from their fellow characters. At first, Mr. Lafkowitz is described in a way that would not immediately label him as threatening. "He was such a small man himself, with a weary look when he was not holding his violin.

His eyebrows curved high above his sallow, Jewish face as though asking a question, but the lids of his eyes drowsed languorous and indifferent" (76). Although the patriarchal power that Mr. Lafkowitz wields is veiled behind his gentle demeanor and his "voice almost like a woman's" (75), this nod to the Jewish effeminacy that was foregrounded in the portrayal of Morris Finestein gives way to Mr. Lafkowitz's lecherous suggestions to Frances that her interpretation of Bach lacks emotion. He stops her playing by asking, "Do you know how many children Bach had?" Frances responds, "A good many. Twenty some odd." This sets Frances up for Mr. Lafkowitz's punch line: "'Well then—' The corners of his mouth etched themselves gently in his pale face. 'He could not have been so cold—then'" (83).

Likewise, Mr. Bilderbach's ways of connecting with Frances seem inappropriately sexualized. Despite the fact that he reproaches Mr. Lafkowitz for his remark about Frances's performance, Mr. Bilderbach's paternalistic relationship with Frances similarly signals the presence of an erotically-charged domination. Petry points out that it seems questionable that a fifteen-year-old girl would spend the night at her teacher's house following her lesson and that a teacher would have a dress custom made for his student. She notes that "Bilderbach's most casual remarks often sound like a man speaking to his mistress" (34) and that his seemingly reassuring words to Frances when she cannot perform, "a teacher trying to soothe his student," seem more akin to those of a "lover trying to console his mistress for a lack of sexual responsiveness" (35). Furthermore, the sexual relationship implied here is not an egalitarian one, for it reeks of the possessiveness that Mr. Bilderbach reveals in his claim to Frances that "I know you so well—as if you were my own girl" (88).

These wavering representations of the Jewish man indicate the extent to which white racialization is destabilized by the introduction of the European immigrant. He is, on the one hand, caricatured in "The Ballad of the Sad Café" as the "quick, skipping little Jew," a feminized victim. But—when given voice and phallic power in "Wunderkind"—he is transformed into a victimizer, figure of authority, and pedagogue, who abuses his status by inflicting patriarchal violence onto his young student. This examination of ethnic difference from within the category of whiteness demonstrates that even within the purportedly strict and confining definitions of "white," there must be a tendency for those definitions to shift and expand. He is both self and other, not white (or powerful) enough and powerfully white, both object and perpetrator of subjugation for those whose notions of whiteness are challenged by his presence.

Another European immigrant, also a music teacher, is the subject of "Madame Zilensky and the King of Finland." In this text, the protagonist is Mr. Brook, the chair of the music department at Ryder College. He has successfully recruited Madame Zilensky, a very well respected teacher and composer from Finland, to join his department. In addition to making her feel welcome professionally, Mr. Brook takes it upon himself to develop a more intimate, non-professional relationship with Madame Zilensky, doing such personal favors as finding her a house next to his own and offering to replace her lost metronome. This foray into her personal affairs leads him to inquire about her children and her past.

Mr. Brook is undecided about where Madame Zilensky stands in his perception of her. She is an imposing presence, commanding respect from both students and colleagues. Despite being a foreigner, her Nordic stock would have made her an ideal immigrant for the likes of Richard Hathaway Edmonds and the readers of the *Manufacturers' Record*. McCullers describes her as having "something that was noble and abstract that made Mr. Brook draw back a moment and stand nervously undoing his cuff links" (104). At the same time, her eccentricities start to weigh increasingly on Mr. Brook, who has made some investment in understanding her not merely on a collegial but also on a personal level. At first, he attributes her absent-minded, off-hand comments as being the effects of "the confusion of getting herself and her family out of Europe" (103). Eventually, his initial awe and captivation with his newest colleague disintegrates following a series of startling revelations about her personal history, and he resolves to develop a paternalism in his interactions with her, "look[ing] on Madame Zilensky as a doctor looks on a sick patient" (109).

Exactly what Mr. Brook is trying to "cure" in Madame Zilensky is unclear. He begins to feel troubled about her presence after she reveals to him that three different men fathered her three sons. Adding to the allure of internationalism that she already carries, all of these men were of a different national origin. The narrator states, "Mr. Brook really did not care one way or the other. He had no prejudices; people could marry seventeen times and have Chinese children so far as he was concerned" (107). Although Mr. Brook's nod towards progressive ideals of heterosexuality is broached in the above passage, addressing such issues as serial monogamy and miscegenation,[3] his discomfort with what he sees as Madame Zilensky's sexual impropriety becomes evident immediately afterwards. He wonders whether having Madame Zilensky on the faculty will result in him being similarly embarrassed as in an incident last year when the harp teacher eloped with a garage mechanic.

It is interesting—especially in a work of southern fiction published the same year as *Absalom, Absalom!*—that a union across class lines is more worrisome than one that crosses the racial divide. The turn McCullers chooses to make here shifts the panic from miscegenation onto what become the more pressing concerns of inappropriately marrying within one's own race by "marrying down." There is, however, no indication that any of Madame Zilensky's former partners were from a different class background, and there is even some indication of class parity in that at least one of them was also a musician. Mr. Brook's conflation of downward class mobility with Madame Zilensky's refusal to heed traditional standards of white feminine propriety by marrying only once and staying married is not arbitrary but, in fact, reveals deep-seated concerns about the continuing importance of lineage to proper white families. Even if the threat of miscegenation is not an issue here or has, at least, receded into the background, the emphasis remains on keeping the vessel of a family's descendants, the white woman, intact and uncontaminated. As a well-respected white woman who has not heeded the standards of the society in which she has made her new home, Madame Zilensky disturbs Mr. Brook who, despite his claim to having no prejudices, cannot reconcile his professional admiration for her with his disapproval of her sexual history.

In order to compensate for his sense of dissonance, Mr. Brook draws the conclusion that Madame Zilensky "was a pathological liar. Almost every word she said outside of class was an untruth. . . . The woman was simply a pathological liar, and that accounted for everything" (109). He begins to preoccupy himself with finding details that could indicate the discrepancies between what Madame Zilensky says about herself and what actually might have happened. Mr. Brook ferrets out and clings to small particulars to support his conviction, such as his observation that all of Madame Zilensky's children look alike despite having different fathers. He distrusts the stories she tells about her well-traveled past. "She was a great globe-trotter, and her conversations were incongruously seasoned with references to far-fetched places. . . . Yet, without exception, there was something queer, in a slanted sort of way, about every episode she mentioned. If she spoke of taking Sammy to the barbershop, the impression she created was just as foreign as if she were telling of an afternoon in Bagdad" (107–108). He eventually makes the diagnosis that Madame Zilensky's compulsion to lie stems from her insular lifestyle as a hard-working and prolific musician, and "through the lies, she lived vicariously. The lies doubled the little of her existence that was left over from work and augmented the little rag end of her personal life" (109).

It is through his perception of Madame Zilensky's need to concoct falsehoods about herself that Mr. Brook reveals the most about himself and his tendency to project his own anxieties onto the figure of the improperly raced white woman. The story's ending instills some doubt in Mr. Brook's ability to trust his own judgment and senses when, to his astonishment, he sees a dog running backwards. He "watched the Airedale until it was out of sight, then resumed his work on the canons which had been turned in by the class in counterpoint" (112). Also weighed down by his work as a musician, he tells lies to himself as a way of living vicariously, producing the type of discourse he deems ideal through the fictions that may be more comforting than any type of truth, however mediated. Through this maneuver, he is able to quell the sense of dissonance created by the white woman whose essence he cannot pin down, who generates both reverence and shock, and he resolves his internal conflict concerning Madame Zilensky through projecting it onto her. If he feels a type of inferiority concerning the stories about her expansive and worldly past, he settles it by attributing it to her tendency to lie resulting from her actual constriction and immobility. Ultimately, it is Mr. Brook who is left in his office over a stack of student assignments, insecure about his provincialism. And in this cloistered state, he fabricates a safe, internal world that reconciles his contradictions.

The contradictions surrounding the presence of European immigrants in McCullers' short fiction force whiteness to face its own contradictions and the lies that it tells itself in order to remain uncontested. But, as Mr. Brook's situation reveals, these lies—which project whiteness's own anxieties onto others—eventually implode under the pressure generated by itself and its own insularity. The eastern European Jewish men in "The Ballad of the Sad Café" and "Wunderkind" do not occupy a comfortable space in whiteness or in patriarchy. The Nordic woman in "Madame Zilensky and the King of Finland" likewise challenges the South's ideals of white sexual propriety. No longer can "white" be a monolithic term, and neither can it remain the unquestioned given. This expansion of the label "white" in McCullers' collection of stories denaturalizes whiteness and provides a more nuanced understanding of racial position. By introducing the possibility of ethnic difference among whites, McCullers opens up new space for conceptualizing race.

Notes

1. Sander Gilman addresses the complexities between the state of being white, the state of being Jewish, and the (in)ability within the category of "white" to fully encompass the category of "Jewish." He points toward the history of Jews having been perceived as being racially inferior and, thus, black in the scientific literature of the nineteenth century as a way to complicate the present day understanding of Jews being white.

2. It is interesting to consider the implications of setting "Wunderkind" in Cincinnati. Originally, my article was to have incorporated McCullers' "The Sojourner" and "A Domestic Dilemma" in addressing southern white migration to the North in conjunction with European immigration to the South. Connections can be made between the rhetorics of assimilation and adjustment in both international emigration and northward migration. Also, the question of what constitutes "southern literature" is a possible topic for exploration here. Is it literature written about the South? Is it literature written by southerners? Who is a southerner? Did McCullers cease being a southern writer when she migrated to the

North? Do these very questions indicate a de-regionalization of southern literature? Such questions, though provoking, are beyond my scope here.

     3. It is difficult to determine whether or not "Chinese" in the above passage is interchangeable with "black," a fact that complicates Mr. Brook's seemingly progressive stance on interracial unions. Certainly, there were anti-miscegenation laws that prohibited marriages between Mongols and Caucasians, just as there were laws against marriages between blacks and Caucasians. However, there was some ambivalence as to how biracial Chinese–white offspring should be raced. The "one-drop rule" that applied to the classification of biracial black–white people did not always apply to biracial Chinese–white people. The children of Chinese men and white women were sometimes considered Chinese, sometimes white. The child of a Chinese father and a black mother was designated a "mulatto" in much the same way that a child of a white father and black mother would have been classified. For a fuller discussion, see Cohen.

Works Cited

Cohen, Lucy. *Chinese in the Post–Civil War South: A People Without History*. Baton Rouge: Louisiana University Press, 1984.

Collins, William J. "When the Tide Turned: Immigration and the Delay of the Black Migration." *Journal of Economic History* 57.3 (1997): 607–632.

Gilman, Sander. *The Jew's Body*. New York: Routledge, 1991.

Ignatiev, Noel. *How the Irish Became White*. New York: Routledge, 1991.

Mandle, Jay R. "The Plantation Economy Mode of Production in the Postbellum South." *Plantation Society in the Americas* 2.3 (1989): 279–294.

McCullers, Carson. *The Ballad of the Sad Café and Other Stories*. 1936. New York: Bantam, 1971.

Petry, Alice Hall. "Carson McCullers's Precocious 'Wunderkind.'" *Southern Quarterly* 26.3 (Spring 1988): 31–39.

Silverman, Jason H. "The 'Divided Mind of the New South' Revisited: Richard Hathaway Edmonds, *The Manufacturers' Record*, and the Immigrant." *Southern Studies* 26.1 (1987): 41–51.

Synott, Martha G. "Replacing 'Sambo': Could White Immigrants Solve the Labor Problem in the Carolinas?" *Proceedings of the South Carolina Historical Association* (1982): 77–89.

SARAH GLEESON-WHITE

Revisiting the Southern Grotesque: Mikhail Bakhtin and the Case of Carson McCullers

"Any form of art can only develop by means of single mutations by individual creators. If only traditional conventions are used an art will die, and the widening of an art form is bound to seem strange at first, and awkward. Any growing thing must go through awkward stages. The creator who is misunderstood because of his breach of convention may say to himself, 'I seem strange to you, but anyway I am alive.'"

—Carson McCullers, "The Vision Shared"

Writers of the "southern grotesque" or "southern gothic"[1]—for example, Eudora Welty, William Faulkner, Carson McCullers, Truman Capote, and Flannery O'Connor—conjure up the strange worlds of freakish outsiders placed in lovelorn barren landscapes, penetrating heat, and closed spaces, with themes of miscegenation, sexual deviance and bloody violence. Perhaps not surprisingly, critical readers have, on the whole, concurred that the southern grotesque aligns itself with a gloomy vision of modernity, according to which the soul of man is both aimless and loveless. The grotesque worlds of southern literature, it is argued, allegorize the human condition itself as existential alienation and angst.

In my view, however, these accounts of the southern grotesque do not tally with the type of art which McCullers describes in the prefatory quotation above, as well as in other essays (for example, "The Russian Realists

From *Southern Literary Journal* 33, no. 2 (Spring 2001): pp. 108–23. © 2001 by the University of North Carolina Press.

and Southern Literature" and "The Flowering Dream: Notes on Writing")
and the fiction itself. McCullers, like O'Connor in "Some Aspects of the
Grotesque in Southern Fiction," accentuates the vitality of the grotesque
vision. Without wanting to dismiss the real pain that is so often at the
heart of the southern grotesque, including McCullers' writings, I want to
suggest that the grotesque is not limited to an alienating modernity. Rather,
it is to do with the affirming qualities and practices of growth, promise and
transformation.

What I am advocating, then, is a crucial need to revisit the grotesque.
In doing so in this essay, I note different theories of the grotesque, and
find Mikhail Bakhtin's conceptualization of it the most fruitful not
only for describing the dynamics of McCullers' grotesque subjects,
but also for promising a radically new construction of how we read the
southern grotesque.[2] I then perform a reading of McCullers' novels of
adolescence—*The Heart Is a Lonely Hunter* (1940) and *The Member of the
Wedding* (1946)—as an example of how we might reframe what I suggest
are limited readings of the southern grotesque. Julia Kristeva first brought
Bakhtin to the attention of western scholars with her 1969 essay, "Word,
Dialogue and Novel." With the translation into English of *Rabelais and His
World* in 1968, and *The Dialogic Imagination* and *Problems of Dostoevsky's
Poetics* in the early 1980s, Bakhtin became a key name in literary studies,
particularly in response to his theory of the novel. *Rabelais and His World*,
Bakhtin's reading of *Gargantua* and *Pantagruel*, contains a revolutionary
conceptualization of the grotesque that I suggest can free not just
McCullers' fiction but much southern writing from the almost paralyzing
burden of more traditional accounts of the grotesque, to celebrate, instead,
McCullers' pronouncement, "but anyway I am alive."

As I have noted, most readers of the southern grotesque submit that
it allegorizes a kind of existential anguish. William Van O'Connor accounts
for the grotesque in southern writing as a response to a world of violence
and upheaval; Joseph Millichap makes a connection between the grotesque
and a dark modernism; and Leslie Fiedler, in *Love and Death in the American
Novel* (1960), links the grotesque with terror and violence. More specifically,
McCullers' worlds are said to represent alienation, loneliness, a lack of human
communication, and the failure of love.[3] Although there is no denying the
validity of these constructions of the southern grotesque, I do not think
they tell the full story. The grotesque can also offer greater possibilities
for representation and knowledge, and McCullers' own definition of the
grotesque is dynamic in its emphasis on creative tension: "The technique
is briefly this: a bold and outwardly callous juxtaposition of the tragic with
the humorous, the immense with the trivial, the sacred with the bawdy, the
whole soul of a man with a materialistic detail" ("Russian Realists" 258).

No critics theorize in any way the category "grotesque," merely equating it with the gothic and the strange. Alan Spiegel's much overlooked 1972 article, "A Theory of the Grotesque in Southern Fiction," is the exception. Spiegel convincingly argues that "the grotesque, as it appears in Southern fiction, refers neither to the particular quality of a story . . . nor to its mood . . . nor to its mode of expression. . . . The grotesque refers rather to a *type of character*," defined by either physical or mental deformity (428). "Deformed" characters are of course ubiquitous in southern fiction: Faulkner's mute, Benjy (*The Sound and the Fury* [1929]); McCullers' "brokeback," Cousin Lymon (*The Ballad of the Sad Café* [1951]); O'Connor's cripple, Hulga Hopewell ("Good Country People," *A Good Man Is Hard to Find* [1955]); and Capote's transvestite, Randolph (*Other Voices, Other Rooms* [1948]). It is this collection of outsiders—whose "difference" spectacularly appears on the body—that invites the classification of much southern literature as grotesque.

Bakhtin's construction of the grotesque likewise emphasizes corporeality, more specifically, corporeal contortion. In Bakhtin's account, the body is a body of excess, and so it queries borders and neat categories. Perhaps most importantly, it is a body in flux, in a constant process of reformation and reemergence: it is becoming. Strictly opposed to the aesthetics of the grotesque is the classic body and its accompanying poetics of closure, coherence, and stasis. The grotesque, then, by its very nature, unnerves the world of classic identity and knowledge, for it tests the very limits of the body and thus of being. Crucially, Bakhtin celebrates this strange body, for it is a site of production: "the grotesque . . . discloses the potentiality of an entirely different world, of another order, another way of life" (*Rabelais* 48). This is the invigorating aspect of the Bakhtinian grotesque: it is transgressive because it challenges normative forms of representation and behavior; it disturbs because it loves the abject and will not rest; it is always in a state of becoming. The carnivalesque grotesque, then, is a strategy of resistance.

Because the grotesque that Bakhtin celebrates is a positive mode of ontological representation, it sharply contrasts with not only traditional responses to the southern grotesque, but also with earlier aesthetic theories of the grotesque more broadly. For example, in Wolfgang Kayser's *The Grotesque in Art and Literature* (1957), there is, Bakhtin writes, "no room for the material bodily principle with its exhaustive wealth and perpetual renewal" (*Rabelais* 48). Connected with this is that, for Kayser, the grotesque portrays a world of violence and fear, alienation and despair, a world in which all that is familiar becomes hostile (reminiscent of Freud's uncanny). Unlike Bakhtin, who draws on the folk humor and carnival of the Middle Ages, Kayser draws on Romantic and modernist angst for his theory of the grotesque, just as do readers of much southern literature. In sum, this more conventional form of the grotesque "expresses not the fear of death but the fear of life" (Bakhtin, *Rabelais* 50).

The grotesque as it appears in McCullers' texts has much in common with Bakhtin's account, an account that illuminates both the oddness of embodiment, as well as resistance. McCullers shares Bakhtin's preoccupation with the body, in her ubiquitous descriptions of disease and death, deformity and disability, strange physical desires, and even stranger gender configurations. Both McCullers and Bakhtin endured severe physical disability and pain throughout their lives. While osteomyelitis plagued Bakhtin, leading to the amputation of his right leg, McCullers suffered a series of strokes that in 1947 left her paralyzed down one side of her body, until the final massive stroke that ended her life twenty years later. Virginia Spencer Carr, in her biography of "the lonely hunter," claims that McCullers also suffered psychosomatic hysterical symptoms. It is perhaps not surprising, then, that the body features so strongly in both writers' works; they experienced first-hand the immediacy of embodiment, both its limitations and its strange possibilities.

McCullers' novels, plays, and short stories, like Sherwood Anderson's *Winesburg, Ohio*, present us with physically freakish characters—giants, dwarfs, mutes, androgynes, and so on—reflecting her own self-styled freakishness and the exploration of gender and sexual identity that she carried out in her own life: she considered herself an "invert" and felt she was "born a man" (Carr, *Lonely Hunter* 167, 159).[4] It is her perhaps least obviously "deformed" characters on whom I want to focus as grotesque figures of resistance: the tomboys, Mick Kelly (*The Heart Is a Lonely Hunter*) and Frankie Addams (*The Member of the Wedding*). McCullers' young girls are particularly amenable to an exploration of the grotesque since historically women have been perceived as freakish lesser men—Adam's rib—and their bodies culturally represented as abjected and amorphous. The female adolescent is perhaps even more grotesque than her adult counterpart for not only is she female, but also she is in that liminal state between childhood and adulthood and, in the case of Mick and Frankie, between masculine and feminine gender identification. The fact that the girls are on the threshold and so "unfixed," means that they promise new configurations of human being in terms of becoming, and so resist the strictures of limits. And this resistance, I would argue, is only underscored in the context of McCullers' South, in which modes of behavior—particularly gender and racial roles— were so narrowly circumscribed and against which McCullers sets up tropes of freakishness, gigantism, and flight to describe recalcitrant adolescence.

Early readers of McCullers' adolescent girls position Mick and Frankie with their male literary counterparts—such as Huck Finn and Holden Caulfield—as "sensitive youths," gender-neutral exemplars of the universal experience of initiation into adulthood and of the modern hero as rebel-victim.[5] Yet, once McCullers' adolescent girls stopped being read as Everymen, they became somehow "freakish" in their apparent reluctance to submit to the ideal of womanhood.[6] And in the 1970s, feminist accounts of McCullers' novels began to explore female adolescence as a category in need of its own terms of description and experience and to highlight the specific constraints of entering womanhood in southern society.[7] Louise Westling and Barbara White, for example, concluded that Mick and Frankie's story is the story of "female limits." However, I want to suggest that McCullers' portraits of grotesque adolescence challenge the very notion of female limits. A new account of the grotesque reveals that female adolescence might, rather, embody the possibility of endless metamorphosis; that is to say, the promise of childhood need not die out with Mick and Frankie's entry into adulthood.

While Westling and White tackled the category of the grotesque in terms of a fraught female identity in McCullers' novels, Mab Segrest, discussing southern writing more broadly, contends that the grotesque is dangerously entangled with both racism and patriarchy in the South: "Both patriarchy and racism depend on creating a category of the Other—or freak, not 'normal like me.' In southern racism, it is the black person; in patriarchy, the female" (27). Similarly wary of the risks of the grotesque, Karen Sosnoski and Ann Carlton have sought to reject the term altogether in their respective accounts of McCullers' women.

All these responses have something valid to add to the body of McCullers criticism, not least of all their observations on the felt "freakishness" of the adolescent, particularly female, experience. However, there are also problems, or oversights, contained within them. By concentrating on "female limits," these responses overlook both the very creative challenge the girls provide to normative identity politics and the powerful literary tropes that *The Heart Is a Lonely Hunter* and *The Member of the Wedding* employ to suggest this challenge. As I have already noted, because the young tomboys are liminal, they embody a kind of dynamism and active potential. It is for this reason that adolescents in general bear the weighty burden of the investment society as a whole places in them: they embody the new generation, the future as hope and possibility. It is this configuration of adolescence—as plastic—that grotesque representation can so well accent, and thus highlight the extremely subversive nature of McCullers' creative project. Her novels of resistance present us with unsettled identities and so push the very boundaries of how we understand human being. And they do so by employing the expansive tropes of freakishness and flight, set against the background of a debilitating ideal femininity, that is, "Dixie's Diadem" (Jones), the southern belle.

The image of the southern belle and lady ruled all notions of white southern womanhood and femininity, even in the postbellum New South, although such an ideal became more and more transparent with the changing status of women in the 1940s and 1950s. In *The Member of the Wedding*, the "southern lady" is imaged in the neighborhood club members, whom Frankie watches from the kitchen window "passing slowly before the arbor. The long gold sun slanted down on them and made their skin look golden also, and they were dressed in clean, fresh dresses" (38). Janice, Frankie's brother's fiancée, who is "small and pretty" (38), provides another example of gracious femininity for Frankie to ideally emulate. For Mick Kelly, it is her girlish older sister who provides the role-model. Etta "primps" and thinks about movie stars while practicing her chin exercises before the mirror (*Heart* 40–41). A more parodic image of this southern debutante is Biff Brannon's four-year-old niece, Baby Wilson, who, like Truman Capote's Miss Bobbitt in "Children on Their Birthdays" (*A Tree of Night and Other Stories* [1950]), is hideous in her femininity. Baby wears "a little white dress with white shoes and white socks and even small white gloves" (114), or a little pink tutu so that with "her yellow hair she was all pink and white and gold—and so small and clean that it almost hurt to watch her" (146–147).

What comes out so powerfully in McCullers' descriptions of ideal femininity is the dual emphasis on cleanliness and smallness, suggesting that the female body is both inherently dirty and in need of containment. Accordingly, Berenice, the Addams' cook, instructs Frankie to "get clean for a change. Scrub your elbows and fix yourself nice. You will do very well" (*Member* 28). Both tomboys attempt to clean themselves up in order to become proper women—Frankie for her date with the soldier (133) and Mick for her prom party (*Heart* 97). The need to "get clean" chimes with cultural perceptions of the unruly grotesque female body, associated with the abject, and captured in Mick's graffiti of "a very bad word—*pussy*" (36–37), written in big bold letters amongst sacred names like Mozart. Here, Mick is also making a connection between the unclean female body and sexuality; she has internalized cultural perceptions which construct femaleness as obscene, as pornographic: sex *is* womanliness. It is no wonder, then, that when Mick has her first encounter with "adult" sexuality, with Harry Minowitz, it leaves her feeling powerless, as if "her head was broke off from her body and thrown away" (243). And Frankie tries to "forget" the "unknown sin" committed with Barry MacKean (*Member* 33).

Just as the young tomboys engage, even if unwittingly, in a politics of purification, they also confront—both literally and figuratively—the diminutive status of classic femininity. Firstly, as I have noted, representations of ideal femininity in McCullers' novels stress petiteness, thus setting up femininity as a kind of arrested development, a stuntedness and child-like powerlessness. Secondly, that femininity is ideally pocket-sized, presenting the perfect woman as a miniature and as something to be collected and hoarded. Baby Wilson, for example, who is depicted as a fairy-child with her pink tutu and golden hair, resembles the "minute perfection of detail and a cultured form of nature" that Susan Stewart explores (112). Representing femininity in terms of the miniature is reminiscent of the containment inherent in the aesthetics of the classic body. Thus, implicit in notions of southern daintiness, exemplified by Janice and parodied in Baby, is not only a loss of power but also a sense of limits.

Mick and Frankie most obviously resist the feminine world of the fairy-like southern belle through their overt tomboy behavior and appearance and, of course, through their use of masculine names. While tomboyishness may have been acceptable in the preadolescent southern girl, at puberty, she was expected to cultivate her charm to become a gentlewoman, in other words, to shed her boyishness for womanliness. Since both girls persevere with their masculine ways, Berenice feels compelled to advise Frankie to "change from being so rough and greedy and big. . . . You ought to fix yourself up nice in your dresses" (*Member* 98), and Etta tells Mick, "it makes me sick to see you in those silly boy's clothes. Somebody ought to . . . make you behave" (*Heart* 41)—that is, somebody ought to make her become a true woman. Notably, both Berenice and Etta stress the need to contain the young girls, if they are ever to amount to anything. It seems that the highly oppressive burden of social expectation cannot accommodate the girls' becoming, their difference.

The atmosphere of containment, a result of such social demands for "normality," is further registered in both texts through the constant allusions to heat and to small enclosures, creating an often terrifying panic in both tomboys and readers. Berenice sums up this sense of capture: "We all of us somehow caught. We born this way or that way and we don't know why. . . . And maybe we wants to widen and bust free. But no matter what we do we still caught" (*Member* 141).[8] This all-pervasive atmosphere of claustrophobia manifests itself in the many "captivity" tropes, from ostensibly benign places of confinement—a house, a room, a small town—to the more sinister prisons and asylums that feature so often in McCullers' fiction. Seemingly trapped in the kitchen or the small town streets, Frankie even envies the prisoners in the town jail, for it "was better to be in a jail where you could bang the walls than in a jail you could not see" (84). Mick describes this sense of captivity as "like the ceiling was pressing slowly down towards her face" (*Heart* 273) and dreams that she is "swimming through great crowds of people. . . . The biggest crowd in the world. And sometimes . . . I'm knocking them all down . . . and other times I'm on the ground and people are trompling all over me" (38–39). Furthermore, both narratives take place in hot southern summers, and Frankie makes a direct association between heat and entrapment when she observes "the bars of sunlight [which] crossed the back yard like the bars of a bright strange jail" (*Member* 95). In contrast to the oppressive heat of the small hometowns, both Mick and Frankie dream of the cool of other climes: for Frankie, this is Alaska; for Mick, Switzerland. Thus, heat only intensifies the already-stifling atmosphere created by the streets of the monotonous southern towns and the enclosed spaces, such as the ubiquitous kitchens or cafés that the tomboys frequent.

With such demands and role models before them, manifested in oppressive images of miniatures, heat and claustrophobia, both Mick and Frankie "freak out." Mick wants to "knock down all the walls of the house and then march through the streets as big as a giant" (*Heart* 220), and Frankie "did things and got herself into real trouble. She broke the law. And once having become a criminal, she broke the law again, and then again" (*Member* 33). The girls' desire to "bust free" resembles the impulse of the grotesque that cannot endure the contours of normal—classic—identity. And because the girls resist such normative claims in the high stakes of identity, they identify, and are identified, with the figures of the freakshow, whom Frankie encounters at the Chattahoochee fair: the Giant, the Fat-Lady, the Midget, the Wild Nigger, the Pin Head, the Alligator Boy, and the Half-Man Half-Woman. It turns out that Frankie, who has already sensed her association with freakishness (*Member* 8–9), "was afraid of all the Freaks, for it seemed to her that they had looked at her in a secret way and tried to connect their eyes with hers, as though to say: we know you" (27).

In fact, both Frankie and Mick are grotesque through less overt allusions to the freaks, particularly the Half-Man Half-Woman and the Giant. Both girls resemble the Half-Man Half-Woman, that "morphodite and a miracle of science" (*Member* 27), in their defiance of neat and proper gender assignment. As young tomboys, they are hybrid figures, neither wholly masculine nor wholly feminine, but both. The image of hermaphroditism powerfully suggests their failure, or perhaps inability, to conform to normative gender practices, that is, to the role of the southern belle. And because they fail in the gendering stakes, they internalize society's act of branding them "freaks." Further, as several commentators have noted (Westling 143, 111; Fiedler, *Freaks* 30), the androgynous Half-Man Half-Woman also conjures up the unease of the adolescent confronted with a strange, emerging sexuality and changing body, as well as the problems of correct gender identification and behavior. O'Connor also deploys the freakshow Hermaphrodite in "A Temple of the Holy Ghost" to suggest the horror of the adolescent's changing pubescent body.

More challenging, I think, in McCullers' portrayal of female adolescence, is the association of the young girls with the freakshow Giant, an essentially grotesque figure.[9] Both Frankie and Mick worry about their extreme height: Frankie estimates that "she would grow to be over nine feet tall," a thought that terrifies her for she knows that "a lady who is over nine feet tall . . . would be a Freak" (*Member* 25) and would never "get married or go to a wedding" (27). Mick similarly experiences her stature as a hindrance to social poise and acceptance: on the night of her party, she acknowledges that "no boy wanted to prom with a girl so much taller than him" (*Heart* 101). And the healthy appetites of both girls only enhance their resemblance to giants (*Heart* 144; *Member* 29, 34, 126). Both Portia, the Kellys' cook, and Berenice warn the girls to cut down on their food intake, as greediness is unladylike and may increase their already freakish height.

Gigantism defies the more appropriate, delicate height of "ladies," something that is particularly striking when we compare Mick and Frankie with the petite Janice and Baby Wilson. As Lori Merish has argued, "cuteness," an epithet which the Shirley Temple-like Baby clearly embodies, "aestheticizes the most primary social distinctions, regulating the (shifting) boundaries between Selves and Others, cultural 'insiders' and cultural 'outsiders,' 'humans' and 'freaks'" (188). While the emphasis on petiteness enshrines the feminine image of the domesticated "little woman," the giant is a part of the masculine world (Stewart 112), again underscoring the "error" in Mick and Frankie's identity as they stray from the bounds of good taste and appropriate behavior.

Images of freakishness powerfully relay the strangeness of the adolescent experience, in terms of the changing body, sexual anxiety, and social demands for conformity. However, these freakish images are also a part of the more creative process of becoming, the domain of the grotesque. McCullers registers the close alignment of becoming with the liminality of the adolescent in her outline for *The Heart Is a Lonely Hunter*: Mick "is a crude child on the threshold of a period of quick awakening and development. Her energy and the possibilities before her are without limits" ("Author's Outline" 139). Unsurprisingly, both *The Heart Is a Lonely Hunter* and *The Member of the Wedding* contain many images of their protagonists appearing on literal thresholds (*Heart* 20, 48; *Member* 7, 14, 33, 133, 149). When Frankie recounts her dream of standing in a doorway to the clairvoyant Big Mama, she is told that it signals the arrival of change in her life (*Member* 149–150). Because the liminality of adolescence promises becoming, it has the capacity to puncture and expand upon the overwhelming atmosphere of containment against which both narratives are set. The trope of the "unfinished" underscores this promise—of new possibilities, of new worlds. While Bakhtin describes the grotesque body as "unfinished, [it] outgrows itself, transgresses its own limits" (*Rabelais* 25–26), Mick and Frankie are similarly unfinished. In fact, Frankie several times uses, or at least invokes, the epithet "unfinished" to describe herself and the world around her (*Member* 7, 30, 32, 47, 142–143). In McCullers' short story "The Sojourner," John "reads" the image of unfinished music: "There's nothing that makes you so aware of the *improvisation* of human existence as a song unfinished" (29; emphasis added). To be unfinished is to participate in an open-ended subjectivity, a prelude to becoming.

Reconsidering the trope of the freak reveals that it does not merely signal adolescent oddness, in terms of the failure to conform. The Half-Man Half-Woman represents an unfinished form of subjectivity vis-à-vis gender, just as Mick and Frankie fluctuate between boyishness and girlishness throughout their respective narratives. And gigantism has an emphasis not merely on magnitude but, importantly, on growing. The giant is unbridled, expansive, and so resists conformity to enclosed models of being. It is for this reason that the figure of the giant is a threatening figure, and for this reason that Mick wishes to "march through the streets as big as a giant" (*Heart* 38–39). The process of growth reflects Mick's and Frankie's yearnings and actual attempts to push beyond restrictive bounds of finished identity, exemplified, as we have seen, in the oppressive gender regime of the South. Thus, the trope of the giant does not merely describe Mick's and Frankie's painful experience of freakish adolescence; it also challenges configurations of identity as static and limited, for the giant grows beyond what is "normal" and "natural" and might represent the possibility of a new subjectivity in terms of becoming.

Rather than reading the grotesque mode as a kind of existential allegory or rejecting it altogether in describing McCullers' texts, to maintain it is to pinpoint the creativity that I believe is the vital element of McCullers' vision of the human being. In this way, we can focus on the inherent human possibility of transformation, what Gilles Deleuze and Felix Guattari call "lines of flight." Flight lines are literally manifested in the recurrent images of flying throughout McCullers' writings. James Johnson claims that flight was an important image in the novels of adolescence in the decades following the 1930s and represents the adolescent "hero's" desire for escape. In his brief discussion of *The Member of the Wedding*, he writes that "Frankie ran away to avoid facing her humiliation" (7) following the nightmare of the wedding. More recently, feminist discussion of flying has suggested it is a trope of female freedom. In Erica Jong's *Fear of Flying* (1973), for example, flight becomes an expression of the reclamation of female sexuality for one's self; and in *Nights at the Circus* (1984), Angela Carter writes of "the New Age in which no woman will be bound down to the ground" (25). Finally, Mary Russo, who discusses aerialism in *The Female Grotesque*, suggests that flight is "the fantasy of a femininity which defies the limits of the body, especially the female body" (44). Accordingly, flight bears within it the potential for testing limits and stepping out of bounds. Russo's reading of flight in particular suggests the modes of resistance and transformation—not escapism—that I have argued are at the heart of McCullers' grotesque portraits.

McCullers always uses flight images in relation to adolescence, resonating once more with liminality since flight takes place between sky and earth. However, it is not merely females whom McCullers associates with flight. For example, in *Clock Without Hands*, Jester Clane believes that everyone should be able to fly and own a plane (69), and in the short story "Untitled Piece," a glider suggests to both the young boy and his younger sister the "expectancy" of a journey (112): "it was as though they had never wanted anything except this glider and its flight from the earth up toward the blue sky" (113). And in "Author's Outline of 'The Mute'," (which became *The Heart Is a Lonely Hunter*), both Mick and Harry are "made restless by the abundance of undirected energy. In the spring they try to construct a glider together in the Kellys' backyard, and although because of inadequate materials they can never get the contraption to fly, they work at it very hard together" (140–141).

In *The Heart Is a Lonely Hunter* itself, Mick, while standing on the roof of an empty house, with her arms spread out "like wings," decides that she will one day invent "flying machines" (33–34). And Frankie, like Jester Clane, plans an ideal world in which everyone is entitled to "an aeroplane and a motorcycle" (*Member* 115) and dreams of "flying aeroplanes" in the war. Mick's and Frankie's desire to carve out new lines of flight belongs to the girls' respective wishes to be foreign (*Heart* 106) and to be "somebody else except me" (*Member* 12). Mick considers becoming an inventor, or "a great world-famous composer . . . and conduct all of her music herself" (*Heart* 211). Significantly, her dreams are no vain desires, evidenced by her decision to take mechanical shop over typing class, her attempt to make a violin (43), and her sacrificing of lunch money to pay for piano lessons (144). Frankie's desires involve wanting to run away and join the war (*Member* 30–31), going to Hollywood (175), and becoming "a great poet—or else the foremost authority on radar" (186). Frankie's creative yearning for other ways of being is underscored by her various name changes: from the regular Frances; to the tomboy-of-action Frankie; to the dreamy F. Jasmine. Flight images, then, reflect the young girls' desire to "bust free," to soar to new heights, and to create new forms of subjectivity.

There is, of course, always an immanent risk in flight, which the Greeks called hubris and which is epitomized in the fateful flight of Icarus. In McCullers' novels of adolescence, Mick's paintings of failed flight—"Sea Gull with Back Broken in Storm," and another illustrating "an airplane crashing down and people jumping out to save themselves" (*Heart* 42)— suggest risk-taking and its deadly consequences. And, standing on a roof-top, "where everybody wanted to stand," Mick feels that "there was something about getting to the very top that gave you a wild feeling and made you want to yell or sing or raise up your arms and fly." However, pondering that "if you lost grip and rolled off the edge it would kill you" (33–36), Mick is acknowledging the painful hazards of "other" ways of being.

In this preliminary revision of the grotesque, I have argued that McCullers' novels construct adolescent subjectivity in the grotesque realms of becoming—in terms of gigantism and flight—and in doing so, challenge those normative demands for identity which seek to constrain the promise of adolescence. And it is at the location of the body that transgression takes place, signified by attempts to "master" the young girls through disciplines of appropriate fashion, behavior, and desires, as well as the ever-present threat of being branded a "freak." At the same time, the novels seem to warn of the dangers of "flights of fancy," for those who fail to conform to prescriptive modes of behavior are painfully punished and ostracized. In McCullers' next novel, *The Ballad of the Sad Café*, we witness the full effects of grotesque transgression: the image of the Amazonian Miss Amelia Evans immured in the boarded-up café literally encloses her narrative. Amelia's fate would seem to dramatize the responses of many commentators to McCullers' grotesque adolescents, in similar attempts at closure, entangled with notions of "female limits." By re-mapping the field of the grotesque, in this case by deploying Bakhtin's conceptualization, we can finally consider McCullers' literary output as an affirmation of creativity. *The Heart Is a Lonely Hunter* and *The Member of the Wedding* are not merely fictional accounts of volatile childish rebellion; they are, rather, powerful narratives of the dynamics of being human. While I hope that this strategic rereading of the grotesque might lead to a complete overhaul of how we read much southern literature, we are yet left to wonder at McCullers' radical expressions of gigantism and aerialism, emerging as they do from a culture of feminine stuntedness and submission.

Notes

1. "Gothic" and "grotesque" have long been used interchangeably to describe southern writing. In this essay, I use "grotesque" to distinguish the literature from tales of the supernatural which "gothic" invokes.

2. Patricia Yaeger has already opened the way for new accounts of Eudora Welty's grotesque, side by side with Bakhtin, in "Edible Labor," *Southern Quarterly* 30.2–3 (1992): 150–159; and "Beyond the Hummingbird: Southern Women Writers and the Southern Gargantua," *Haunted Bodies: Gender and Southern Texts*, eds. Anne Goodwyn Jones and Susan V. Donaldson (Charlottesville: UP of Virginia, 1997), 287–318.

3. See for example, Frank Baldanza, "Plato in Dixie," *Georgia Review* 12.2 (1958): 151–167; Ihab Hassan, "Carson McCullers: The Alchemy of Love and Aesthetics of

Pain," *Modern Fiction Studies* 5.4 (1959–1960): 311–26; Chester Eisinger, "Carson McCullers and the Failure of Dialogue," *Fiction of the Forties* (Chicago: U of Chicago P, 1963), 243–258; Frances Freeman Paden, "Autistic Gestures in *The Heart Is a Lonely Hunter*," *Modern Fiction Studies* 28.3 (1982): 453–463; Donna Bauerly, "Themes of Eros and Agape in the Major Fiction of Carson McCullers," *Pembroke Magazine* 20 (1988): 72–76; Adelaide Frazier, "Terminal Metaphors for Love," *Pembroke Magazine* 20 (1988): 77–81; Leroy Thomas, "Carson McCullers: The Plight of the Lonely Hunter," *Pembroke Magazine* 20 (1988): 10–15; Mary Whitt, "The Mutes in Carson McCullers' *The Heart Is a Lonely Hunter*," *Pembroke Magazine* 20 (1988): 24–29; Raphael Johstoneaux, "The Forces of Dehumanization: *Reflections in a Golden Eye*," *Encyclia* 66 (1989): 97–104; Mary McBride, "Loneliness and Longing in Selected Plays of Carson McCullers and Tennessee Williams," *Modern American Drama: The Female Canon*, ed. June Schlueter (Rutherford, NJ: Fairleigh Dickinson UP, 1990), 143–50; and Ruth Vande Kieft, "The Love Ethos of Porter, Welty, and McCullers," *The Female Tradition in Southern Literature*, ed. Carol Manning (Urbana: U of Illinois P, 1993), 235–258.

4. Virginia Spencer Carr writes that McCullers had a passing acquaintance with Anderson (*Lonely Hunter* 145). Oliver Evans compares *The Heart Is a Lonely Hunter* to "Queer," and a scene in *The Ballad of the Sad Café* to "The Egg," *Winesburg, Ohio* (Carr, *Understanding McCullers* 54, 135). I compare "Hands" with *The Heart Is a Lonely Hunter*— vis-à-vis homosexual desire—in "Grotesque Subjects: A Reading of Carson McCullers" (Diss. U of New South Wales, 1997).

5. See Ihab Hassan, "The Idea of Adolescence in American Fiction," *American Quarterly* 10.3 (1958): 312–324; *Radical Innocence: Studies in the Contemporary American Novel* (Princeton: Princeton UP, 1961); and "The Character of Post-War Fiction," *The English Journal* 51.1 (1962): 1–8. See also Leslie Fiedler's chapter "Adolescence and Maturity in the American Novel" in *An End to Innocence: Essays on Culture and Politics* (Boston: Beacon, 1966), 191–210; Frederic Carpenter, "The Adolescent in American Fiction," *The English Journal* 46.6 (1957): 313–319; and James Johnson, "The Adolescent Hero: A Trend in Modern Fiction."

6. See for example, Maureen Howard, "Introduction," *Seven American Women Writers of the Twentieth Century: An Introduction*, ed. Maureen Howard (Minneapolis: U of Minnesota P, 1963), 3–27; Irving Buchen, "Carson McCullers: A Case of Convergence," *The Bucknell Review* 21 (Spring, 1973): 15–28; Ann Carlton, "Beyond Gothic and Grotesque: A Feminist View of Three Female Characters of Carson McCullers," *Pembroke Magazine* 20 (1988): 56, 58; Richard Cook, *Carson McCullers* (New York: Frederick Ungar, 1975), 64; Fiedler, *An End to Innocence* 203; Linda Huf, "The Heart Is a Lonely Hunter: Carson McCuller's [sic] Young Woman with a Great Future Behind Her," *A Portrait of the Artist as a Young Woman: The Writer as Heroine in American Literature* (New York: Ungar, 1983), 111; Margaret B. McDowell, *Carson McCullers* (Boston: Twayne, 1980), 85; Sosnoski 86; and Westling 111, 115.

7. See for example, Elaine Ginsberg, "The Female Initiation Theme in American Fiction," *Studies in American Fiction* 3 (1975): 27–38; Westling; Huf; Katherine Dalsimer, "Preadolescence: *The Member of the Wedding*," *Female Adolescence: Psychoanalytic Reflections on Works of Literature* (New Haven: Yale, 1986), 13–26; Constance M. Perry, "Carson McCullers and the Female *Wunderkind*," *Southern Literary Journal* 19 (1986): 36–45; Alice Hall Petry, "Carson McCullers's Precocious 'Wunderkind'," *Southern Quarterly* 26.3 (1988): 31–39; and White.

8. Importantly, Berenice adds that she is "caught worst" because she is "black.... Everybody is caught one way or another. But they done drawn completely extra bounds

around all colored people. . . . Sometimes it just about more than we can stand" (McCullers, *Member* 141). In *Winesburg, Ohio,* Anderson also portrays his grotesques as trapped: men and women grab hold of one truth "but the moment one of the people took one of the truths to himself, called it his truth, and tried to live his life by it, he became a grotesque and the truth he embraced became a falsehood" ("The Book of the Grotesque," *Winesburg, Ohio* 24). While for Anderson the experience of being trapped might be symbolic of some form of psychic alienation or anguish, I want to stress that for McCullers, it is primarily a bodily experience.

9. See Yaeger's "Beyond the Hummingbird" for her account of gigantism in Welty.

WORKS CITED

Anderson, Sherwood. *Winesburg, Ohio.* 1919. London: Picador, 1988.
Bakhtin, Mikhail. *The Dialogic Imagination: Four Essays by M. M. Bakhtin.* Trans. Caryl Emerson and Michael Holquist. Austin: U of Texas P, 1981.
———. *Problems of Dostoevsky's Poetics.* 1929. Ed. and trans. Caryl Emerson. Minneapolis: U of Minnesota P, 1984.
———. *Rabelais and His World.* 1965. Trans. Helene Iswolsky. Bloomington: Indiana UP, 1984.
Carlton, Ann. "Beyond Gothic and Grotesque: A Feminist View of Three Female Characters of Carson McCullers." *Pembroke Magazine* 20 (1988): 54–62.
Carr, Virginia Spencer. *The Lonely Hunter: A Biography of Carson McCullers.* New York: Carroll and Graf, 1975.
———. *Understanding Carson McCullers.* Columbia: U of South Carolina P, 1990.
Carter, Angela. *Nights at the Circus.* London: Chatto and Windus, 1984.
Deleuze, Gilles, and Felix Guattari. *Kafka: For a Minor Literature.* Trans. Dana Polon. Minneapolis: U of Minnesota P, 1986.
Fiedler, Leslie. *Freaks: Myths and Images of the Secret Self.* London: Penguin, 1978.
Johnson, James William. "The Adolescent Hero: A Trend in Modern Fiction," *Twentieth Century Literature* 5.1 (1959): 3–11.
Jones, Anne Goodwyn. "Dixie's Diadem." *Tomorrow is Another Day: The Woman Writer in the South, 1859–1936.* Baton Rouge: Louisiana State UP, 1981. 3–50.
Kayser, Wolfgang. *The Grotesque in Art and Literature.* 1957. Trans. Ulrich Weisstein. Gloucester, MA: P. Smith, 1968.
Kristeva, Julia. "Word, Dialogue and Novel." *Desire in Language: A Semiotic Approach to Art and Literature.* 1969. Trans. Thomas Gora, Alice Jardine, and Leon S. Roudiez. New York: Columbia UP, 1980.
McCullers, Carson. "Author's Outline of 'The Mute' (*The Heart Is a Lonely Hunter*)." *The Mortgaged Heart.* London: Penguin, 1972. 136–159.
———. *Clock Without Hands.* 1961. London: Penguin, 1965.
———. "The Flowering Dream: Notes on Writing." *The Mortgaged Heart.* London: Penguin, 1972. 280–287.
———. *The Heart Is a Lonely Hunter.* 1940. London: Penguin, 1961.
———. *The Member of the Wedding.* 1946. London: Penguin, 1962.
———. "The Russian Realists and Southern Literature." *The Mortgaged Heart.* London: Penguin, 1972. 258–264.
———. "The Sojourner." 1951. *The Ballad of the Sad Café.* London: Penguin, 1963. 121–133.
———. "Untitled Piece." *The Mortgaged Heart.* London: Penguin, 1972. 111–135.

Merish, Lori. "Cuteness and Commodity Aesthetics: Tom Thumb and Shirley Temple." *Freakery: Cultural Spectacles of the Extraordinary Body*. Ed. Rosemarie Garland Thomson. New York: New York UP, 1996. 185–203.

Millichap, Joseph. "Distorted Matter and Disjunctive Forms: The Grotesque as Modernist Genre." *Arizona Quarterly* 33 (1977): 339–347.

O'Connor, Flannery. "Some Aspects of the Grotesque in Southern Fiction." *Mystery and Manners: Occasional Prose*. Ed. Sally and Robert Fitzgerald. New York: Noonday, 1994. 36–50.

O'Connor, William Van. "The Grotesque: An American Genre." *The Grotesque: An American Genre and Other Essays*. Carbondale, IL: Southern Illinois P, 1962. 3–19.

Russo, Mary. *The Female Grotesque: Risk, Excess and Modernity*. New York: Routledge, 1994.

Segrest, Mab. "Southern Women Writing: Toward a Literature of Wholeness." *My Mama's Dead Squirrel: Lesbian Essays on Southern Culture*. Ithaca, NY: Firebrand, 1985. 19–42.

Sosnoski, Karen. "Society's Freaks: The Effects of Sexual Stereotyping in Carson McCullers' Fiction." *Pembroke Magazine* 20 (1988): 82–88.

Spiegel, Alan. "A Theory of the Grotesque in Southern Fiction." *The Georgia Review* 26 (1972): 426–437.

Stewart, Susan. *On Longing: Narratives of the Miniature, the Gigantic, the Souvenir, the Collection*. Durham: Duke UP, 1993.

Westling, Louise. *Sacred Groves and Ravaged Gardens: The Fiction of Eudora Welty, Carson McCullers, and Flannery O'Connor*. Athens: U of Georgia P, 1985.

White, Barbara. "Loss of Self in Carson McCullers' *The Member of the Wedding*." *Growing Up Female: Adolescent Girlhood in American Fiction*. Westport, CT: Greenwood, 1985. 89–111.

DOREEN FOWLER

Carson McCullers's Primal Scenes:
The Ballad of the Sad Café

The signature characteristic of Carson McCullers's fiction is her abiding preoccupation with loneliness. Time and again McCullers has acknowledged this preoccupation, and it has become commonplace among critics to observe that a dread of alienation drives her fiction.[1] I call attention to this obsession to note the convergence of southern writer McCullers's perception that unspeakable isolation is the fundamental human condition and French psychoanalyst Jacques Lacan's theory that identity is predicated on alienation. According to Lacan, we are not alone in the beginning because the child perceives itself as part of the mother's body; but to define itself as an "I" separate from the mother, the child must submit to loss—the loss of the mother's body. All of McCullers's works seem to dramatize the estranged condition that Lacan maintains is prerequisite for human subjectivity. Accordingly, we can superimpose Lacan's theory of identity onto McCullers's narratives of loneliness.[2]

Both Freud and Lacan theorize about the unconscious and ultimately claim that what is buried in the unconscious is a guilty desire for a lost presumptive holistic unity. Further, Freud and Lacan propose that repressed material always returns in disguised forms—in dreams, in slips of the tongue, and in literature.[3] McCullers's Ballad of the Sad Café represents, I claim, such a disguised return of buried meanings. The Ballad opens with a dream

From *Critique* 43, no. 3 (Spring 2002): pp. 260–70. © 2002 by Heldref Publications.

image: a ghostlike face peers from the window of a boarded-up house, "like the terrible dim faces known in dreams" (3). This image serves as notice that we are entering the terrain of the unconscious, that like a dream image, McCullers's Ballad constitutes a disguised message from the unconscious mind. Lacan's reformulation of Freud's theory of the unconscious can help us to decipher this message.

Lacan holds that in the beginning, before the formation of identity, in what he calls the imaginary or preoedipal phase, we experience no loneliness, no lack of any kind. In the mother's womb and in the first few months of the child's life, the mother and child exist as one continuous, complete, unbroken circuit; the child does not exist as a separate subject. For identity and cultural meaning to exist, there must be difference, which is predicated upon exclusion. Specifically, the mother must be excluded and must become the first to be Other. (Many others—for example, ethnic, religious, or racial others—follow.) This act of exclusion, which Lacan calls a symbolic self-castration, is the pivotal moment in the emergence of the human subject. At this critical splitting, a desire for a lost imagined integration is driven underground; and, in the words of Terry Eagleton, this buried guilty desire "just is what is called the unconscious" (165). This repression marks the newly constituted subject's entry into the symbolic order, a register of being that overlays the imaginary and is based in absence. The self, then, is born through a division and comes into being fragmented. This narrative of identity as the consequence of loss offers a way to read McCullers's Ballad. In fact, the events of the novella appear repeatedly to stage the disguised return and the subsequent repression of the desire to overcome loss.

A rejection of the feminine, identified with the maternal, characterizes both Lacan's symbolic order and the world of McCullers's Ballad before Lymon's arrival. Panthea Broughton was the first to observe that The Ballad reflects a culture "in flight from the feminine" (41). Miss Amelia, who denies her femininity, is a case in point. As countless critics have observed, before Lymon's appearance, Miss Amelia is masculine not only in her appearance but also in her behavior. In stark antithesis to the feminine maternal, she is domineering, ruthless, aggressive, and exploitative. Both Broughton and Suzanne Morrow Paulson demonstrate that these are the qualities that this culture admires and aspires to. Paulson, in particular, richly documents that Miss Amelia's town is not only "male-dominated" but is also intent on "the murder of the feminine" (188). Arguably, the androcentrism of Miss Amelia's community reflects our own social order writ large, which Lacan submits is male-centered (or phallocentric) because the symbolic order, the register of language, law, and culture, is based in absence, an absence identified with the maternal body.[4] In the constitutive moment, the child rejects the mother and takes for the object of desire the father as presumed originator of being.[5]

In other words, Paulson's characterization of Carson McCullers's fictional world, namely that "[e]veryone wants to be the father and to belong to the gang" (194), is also a disturbingly accurate description of Lacan's symbolic order, the order of cultural exchange: one need only read "father-become-Father" for "father" and "symbolic order" for "gang."

This rigid cultural repression of the feminine is relaxed, however, when Lymon appears, and Miss Amelia takes him in. It is noteworthy that Lymon claims to be related to Miss Amelia through his dead mother who he alleges is the half-sister of Miss Amelia's dead mother. Lymon is associated with the dead mother or, in Lacanian terms, the displaced mother of earliest memories. Perhaps that is why Miss Amelia, who is a "solitary" person and was never known to invite anyone to eat with her "unless she was planning to trick them in some way, or make money out of them" (11), now adopts a nurturing attitude toward Lymon. The narrator explains the peculiar tie that develops between Lymon and Miss Amelia in terms of love and observes that "the beloved is only a stimulus for all the stored up love which has lain quiet within the lover for a long time hither to" (26). What the narrator identifies as "falling in love" is another way of naming a disguised eruption of a long-buried desire. The lover's "stored up love" may represent metaphorically what Lacan calls the repressed, the desire for incorporation that was driven underground at the moment of splitting. What Lymon serves to trigger, then, may be a repressed desire to heal the split subject.

The theories of Nancy Chodorow offer a way to interpret Miss Amelia's attachment to Lymon. Chodorow maintains that all adults "look for a return to this emotional and physical union [experienced with the mother before the entry into language and culture]" and that women seek to reproduce this union by becoming mothers themselves (199). Undeniably, Miss Amelia adopts a maternal role toward the child-like Lymon.[6] She carries Lymon on her back and sits by his bedside until he falls asleep. As for Lymon, the narrator is at pains to point out his child-like qualities: he reaches only to the belt buckle of most men; he sucks on candy instead of snuff; and he has "an instinct which is usually found in small children, an instinct to establish immediate vital contact between himself and all things in the world" (20). Thus the relationship between Miss Amelia and Cousin Lymon appears to attempt to reproduce the presumptive unity and integration experienced in an earlier phase of development—the mirror stage.

The mirror stage is an intermediate phase between the imaginary and the symbolic. There can be no reenactment of existence in the imaginary because in that stage the child exists as "an uncognized, material, somatic existence" (Mellard 12). In the mirror stage, the child begins the work of constructing an "I." In the intermediate mirror stage, subjectivity is based in identification with the mother whereas, in the later symbolic phase, identity is predicated upon alienation. The child begins to locate a self, and this sense of self is bestowed on the child by the mother; that is, the mother is the mirror that gives the child a sense of a unified self.

The image is the language of the unconscious, and in The Ballad an image appears to signal covertly the return of mirror-stage fusion. On the evening that the café has its origin, when Miss Amelia first permits her customers to buy and drink whisky in "the warm, bright store" (21), she [. . .] stood most of the evening in the doorway leading to the kitchen" and "most of the time her eyes were fastened lonesomely on the hunchback" (23). A doorway is a frame and, as a frame, suggests a mirror. Looking out from the doorframe, Miss Amelia sees Lymon on the other side as her mirror image, the identificatory imago of mirror-stage fusion.

Miss Amelia's ambivalent feelings on that evening—according to the narrator, "there was in her expression pain, perplexity and uncertain joy" (23)—can also be interpreted in terms of mirror-phase identification. Although in this intermediate stage, identity is based on identification and the yawning gap of the oedipal phase has not yet opened up, nevertheless, in the mirror phase there is not the complete incorporation of the imaginary: There is a distance between the self and the identificatory imago. That space may explain why Miss Amelia wears, in the narrator's words, "the lonesome look of the lover" (23). What the narrator calls "lonesome" Lacan would identify as a repressed desire for incorporation, which has now surfaced disguised. Such desire would cause the lover, in the narrator's words, to "crave any possible relation with the beloved, even if this experience can cause him only pain" (27). The satisfaction of the desire for incorporation would indeed cause the beloved "pain"; it would efface the difference that constitutes identity. Thus the beloved "fears and hates the lover" (27) with good reason: The lover's desire for assimilation threatens the beloved's sense of identity.

A Lacanian framework also provides a fresh way to read the meaning of the café that comes into being as a result of Miss Amelia's relationship with Cousin Lymon. The café is a manifestation of this momentary relaxation of repression. During its brief existence, the people of Miss Amelia's town converge. The café becomes the "warm bright center point of the town" (54); that is, it is a symbol of unity, community, and integration as opposed to the fragmentation that characterizes the postoedipal subject. Interestingly, the café is associated with warmth and the color red. Miss Amelia makes red curtains for the windows; "the great iron stove at the back of the room roared, crackled, and turned red" (54). The emphasis on warmth and the color of blood associates the café with the body; and it is the body, particularly a somatic unity with the mother, that is displaced, leaving a void on accession to the symbolic plane. The café of McCullers's title, then, is the site of a return of a buried desire for a time before alienation and division.[7]

At this juncture, the narrative itself enacts a return in the form of a flashback that the narrator describes as "a curious episode" from "long ago" (27). We are told that Marvin Macy fell in love with Miss Amelia, and they married. I read Marvin Macy's love for Miss Amelia, like Miss Amelia's for Cousin Lymon, as a disguised emergence of a desire that was repressed at the constitution of subjectivity. Once again, Chodorow's theory can be usefully invoked. According to Chodorow, men seek to reenact the "emotional and physical union" that characterized the mother-child relationship in the preoedipal phase by taking wives as substitutes for the rejected mother (199). Applying that thesis to this episode, we can say that Marvin marries Miss Amelia in an attempt to replace the banished mother of the imaginary plane.

Their ten-day marriage, I suggest, is an attempt to reenact mirror-stage identification. Here, also is an image in the text that signifies a return to the mirror phase of development. According to the narrator, Marvin delays "declaring himself" to Miss Amelia for two years. During those years, while he improved himself, "[h]e would stand near the door of her premises his cap in his hand, his eyes meek and longing and misty gray" (29). Standing framed in the door, Marvin sees Amelia on the other side as if she were his mirror image; and he longs for greater intimacy, for total immersion.

This craving for assimilation surfaces on Miss Amelia and Marvin's disastrous wedding night. In psychoanalytic terms, Marvin longs for the incorporation of the imaginary phase and seeks it in the marriage bed. Marvin Macy, the lover, urgently desires what Miss Amelia, the beloved, dreads—the obliteration of distinctions that sexual coupling figures. Thus the unsuccessful outcome of their wedding night is a foregone conclusion.

At another level, Marvin's failure to bring his beloved bride to bed constitutes an abortive primal scene and prefigures the climactic primal scene that is played out at the novella's conclusion. A primal scene, Freud explains, is a child's buried memory of having witnessed parental intercourse. In his later writing, Freud acknowledges that the child may not be remembering an actual witnessed event but may be experiencing a dream or fantasy memory, that is, an archetypal image out of the unconscious mind. This image reflects the child's oedipal desires and his or her related castration anxiety. In the primal tableau, the child observes the father fulfilling the child's desire both to possess and to master the powerful mother. As the child interprets the image of parental intercourse, the father seems to be both satisfying his desire for the mother as well as the mother's desire; paradoxically, the father also appears to be hurting the mother, even castrating her, and the child imagines this is why the mother does not have a penis. This observed tableau serves as a threat to the child: The child will likewise be castrated if she or he continues to desire physical union with the mother. Under the threat of castration, the child renounces the mother; and thus this primal image functions in what Freud calls the oedipal crisis and what Lacan later rewrites as a moment of division that constitutes the fragmented self.

Marvin Macy's failure to consummate his marriage to Miss Amelia represents a failed primal scene. It is a scene of unsuccessful sexual intercourse between a married couple, observed by son-figures, "the young boys who watched through the window on that night" (31). In this evocation of the primal scene, the father-figure, Marvin, is wretchedly unable to play the father's role. As the narrator sagely observes, "A groom is in a sorry fix when he is unable to bring his well-beloved bride to bed with him, and the whole town knows it" (31). Before the watching eyes of the young boys, Marvin is unable to satisfy his desire or the mother's desire; equally important, he fails to appear to disempower the mother. Miss Amelia emerges from the marriage bed as powerful as ever; and Marvin appears to be helpless, as helpless as the watching boys to satisfy or subdue the powerful mother. When, before the child-witnesses, Miss Amelia refuses sexual intercourse, "stomp[s] down the stairs in breeches and a khaki jacket" (31), "slam[s] the kitchen door and give[s] it an ugly kick," and, perhaps most tellingly, "ha[s] a smoke with her father's pipe" (31), she assumes the aspect of the child's fantasy of the phallic mother, the powerful mother of the preoedipal phase, before the appearance of the father. The phallic mother is a child's projection; the child imagines that the mother of the preoedipal stage, who appears to be all-powerful and complete, possesses a penis.

The role of the father in the primal scene is related to what Lacan calls the phallus.[8] The phallus is a difficult Lacanian concept largely because of the connotations the word carries in our culture. In Lacanian terminology, the phallus is not the penis; the phallus is a symbol. It symbolizes the critical moment in the development of subjectivity, the moment when the child, in obedience to the Law of the Father, performs the symbolic self-castration that constitutes identity. Given that the primal scene is an image out of the unconscious for this constitutive moment, the phallus signifies the father's role in this tableau, and in this first rendition of the primal scene in The Ballad, Marvin Macy fails to represent the phallus. However, both before and after his fall into loving abjection with Miss Amelia, Marvin, who comes between Miss Amelia and Cousin Lymon, is identified in the text with images that align him with the phallic signifier; specifically, he is infamous for having performed acts of mutilation that symbolize castration. The narrator relates that, as a boy, "for years," Marvin "carried about with him the dried and salted ear of a man he had killed in a razor fight" and that he "had chopped off the tails of squirrels in the pinewoods just to please his fancy" (27-28). In my reading, without his conscious knowledge, Marvin "fanc[ies]" cutting off body-parts of squirrels and people because such acts of mutilation symbolize the severing that constituted identity; they symbolize the always mythical power of the phallus.[9]

Miss Amelia cannot fathom Cousin Lymon's obsession with Marvin Macy, but if we read Marvin in terms of phallic signification, Lymon, who is reenacting with Miss Amelia mirror-stage fusion, desires a representative of the phallic Other, the Other who intervenes in the dyadic relation and ordains subjectivity and loss. "Man's desire," Lacan writes, "is the desire of the Other" (Écrits 289). By this, Lacan means that we look to accede to the place of the Other, the place of the constitution of the self, the privileged signifier that appears to hold all signifieds in thrall but does not.[10] When Lymon attempts to explain his fascination with Marvin Macy to Miss Amelia, she is mystified, but Lymon's words imply that he is drawn to Marvin because of his difference: "'Oh Marvin Macy,' groaned the hunchback, and the sound of the name was enough to upset the rhythm of his sobs so that he hiccuped. 'He has been to Atlanta. [. . .] He has been to the penitentiary,' said the hunchback, miserable with longing" (53). Macy is from a world outside of the closed unit that Lymon and Miss Amelia form. For Lymon, the penitentiary in Atlanta figures the place of the Other, and he "long[s]" to accede to this place that he mistakenly imagines exists outside of loss.

All of McCullers's Ballad has been building inexorably toward one climactic event, the battle between Miss Amelia and Marvin. In the psychoanalytic narrative, there is one moment that matters, the moment when the desire for the mother is repressed and the father takes the mother's place as the object of desire. This crucial development in the construction of the ego appears transformed in McCullers's Ballad as the epic battle between Marvin Macy and Miss Amelia, which, in turn, takes the form of the novella's second and final primal scene.

The Ballad's second reenactment of the primal scene[11] inverts the traditional formula. Whereas in the traditional primal scene the child-viewer reads sexual coupling as a violent struggle, in McCullers's version, a violent struggle takes on the appearance of sexual coupling. The fight is evoked in distinctly sexual terms; as one sexual image after another appears, we inevitably recall that Miss Amelia and Marvin are still husband and wife but have not as yet sexually consummated their marriage. It is as if this fight is that consummation:

> And now that Miss Amelia and Marvin were locked in a hold
> together the crowd came out of its daze and pressed closer. For
> a while the fighters grappled muscle to muscle, their hipbones

braced against each other. Backward and forward, from side to
side, they swayed in this way. (67)

This blurring of sex and struggle, which obtains in both the primal scene
and in McCullers's disguised representation of the primal drama, implies a
disturbing unconscious knowledge that love is aligned with power and sex
with violence. The psychoanalytic narrative of identity offers a way to interpret
this troubling alignment: love and sexual intercourse figure the dyadic unity
experienced with the mother of the imaginary plane, and this original unity
ends in a traumatic, violent sundering that constitutes the fractured subject.

The climax of the novel is the epic struggle between Miss Amelia and
Marvin; and the climax (in all senses of the word) of the battle is Lymon's
decisive intervention.[12] Just as Miss Amelia seems to have won the battle,
just as she has Marvin pinned and her hands encircle his throat, Lymon
"sailed through the air as though he had grown hawk wings," lands on Miss
Amelia's back, and "clutche[s] at her neck with his clawed little fingers" (68).
As a result, Miss Amelia is defeated. At one level, Lyman's intervention
signifies the moment of primary repression, the moment when the child
rejects the mother. Although the Law of the Father requires this separation,
it is not the father, but the child who disrupts the original dyadic unity.
Thus Lymon's act of betrayal can be read as a disguised image for the child's
renunciation of the mother, a necessary step in the formation of identity.

At the same time, Lymon's mythic soaring flight and hawklike descent
invites a complementary reading. The fight takes the form of a primal
scene—a scene that makes palpably evident the father's terrible power and
precipitates the child's rejection of the mother. In this reenactment of the
primal scene, however, as in the failed primal scene on the wedding night, it
appears that the mother-figure is stronger than the father-figure. Describing
the terrible contest between Miss Amelia and Marvin, the narrator twice
avers that Miss Amelia is "the stronger":

> Now the test had come, and in these moments of terrible
> effort, it was Miss Amelia who was the stronger. Marvin Macy
> was greased and slippery, tricky to grasp, but she was stronger.
> Gradually she bent him over backward, and inch by inch she
> forced him to the floor. It was a terrible thing to watch and their
> deep hoarse breaths were the only sound in the café. At last she
> had him down, and straddled; her strong big hands were on his
> throat. (67)

Once again, Marvin Macy is unable to play the father's part in the
primal drama, and at the critical moment, "just as the fight was won" (67) by

Miss Amelia, Lymon appears to assume supernatural powers and succeeds where Marvin had failed. In this reprise of the primal scene, Lymon, the watching child-figure, assumes the role of father. He symbolically enacts the father's power both to copulate with the mother and to disempower her. When he sails through the air and "land[s] on the broad strong back of Miss Amelia," he assumes the father's position in the act of anal intercourse;[13] and after this figurative intercourse, Miss Amelia is "beaten" and "lay sprawled on the floor, her arms flung outward and motionless," the picture of total abjection (68).

The battle between Marvin and Miss Amelia, which simulates sexual intercourse, ends in a metaphorical sexual consummation, but it is Lymon who experiences this consummation. Observing the fight, Lymon exhibits signs of sexual arousal: "the excitement had made him break out in a rash, and his pale mouth shivered" (67). At the moment when Lymon seems to assume supernatural powers and springs onto Miss Amelia's back from twelve feet away, he utters a cry "that caused a shrill bright shiver to run down the spine" (67). Lymon's cry is the cry of a man experiencing orgasm or, in Lacanian terms, jouissance. Jouissance is ultimate sexual enjoyment; in French, jouissance literally means orgasm. It is the forbidden satisfaction of the sexual drive that Lacan, following Freud, defines as a drive toward self-completion through the Other. Jouissance is the always momentary rapture experienced in attempting to reclaim the missing phallus. Lacan uses the sexual term jouissance for this ecstasy because sexual intercourse also enacts our desire to have the phallus. In sexual intercourse, the woman is the fetish object substituting for the missing phallus and allowing the man to conceal his phallic lack (Lee 180). Thus jouissance, identified with the mythical phallus, is a momentary feeling of empowerment and completion. Lymon experiences this rapturous sense of fulfillment when he ritually enacts the satisfaction of the child's forbidden desire to accede to the place of power, to take the father's place and restore the phallus that can connect us with the mother. To represent jouissance, McCullers imaginatively invokes Lymon's orgiastic cry, his ejaculatory leap, and his coital "land[ing]" on Miss Amelia.

Immediately following this moment of triumph Lymon "disappears" (68). The narrator seems hard-pressed to account for this disappearance; however, from a psychoanalytic point of view, it is the inevitable consequence of Lymon's forbidden jouissance. Jouissance marks the moment of violating the law against a narcissistic merging[14] and momentarily overcoming lack; however, because identity is defined by absence, where there is no lack, there is no subject. Jouissance marks the dissolution of the separate subject and a return to an imaginary unity that preceded subjectivity. It is, Lacan says, "de trop" (Écrits 319); it is too much; it is the last gasp of the subject as it dissolves into an imaginary relation with the Other. Accordingly, immediately after exhibiting signs of sexual excitation and ritually reenacting the restoration of the forbidden phallic signifier, Lymon temporarily at least "slip[s] out" of view (68).

The novella ends with Miss Amelia's defeat. To drive home that defeat, following the fight, Marvin and Lymon do "everything ruinous they could think of without actually breaking into the office where Miss Amelia stayed the night" (69). The list of "ruinous" deeds—from taking the curios in Miss Amelia's private cabinet to setting out a poisoned dish of her favorite food—suggests that Marvin and Lymon perform every act they can think of to enact ritually the castration of the mythic phallic mother of the preoedipal stage. And then, the narrator tells us, Lymon and Macy go away, opening up the alienation that characterizes the "I" in the symbolic order.

The conclusion of this love story is written in our cultural memory. There can be only one outcome. Both McCullers's subtext and the psychoanalytic narrative propose that all love is in some way an attempt to reenact the first love, and this mother-child relationship must give way to the Law. The imaginary must give way to the symbolic; the mother must give way to the Father.[15] When a desire for return slips past unconscious censors and is recognized, it must be repressed again. Miss Amelia's terrible defeat at the hands of Lymon and Marvin symbolizes this repression. Also it reenacts the all-important moment, the moment of primary repression when a representative of the sign of difference appears and the mother is excluded. The events of The Ballad conform to a primal script. Repeatedly throughout the novella a forbidden desire for a lost presumptive wholeness reasserts itself—and is repressed. When Marvin takes his new bride to bed, when Miss Amelia lives with Lymon and "mothers" him, when Lymon ritually enacts a narcissistic merging with the lost mother—all these acts are disguised formulations of a desire to heal the split subject and to restore the missing part lost long ago in an explosive moment of division, the founding moment. Endlessly this desire is repressed and endlessly it returns because, according to Freud, repression, by its very nature, leads to exactly what repression was meant to prevent, the return of the repressed. The desire to break out of human isolation is doomed; at the same time, that desire will never die. Carson McCullers's fable, The Ballad of the Sad Café, is an expression of a forbidden undying desire no longer to be alone.

Notes

1. In the preface to The Square Root of Wonderful, for example, McCullers writes: "My central theme is the theme of spiritual isolation. Certainly I have always felt alone" (viii). Two critics who have articulated McCullers' concern with loneliness particularly eloquently are Harold Bloom and Oliver Evans. In the words of Bloom, a "fear of insulation"

is "the enabling power of McCullers's imagination" (2). Evans writes: "What she conceives to be the truth about human nature is a melancholy truth: each man is surrounded by a 'zone of loneliness,' serving a life sentence of solitary confinement" (126).

2. I am not proposing that McCullers was influenced by Lacan. Almost certainly McCullers did not know his work. Jacques Lacan's theories were not widely circulated in the United States until the publication of Écrits in 1966, and The Ballad of the Sad Café was written in the summer of 1941. But a writer does not need a formal knowledge of a theory for meanings that are interpretable by that theory to figure in his or her work. Freud frequently reiterated the dictum that poets often "discover" what philosophers and others come to theorize about later.

3. In his famous essay, "Repression" (1915), Freud states that "repression itself [...] produces substitutive formations and symptoms, [...] indications of a return of the repressed." Echoing Freud, Lacan states flatly, "repressed, it reappears" (Écrits 311.)

4. Lacan states that "there is woman only as excluded by the nature of things which is the nature of words" (Feminine Sexuality 144). Lacanian interpreter Jonathan Scott Lee explains that Lacan means that "woman finds herself systematically excluded from reality as constructed in terms of the androcentric symbolic order" (177). Jacqueline Rose cautions against interpreting Lacan's statement to mean that women are excluded from language. She writes: "Woman is excluded by the nature of words, meaning that the definition poses her as exclusion. Note that this is not the same thing as saying that woman is excluded from the nature of words, a misreading which leads to the recasting of the whole problem in terms of woman's place outside language, the idea that women might have of themselves an entirely different speech" (49).

5. It is noteworthy that this Lacanian paradigm is played out in Miss Amelia's life. Her mother is erased in the text (she is mentioned only once—on Miss Amelia's wedding day, she wears her dead mother's wedding dress) and is replaced by her father, whom, even in death, Miss Amelia appears to revere. Miss Amelia, then, may be read as the child who has renounced the mother and identifies with the phallic father and with the Law that forbids merger.

6. Applying a Freudian perspective, Gilbert and Gubar suggest that Lymon represents "the (false) baby as phallus, whose deformity and fake masculinity represent the deformity and fakery that (as Miss Amelia must learn) are associated with her own self-deluding male impersonation" (150).

7. Before Lymon's appearance, the world of The Ballad can be read to reflect an imbalance between the imaginary and the symbolic, that is, a culture in which the order identified with the Law that stands for exclusion is dangerously ascendant. The two orders are dependent on one another, and theorists argue that there needs to be a balance between them. Lacanian interpreters, particularly feminist ones, have labored to show what Jane Gallop calls "the positive and necessary function" of the imaginary. According to Gallop, "the imaginary embodies, fleshes out the skeletal symbolic" (Daughter's Seduction 149). Laplanche calls the imaginary "the vital order" (125). The passage into subjectivity, however, is a passage away from the imaginary and into the symbolic; and the imaginary, identified with the rejected mother-child relation and an original formlessness, is resisted and subordinated as we accede to what Jane Gallop calls "the ethical imperative [...] to disrupt the imaginary to reach the symbolic" (Reading Lacan 59).

8. The phallus stands for the loss that is constitutive of identity, and it is associated with the father-become-Father who ordains this separation. Because this moment of splitting constitutes identity and because the father ordains it, the child associates the phallus with power, the power to constitute the self. But, as Jacqueline Rose points out,

"this is the ultimate fantasy" (32). The phallus cannot confer complete identity; the phallus is merely a symbol for the rupture that made identity possible. However, human beings continue to identify the phallus with the power to make good our loss.

9. Although they do not apply a Lacanian methodology, Gilbert and Gubar seem to imply a similar reading of Marvin's symbolic role in the text. They write that Miss Amelia is "caught between two phallic beings, the one exploitative, the other vengeful" (150).

10. Lacan defines the Other as the always posited but never grasped original signifier of being. We look to the Other to guarantee meaning, but, in Lacan's words, "there is no Other of the Other" (Écrits 311); that is, there is no transcendental or fixed sign that imbues our cultural signifiers with meaning.

11. Gilbert and Gubar have observed that the struggle between Miss Amelia and Marvin takes the form of a primal scene. They state that "the spectacular fight in which Marvin Macy and Miss Amelia engage before a mass of spectators [. . .] is the primal scene of sexual consummation which did not take place on their wedding night" (151).

12. Gilbert and Gubar offer several provocative other interpretations of Lymon's decisive intervention in the struggle. Each of them resonates interestingly with my own. In one Freudian reading, they interpret Miss Amelia as being punished for "penis envy." In another, the fight signals the moment when she is forced to confront her desire for Marvin Macy. In the third, Miss Amelia is the medium for a homosexual bonding between Lymon and Macy. It should perhaps also be explained that Gilbert and Gubar's purpose is to reveal that McCullers has "internalized just the horror at independent womanhood which marks the writings of literary men from Faulkner to Wylie" (147). I would modify that statement and say that McCullers has psychically internalized an exclusionary model of identity and the social order.

13. Freud uncovers the primal scene in the course of analyzing a patient identified as the Wolf Man, who, as a child, either witnessed his parents engaged in coitus a tergo or imagined such a scene after having observed animals copulating. For a full discussion of the primal scene, see Freud's case study of the "Wolf Man," Standard Edition 17:36, 77–80, 107–09. See also Brooks, "Fictions of the Wolf Man: Freud and Narrative Understanding" in Reading for the Plot.

14. All attempts to restore the phallus are prohibited by the Law of the Father. In fact, Lacan writes that the Law is the Law against jouissance: "But we must insist that jouissance is forbidden to him who speaks as such, although it can only be said between the lines for whoever is subject of the Law, since the Law is grounded in this very prohibition" (Écrits 319).

15. In the words of Terry Eagleton, "The presence of the father, symbolized by the phallus, teaches the child that it must take up a place in the family which is defined by sexual difference, by exclusion (it cannot be its parent's lover) and by absence (it must relinquish its earlier bonds to the mother's body)" (167).

Works Cited

Bloom, Harold. Introduction. Carson McCullers. Ed. Harold Bloom. New York: Chelsea, 1986.

Brooks, Peter. Reading for the Plot: Design and Intention in Narrative. New York: Knopf, 1984.

Broughton, Panthea. "Rejection of the Feminine in Carson McCullers's The Ballad of the Sad Café." Twentieth Century Literature 20 (January 1974): 34–43.

Chodorow, Nancy. The Reproduction of Mothering: Psychoanalysis and the Sociology of Gender. Berkeley: U of California P, 1978.

Clark, Beverly Lyon and Melvin J. Friedman, eds. Critical Essays on Carson McCullers. New York: Hall, 1996.

Eagleton, Terry. Literary Theory: An Introduction. Minneapolis: U Minnesota P, 1983.

Evans, Oliver. "The Case of Carson McCullers." Clark and Friedman 124–28.

Freud, Sigmund. The Standard Edition of the Complete Psychological Works of Freud. Ed. and trans. James Strachey. 24 vols. London: Hogarth, 1961.

Gallop, Jane. The Daughter's Seduction: Feminism and Psychoanalysis. Ithaca: Cornell UP, 1982.

———. Reading Lacan. Ithaca: Cornell UP, 1985.

Gilbert, Sandra M. and Susan Gubar. "Fighting for Life." Clark and Friedman 147–54.

Lacan, Jacques. Écrits: A Selection. Trans. by Alan Sheridan. 1966. New York: Norton, 1977.

Laplanche, Jean. Life and Death in Psychoanalysis. Trans. by Jeffrey Mehlman. Baltimore: Johns Hopkins UP, 1976.

Lee, Jonathan Scott. Jacques Lacan. Amherst: U of Massachusetts P, 1990.

McCullers, Carson. The Ballad of the Sad Café and Other Stories. New York: Bantam, 1971.

———. Preface. The Square Root of Wonderful: A Play. Boston: Houghton, 1971.

Mellard, James M. Using Lacan, Reading Fiction. Urbana: U of Illinois P, 1991.

Mitchell, Juliet, ed. Feminine Sexuality: Jacques Lacan and the "Ecole Freudienne." Ed. and trans. Jacqueline Rose. New York: Norton, 1992.

Paulson, Suzanne Morrow. "Carson McCullers's The Ballad of the Sad Café: A Song Half Sung, Misogyny, and 'Ganging Up.'" Clark and Friedman 187–205.

Rose, Jacqueline. Introduction. Mitchell 27–57.

BETTY E. McKINNIE AND CARLOS L. DEWS

The Delayed Entrance of Lily Mae Jenkins: Queer Identity, Gender Ambiguity, and Southern Ambivalence in Carson McCullers's The Member of the Wedding

Despite the importance the South plays in her fiction and drama, Carson McCullers was ambivalent about her native region. Delma Eugene Presley, in "Carson McCullers and the South," and Louis Rubin, in "Carson McCullers: The Aesthetic of Pain," provide insight into the possible sources of her feelings toward the South and the impact these feelings had on her work, yet both critics fail to consider perhaps the most important reason for her desire to escape the South. Our essay, through the examination of an obscure character once proposed then removed from her first novel and only mentioned in a later novel and play, suggests that McCullers's ambivalence comes from her response to the South's homophobia and its strict demands of gendered behavior. We not only furnish a new reading of McCullers as a playwright and as an unconventional Southern woman, but we also encourage a more general reading of queer and gender identity in all of her work. This new key to reading McCullers's response to the South appears in the ghostly form of a "waifish Negro homosexual," Lily Mae Jenkins (McCullers, "Author's Outline" 140).

In 1938, Carson McCullers submitted an outline of her first novel, "The Mute" (published as *The Heart Is a Lonely Hunter*), to Houghton Mifflin as an entry in a first novel contest. The author described "The Mute" in her outline as "the story of five isolated, lonely people in their search for expression and

From *Southern Women Playwrights: New Essays in Literary History and Criticism*, edited by Robert L. McDonald and Linda Rohrer Paige, pp. 61–72. © 2002 by the University of Alabama Press.

spiritual integration with something greater than themselves. One of these five persons is a deaf mute, John Singer and it is around him that the whole book pivots" (125). McCullers describes one of the proposed secondary characters as "an abandoned, waifish Negro homosexual who haunts the Sunny Dixie show where Jake [Blount] works. He is always dancing. His mind and feelings are childish and he is totally unfit to earn his living" (140). McCullers also incorporated in the outline what other characters would say about Lily Mae, including Portia's description of Lily Mae for her father, Dr. Copeland:

> Lily Mae is right pitiful now. I don't know if you ever noticed any boys like this but he cares for mens instead of girls. When he were younger he used to be real cute. He were all the time dressing up in girls clothes and laughing. Everybody thought he were real cute then. (140–41)

In another section of "The Mute" outline, the reader learns why other characters tolerate Lily Mae. McCullers wrote, "Because of [Lily Mae's] skill in music and dancing he is a friend of Willie's. [Lily Mae] is always half starved and he hangs around Portia's kitchen constantly in the hopes of getting a meal. When Highboy and Willie are gone Portia takes some comfort in Lily Mae" (140). Portia says, "[Lily Mae] getting old and he seem different. He all the time hungry and he real pitiful. He loves to come set and talk with me in the kitchen. He dances for me and I gives him a little dinner" (141). According to the outline, after the character Willie returns home from serving a prison sentence, "Willie's story is repeated over and over in sullen monotones. Then this atmosphere begins to change. Willie sits up on the cot and begins to play his harp. Lily Mae starts dancing. As the evening progresses, the atmosphere changes to a wild artificial release of merriment" (143). A few significant details from these descriptions help explain McCullers's intended use of the character of Lily Mae in the proposed novel. As the words used to describe Lily Mae at his introduction suggest—"abandoned," "waifish," "homosexual," "unfit" (140)—he serves as an example of the isolated, shunned, and lonely character; an emblem of the fundamental isolated nature of all humans; a source of solace and commiseration for similarly isolated characters; and an inspiration for pity.

In fact, Portia and other characters, instead of accepting him fully, see Lily Mae only as a distraction from everyday life. The fact that Portia "takes some comfort" from Lily Mae signifies McCullers's depiction of this character as transcendent of rigid gender and sexual boundaries and able to provide comfort to another outsider. Portia uses Lily Mae as a distraction from her own loneliness because she identifies with his status; for example, she works as a domestic servant in a white household. Ultimately Lily Mae functions simultaneously as an insider and outsider: he represents the ambivalence with which the community deals with those outside its rigid boundaries of acceptable behavior, yet he also has value for his shamanistic, curative, or empathetic qualities.

It is perhaps incorrect to describe Carson McCullers as a dramatist, and in many ways the play *The Member of the Wedding* can be seen as an anomaly in the corpus of her work. McCullers penned only two plays and one of these, *The Member of the Wedding*, was an adaptation of her novel by the same name. Her only play written as such, *The Square Root of Wonderful*, was a dramatic and literary failure when it appeared briefly on Broadway in 1957. McCullers wrote of her lack of training in writing for the stage and her adaptation of *Member* in an introduction she wrote for the published version of *Square Root* in 1958:

> Tennessee Williams wrote me about the book and asked me if I could come and spend the summer with him on Nantucket and I accepted the invitation. During that sea-summer lit with the glow of a new friendship he suggested I do *The Member of the Wedding* as a play. I was hesitant at first, knowing nothing about the theatre. I had seen only about ten plays in my life, including high school *Hamlet*s and *Vagabond Kings*. (viii)

If McCullers did not consider herself primarily a playwright, had so little experience with drama, and preferred writing prose, what might explain the strength, skillful nature, and mature drama of *Member* (adapted for the stage in 1946) and the relative weakness, immature style, and haphazard construction of *Square Root* written a decade later? The biographically over-determined nature of the character of Lily Mae Jenkins as well as the inherent struggles with McCullers's identity as a Southerner in writing of her own adolescence in the South might also provide an answer to this question.

Lily Mae Jenkins might not be known to those familiar with *The Heart Is a Lonely Hunter,* for when the novel was published in 1940 the "waifish Negro homosexual" (140) had been removed from the manuscript. Portia turns to other characters for distraction and solace, Highboy does the dancing at the telling of Willie's tale, and other characters (Jake Blount, Portia, Dr. Copeland, and Mick) fill the role of outsider. Six years after the publication of *Heart*, McCullers resurrected Lily Mae Jenkins in her novel then play *The Member of the Wedding*. Unlike the proposed appearance in "The Mute," Lily Mae does not actually appear as a character in *Member;* one of the central characters merely mentions him. Additionally, unlike his appearance in "The

Mute" outline, where he serves various contradictory or ambiguous functions, Lily Mae appears to have a single purpose in *Member*.

The Member of the Wedding dramatizes the story of Frankie Addams, a lonely girl on the brink of sexual maturity, and details her search for a meaningful connection with another human being and the world outside her small Southern hometown. After Frankie Addams has revealed her plan to join her brother and his new bride after their wedding in her "we of me," a social and spiritual unit seen as a solution to her isolation and loneliness, Berenice, the family's cook and housekeeper, attempts to dissuade Frankie from leaving. In a pivotal scene in the play, Berenice attempts to instill in Frankie a reverence for what might be called naturalized monogamous heterosexuality:

> BERENICE: Truly, Frankie, what makes you think they want you taggin' along with them? Two is company and three is a crowd. And that's the main thing bout a wedding. Two is company and three is a crowd.
> FRANKIE: You wait and see.
> BERENICE: Remember back to the time of the flood. Remember Noah and the Ark. (55)
>
> . . . .
>
> FRANKIE: That's all right. But you wait and see. They will take me.
> BERENICE: And if they don't?
> FRANKIE: If they don't, I will kill myself. (55–56)

Frankie believes that death provides the only recourse for non-acceptance of naturalized heterosexuality; committing suicide seems to be her only option, the threat of which underscores (to Berenice) the seriousness of Frankie's desire for a "we of me." Frankie's strong negative response to Berenice, her threat of suicide, and her refusal to accept exclusion from the wedding force Berenice to offer examples of deviant behavior as negative guideposts. Berenice continues:

> BERENICE: . . . I have heard of many a peculiar thing. I have knew men to fall in love with girls so ugly that you wonder if their eyes is straight.
> JOHN HENRY: Who?
> BERENICE: I have knew women to love veritable satans and thank Jesus when they put their split hooves over the threshold. I have knew boys to take it into their heads to fall in love with other boys. You know Lily Mae Jenkins?

FRANKIE: I'm not sure. I know a lot of people.
BERENICE: Well, you either know him or you don't know him.
He prisses around in a girls' blouse with one arm akimbo. Now
this Lily Mae Jenkins fell in love with a man name Juney Jones.
A man, mind you. And Lily Mae turned into a girl. He changed
his nature and his sex and turned into a girl.
FRANKIE: What?
BERENICE: He did. To all intents and purposes . . .
FRANKIE: It's funny I can't think who you are talking about. I
used to think I knew so many people.
BERENICE: Well, you don't need to know Lily Mae Jenkins.
You can live without knowing him.
FRANKIE: Anyway, I don't believe you.
BERENICE: I ain't arguing with you. What was we speaking
about?
FRANKIE: About peculiar things. (57)

Lily Mae functions in this scene solely as an example of the bizarre, of
what society tolerates but does not fully accept. Berenice's suggestion that
"you don't need to know Lily Mae Jenkins. You can live without knowing
him" limits Lily Mae's function in the play to his use as a cautionary model.
Berenice's use of Lily Mae robs him of his subjectivity and underscores the
obviously disposable nature of the sexual transgressive. Louise Westling
writes the following in her essay "Tomboys and Revolting Femininity":
"Images of sexual ambivalence are carefully cultivated throughout the novel
in the Negro transvestite Lily Mae Jenkins. . . . Always such hermaphroditic
or androgynous references are placed in a negative frame, for the novel's
entire movement is toward Frankie's ultimate submission to the inexorable
demand that she accept her sex as female" (127). Later in the same scene
Berenice returns to the lesson she attempts to teach Frankie, saying: "But
what I'm warning is this. If you start out falling in love with some unheard-of
thing like that, what is going to happen to you? If you take a mania like this,
it won't be the last time and of that you can be sure. So what will become of
you? Will you be trying to break into weddings the rest of your days?" (80).

Berenice considers Frankie's "falling in love with a wedding" even
more queer than she views Lily Mae's changed nature. Berenice seems to
associate what Frankie wants to do with what Lily Mae has done because
both are "considered unacceptable behavior by society. Concerned for
Frankie's future, Berenice issues her cautionary tale to persuade Frankie
to conform, to "go along to get along." Her warning to the young girl
illustrates that heterosexuality remains the norm, and resistance to perceived
normalcy is futile.

Lily Mae's proposed roles in "The Mute," his subsequent removal from the work in progress, and his eventual reappearance in McCullers's play and novel, *Member*, can best be explained within the context of McCullers's own struggle with sexual/gender identity and with her ambivalent relationship with her native South. Carson McCullers's living and writing conditions during the periods in which she wrote the works where Lily Mae appears are significant. McCullers wrote the outline for her proposed first novel, "The Mute," and revised the completed manuscript (by then changed to *The Heart Is a Lonely Hunter*) while living with her husband, Reeves McCullers, in Charlotte and Fayetteville, North Carolina, between 1938 and 1940. Upon publication of the novel, Carson and Reeves moved to New York in 1940, where they soon divorced, and Carson became involved with a wide range of friends from international artistic, musical, and literary circles. During this period McCullers also received her "illumination," as she described inspiration in her autobiography, for *Member* (32).

Significantly, McCullers composed *Member* primarily in New York City and in the Yaddo arts colony of Saratoga Springs, New York, between 1940 and 1945. The adaptation of the novel into the play took place under the influence of Tennessee Williams, who, as McCullers recalled, suggested the adaptation and provided friendship and inspiration during the summer of 1946 on Nantucket Island (Carr 270–78).

Lori Kenschaft, in "Homoerotics and Human Connections: Reading Carson McCullers 'As a Lesbian,'" details this period's relevance to McCullers's growing sexual and gender self-concept:

> *The Ballad of the Sad Café* was written in the summer of 1941; *The Member of the Wedding* was an ongoing project from 1939 to 1946. In 1940 McCullers fell in love with Annemarie Clarac-Schwarzenbach, whom she later considered the greatest passion of her life. According to her biographer, McCullers's husband was already accustomed to her frequent crushes on women. That fall they separated and she moved into a group house. Her housemates included Benjamin Britten and Peter Pears, who were life-long lovers, Christopher Isherwood, and W. H. Auden, whose new lover, Chester Kallman, soon moved in. The next summer at Yaddo, McCullers's men's clothes and boyish haircut made her easily identifiable as a "mannish woman." (221)

In her essay "How I Began to Write," McCullers described her feelings about her hometown and her desire to leave for New York as early as age seventeen: "By that winter [1934–35] the family rooms, the whole town, seemed to pinch and cramp my adolescent heart. I longed for wanderings. I longed especially for New York" (*Mortgaged* 251).

The negative reaction by those around her to her androgynous nature and masculine dress proved a likely factor in her desire for escape. In her biography of McCullers, *The Lonely Hunter*, Virginia Spencer Carr explains McCullers's adolescent experience with this cultural anxiety: "When Carson was younger, some of the girls gathered in little clumps of femininity and threw rocks at her when she walked nearby, snickering loud asides and tossing within hearing distance such descriptive labels as 'weird,' 'freakish-looking,' and 'queer'" (29–30).

McCullers articulated her desire to leave the South by including a similar yearning for escape in her characters Frankie Addams and Mick Kelly. As Oliver Evans writes of the autobiographical nature of Mick and Frankie: "Certainly the resemblances between Lula Carson Smith and Mick Kelly are too obvious to be ignored: both are tall for their age, both are tomboys, and the fathers of both are small-town jewelers. The resemblances between Lula Carson Smith and Frankie Addams are stronger still" (18). And as Presley has observed, "For both Mick and Frankie, leaving home would have been a means of escaping the inevitable trap" (105).

Carr reveals the ambivalence McCullers felt about the South: "Her work demanded that she go back from time to time, just as she had told Eleanor Clark at Yaddo a few years earlier that she must periodically return to the South to renew her 'sense of horror'" (313). Indeed, in an interview with *Esquire* magazine McCullers once remarked, "People ask me why I don't go back to the South more often. But the South is a very emotional experience for me, fraught with all the memories of my childhood. When I go back South I always get into arguments, so that a visit to Columbus is a stirring up of love and antagonism" (qtd. in Presley 109).

Negative reaction to characters in her second novel, *Reflections in a Golden Eye*, would confirm any fears McCullers had about the reception of Lily Mae had he remained in "The Mute." In her unfinished autobiography, *Illumination and Night Glare*, McCullers recalls the reaction she faced during a visit to her hometown after the publication of *Reflections*: "'Reflections In A Golden Eye' was just published, and this, with the attendant publicity made quite a stir in town and especially at Ft. Benning, the Army Post nearby. . . . The Ku Klux Klan even called me and said, 'we are the Klan and we don't like nigger lovers or fairies. Tonight will be your night'" (31).

If such a reaction confirmed her anxiety when contemplating the South's reaction to her work, McCullers experienced reinforcement of her positive associations with life in the North. Living with a group that became her personal "we of me" and working in a setting that fostered her political and social progressiveness, McCullers began to fully comprehend the intolerance of the South. As Presley writes, "In Brooklyn, the young Mrs. McCullers found what, in the simple logic of *The Heart Is a Lonely Hunter*, could have saved Mick Kelly: a place where she could relish being different, a sympathetic community in which she could find uncritical acceptance" (103); or as McCullers herself wrote in the essay "Brooklyn Is My Neighbourhood," "That is one of the things I love most about Brooklyn. Everyone is not expected to be exactly like everyone else" (220).

By the time McCullers published *Member*, she also had experienced an acceptance of her lesbianism or bisexuality. Having moved to New York, she discovered a new society that allowed her to pursue any type of relationship she desired. Finding a community that embraced homosexuality helped McCullers reexamine her notions about the South's rigidity and repressiveness. Upon reviewing the South's attitude toward sexual transgression, McCullers perhaps realized the flaws in her thinking about the South and saw her attempts to effect lasting social change there as futile.

McCullers's developing ideas about the racism and intolerance of the South would later be articulated in her final novel, *Clock Without Hands*. According to Virginia Spencer Carr, "The South which Carson depicted in *Clock Without Hands*, as in her earlier works, was sadly lacking in the dimensions of justice and humanity. It was a South she had left but still viewed with the ambivalent feelings of affection and rancor" (493). Presley misunderstands McCullers's reaction to the South Carr describes as an indication of McCullers's lack of knowledge of the South: "In *Clock Without Hands* Mrs. McCullers attempted to go back home, but the South as she described it never existed, and it does not exist in this fiction" (108). However, given her negative experiences with racism and, perhaps most importantly, homophobia, the South that never existed in McCullers's work was a just and accepting South.

In an attempt to come to terms with her isolation as a sexual transgressive in the South, McCullers created characters through whom she could illustrate her frustration. According to Oliver Evans, "The . . . reason Mrs. McCullers has suffered unfavorable criticism is her choice of characters and situations. It must be admitted that her characters are not always the kind one is likely to encounter in ordinary experience, and that the situations in which she places them are frequently uncommon, even implausible" (127). By creating characters who do not seem familiar to us, McCullers creates an effective isolation for these individuals which replicates her own experience as a progressive Southerner in the repressive South.

Despite their significant contribution of detail and biographical background to a consideration of McCullers's relationship with the South and the impact of that relationship on her work, Presley and Rubin fail to consider the reasons McCullers might have had to want to escape her native region. By failing to understand the influence of the South's homophobia on McCullers, Presley appears to blame her for her escape and suggests the unbearably painful life of a queer woman in the South should be credited with at least providing artistic inspiration: "The fact that she was a Southerner was a great burden she struggled to displace very early in her career. Significantly, out of the struggle emerged some literature of the first order. But once she abandoned the landscape of her agony, she wrote works which lack distinction. Her early success and her ultimate failure, I maintain, can be attributed in large measure to this pattern of struggle in her relationship to the South" (99).

Presley also seems to blame McCullers for her continued distrust of the South without recognizing the realities of the South: "Carson McCullers' relationship to the land of her youth reminds us that she engaged in something other than a lover's quarrel with the South. A quarrel between lovers implies that both parties have mutual understanding, mutual respect, as it were" (105). Presley's idea that McCullers's "chief difficulties as a writer stemmed from her disregard of her own past" might be better understood in reverse. McCullers did not abandon the South; the South disregarded her. A flight from a homophobic and misogynistic society seems justifiable for McCullers and many of her fellow queer Southerners: Tennessee Williams and Truman Capote, for example, to name only two of her friends and fellow expatriate Southerners.

In "Carson McCullers The Aesthetic of Pain," Louis D. Rubin posits this explanation for McCullers's desire to move to New York:

> New York was the place of art, of culture, of fulfillment, where the dreams of the lonely provincial could come true. . . . The particular vision of Carson McCullers, the capacity for recognizing and portraying and sympathetically identifying with pain and loneliness, could arise only out of a social situation in which the patterns and forms and expectations of conduct and attitude are very firmly and formidably present, so that the inability or failure to function within those patterns seems crucial. . . . If there is a strong set of expectations, and one is unable to fulfill them and yet be oneself, then one searches out for kindred sufferers, in order to feel less lonely through assurance of their pain as well. (113, 119)

For McCullers and her characters, however, this private distance is one of necessity because of the South's response to difference. The vague "one reason or other" offers an unfortunate eliding of the very significance of the South's intransigent homophobia and racism.

Although very little is known of the process by which McCullers transformed her outline of "The Mute" into the novel *Heart*, at least two plausible explanations exist for her removal of Lily Mae Jenkins. McCullers perhaps removed Lily Mae from the published version of the novel because she believed the South would not tolerate a story of sexual transgression both in the telling of the story of the transgression (by McCullers in the act of writing the novel) and in the record of the transgressive (in the depicted life of Lily Mae Jenkins). Perhaps McCullers believed Lily Mae would be unacceptable to towns such as her native Columbus, Georgia, or that a character like Lily Mae Jenkins, with his multiple social roles, was unimaginable in a place like Columbus.

McCullers's original conception of Lily Mae Jenkins in the South and her removal of him from her first novel and subsequent return to him for her play *Member* are articulations of her ambivalence toward the South and the region's response to gender ambiguity and sexual transgression. With little experience away from her native South and perhaps an inability to imagine a place for Lily Mae in the South, or in her novel, McCullers felt compelled to remove him. Lily Mae's absence might then be simply the editorial removal of a character the author could not imagine in the setting of the work (perhaps not unlike McCullers's inability to imagine her own future in the South). Lily Mae's removal from the novel allows McCullers to spare her character from searching for a resolution to the paradox of Southern queer identity, a paradox fraught with its concomitant ambivalences—and with which McCullers found herself struggling. McCullers's extraction of Lily Mae from the novel was a generous gesture. By removing Lily Mae, McCullers spared him the painful death of spiritual and personal starvation which would have been his fate in the South McCullers knew all too well.

Returning once again to McCullers's introduction to the published edition of her failed play *The Square Root of Wonderful*, one can perhaps see McCullers herself providing answers to the lingering questions as to the source of the power of the adolescent dilemma dramatized in *Member*, for which Lily Mae Jenkins serves as a simulacrum:

> When people ask why I write for the theatre I can only counter with another question. Why does anyone write at all? I suppose a writer writes out of some inward compulsion to transform his own experience (much of it is unconscious) into the universal and symbolical. The themes the artist chooses are always deeply personal. I suppose my central theme is the theme of spiritual isolation. Certainly I have always felt alone. In addition to being lonely, a writer is also amorphous. A writer soon discovers he has no single identity but lives the lives of all the people he creates

and his weathers are independent of the actual day around him. I
live with the people I create and it has always made my essential
loneliness less keen. (viii)

Perhaps the above pronouncement provides not only a clue to the questions
regarding Lily Mae Jenkins's characterization in her novel and play but also
to the questions about McCullers as a dramatist. Perhaps as a recapitulation
of her own childhood drama, *Member* was the only story that McCullers
could successfully dramatize. McCullers might well be said to have been
dramatizing her own adolescent struggles with gender and sexuality and
calling upon unresolved psychic (unconscious) material in her adaptation of
Member rather than merely dramatizing her novel for the stage. Lily Mae
could then be read as one of the characters McCullers created to "live with"
in order to feel her loneliness less keenly. However, this role for Lily Mae
does not consider McCullers's use of Lily Mae as a critique of the South and
does not help explain her wavering use of Lily Mae.

When McCullers reintroduces Lily Mae Jenkins in *Member* and
mercifully leaves him out of sight, she uses him only to reflect negatively
on the South and its lack of imagination in providing a place for such a
character. Had he remained in *Heart*, Lily Mae would have served as a mirror
placed in front of McCullers's face, reflecting a too-painful image of her own
suffering. Instead, McCullers removed him from the novel and recalled him
in *The Member of the Wedding* to serve as an all-too-honest reflection of the
South and its intolerant nature, a South McCullers knew in an all-too-real
way as an intolerant place where her work for change was futile.

Works Cited

Carr, Virginia Spencer. *The Lonely Hunter: A Biography of Carson McCullers*. Garden City,
    NY: Doubleday, 1975.
Evans, Oliver. "The Case of Carson McCullers." *Critical Essays on Carson McCullers*. Ed.
    Beverly L. Clark and Melvin J. Friedman. New York: Hall, 1996. 123–28.
Kenschaft, Lori J. "Homoerotics and Human Connections: Reading Carson McCullers 'As
    a Lesbian.'" *Critical Essays on Carson McCullers*. Ed. Beverly L. Clark and Melvin J.
    Friedman. New York: Hall, 1996. 220–33.
McCullers, Carson. "Author's Outline of 'The Mute' (*The Heart Is a Lonely Hunter*)." *The
    Mortgaged Heart*. Ed. Margarita G. Smith. Boston: Houghton, 1971. 124–49.
———. "Brooklyn Is My Neighbourhood." *The Mortgaged Heart*. Ed. Margarita G. Smith.
    Boston: Houghton, 1971. 216–20.
———. *Clock Without Hands*. Boston: Houghton-Riverside, 1953.
———. *The Heart Is a Lonely Hunter*. New York: Modern Library, 1993.
———. "How I Began to Write." *The Mortgaged Heart*. Ed. Margarita G. Smith. Boston:
    Houghton, 1971. 249–51.

———. *Illumination and Night Glare: The Unfinished Autobiography of Carson McCullers*. Ed. Carlos L. Dews. Madison: U of Wisconsin P, 1999.

———. *The Member of the Wedding* (Play). New York: New Directions, 1951.

———. *The Member of the Wedding*. Boston: Houghton, 1973.

———. *Reflections in a Golden Eye*. Cambridge: Riverside, 1941.

———. *The Square Root of Wonderful*. Introduction. Dunwoody, GA: Berg, 1971. vii–x.

Presley, Delma Eugene. "Carson McCullers and the South." 1974. *Critical Essays on Carson McCullers*. Ed. Beverly Lyon Clark and Melvin J. Friedman. New York: Hall, 1996. 99–110.

Rubin, Louis D., Jr. "Carson McCullers: The Aesthetic of Pain." 1977. *Critical Essays on Carson McCullers*. Ed. Beverly Lyon Clark and Melvin J. Friedman. New York: Hall, 1996. 111–23.

Westling, Louise. "Tomboys and Revolting Femininity." *Sacred Groves and Ravaged Gardens: The Fiction of Eudora Welty, Carson McCullers, and Flannery O'Connor*. Athens: U of Georgia P, 1985. 110–32.

JEFF ABERNATHY

Divided Hearts:
Carson McCullers and Harper Lee
Explore Racial Uncertainty

There was a stage, when we were about thirteen, in which we "went Negro." We tried to broaden our accents to sound like Negroes, as if there were not enough similarity already. We consciously walked like young Negroes, mocking their swinging gait, moving our arms the way they did, cracking our knuckles and whistling between our teeth.

—Willie Morris

I hardly let characters speak unless they are Southern. Wolfe wrote brilliantly of Brooklyn, but more brilliantly of the Southern cadence and ways of speech. This is particularly true of Southern writers because it is not only their speech and the foliage, but their entire culture—which makes it a homeland within a homeland. No matter what the politics, the degree or non-degree of liberalism in a Southern writer, he is still bound to this particular regionalism of language and voices and foliage and memory.

—Carson McCullers

Popular narratives of race in the South appeared more frequently in the wake of World War Two. The pattern of initiation and reversal I have traced took hold in the popular imagination in post-war America, even as civil unrest among African Americans in the Jim Crow South was beginning. In

From *To Hell and Back: Race and Betrayal in the Southern Novel*, pp. 84–106. © 2003 by the University of Georgia Press.

the two decades following the war, racial certainties spun apart in popular culture as in the southern novel. When Elvis Presley recalled his turbulent first days as a rock singer, he remembered what it meant to sound black for a white audience: "[W]hen the record came out a lot of people liked it and you could hear folks around town saying, 'Is he, is he?' and I'm going, 'Am I, am I?'" (qtd. in Marcus, *Mystery Train* 152).

The potential of racial uncertainty characterizes Carson McCullers's *The Member of the Wedding* and Harper Lee's *To Kill a Mockingbird*, both of which repeat the pattern of inversion we have been tracing thus far—an emerging American mythos pertaining to race—in narratives that focus upon the development of adolescent characters through their relationships with marginalized and exotic African American characters. While both novels portray white girls whose mothers are absent and who look to their black servants for counsel, McCullers equips Frankie Addams's black mentor, Berenice, with a degree of autonomy comparable to that of Faulkner's Lucas Beauchamp. Lee, by contrast, portrays African American characters wholly dependent upon the white community.

A SAD AND UGLY ROOM

Frankie Addams of Carson McCullers's *The Member of the Wedding* discovers her identity in moving back and forth between black and white worlds, a theme alluded to by her recurrent name and costume changes. Because her mother has died and she is increasingly alienated from her father, Frankie looks to Berenice, her family's black cook, as moral guide and as model for self-discovery. She vacillates between conflicting desires to remain in the exoticized black world of Berenice's kitchen—territory owned by Frankie's father but ruled by Berenice alone—and to escape to a white one symbolized by her brother's imminent wedding. She fears discovering a marginalized black identity within herself as she moves into adolescence, a time when she will feel compelled to shed all association with blackness. Frankie's attempts to escape the black world that Berenice represents as well as her repeated efforts to return to that world give shape and focus to the broken identity she forms. Frankie perceives Berenice in a series of familiar stereotypes: as Margaret McDowell writes, for Frankie, Berenice is variously "affectionate or stern mother, the primitive seer, and the black queen who once lived with her dream lover" (81). Frankie sees her mentor through the prism of white society's gaze; Berenice, however, persistently attempts to compel Frankie to view her as an individual outside of the socially enforced constructs of self and other.

For Frankie, the black world dominated by Berenice is fractured and incomplete and thus an accurate reflection of her own state of mind. In her romantic notions of joining her older brother and his new wife on their honeymoon, she believes that she has found a path that will lead her to the wholeness she associates with whiteness and away from the childhood world inextricably tied to Berenice and to a marginalized black identity. When Berenice cautiously tries to dissuade Frankie from her plan, Frankie suspects her of jealousy.

From the opening pages of the novel, Frankie feels ill at ease in Berenice's kitchen, for it is a "sad and ugly room" in which the walls are covered with Frankie's cousin John Henry's "queer, child drawings, as far up as his arm would reach" (4). In her longing to escape childhood, she likewise wishes to grow out of her relationship with Berenice: the kitchen soon looks to her "like that of a room in the crazy-house. And now the old kitchen made Frankie sick. The name for what had happened to her Frankie did not know, but she could feel her squeezed heart beating against the table edge" (4). In her departures from the kitchen, Frankie escapes all guilt: it is a place from which Frankie wishes she could "just light out," yet her dependence upon Berenice leaves her unable to do so (6).

Yet Frankie persistently returns to that kitchen, for if she experiences guilt there, she also finds solace. Berenice recognizes Frankie's dilemma throughout, insisting that Frankie confront her own identity. "'You jealous [of the wedding],' said Berenice. 'Go and behold yourself in the mirror. I can see from the color in your eye'" (2). Frankie attempts to understand her own experience through the filter of Berenice's perspective. Immediately after her brother and his fiancée come to visit, Frankie asks Berenice to recount the visit for her once again:

> "Tell me," she said. "Tell me exactly how it was."
> "You know!" said Berenice. "You seen them."
> "But tell me," Frankie said. (26)

Frankie validates her experiences by channeling them through Berenice, and, while she struggles throughout the novel to achieve an identity independent of her mammy, she never quite achieves the goal. "'Tell me,'" Frankie says again. "'Exactly what did they look like?'" Frankie says once Berenice has interpreted the visit for her (27). Winthrop Jordan writes of the need westerners have always felt to see themselves through the experience of the colonized other; for Jordan, the English used "peoples overseas as social mirrors" that reflected the very traits the English feared in themselves (40). Here Frankie reifies her own experience through that of her black companion, reflecting a like dependence in American culture in which the dominant society has always defined itself by the margin, by what it claims not to be.

Despite her stated desire to become a "member of the wedding" and leave with her brother when he marries, Frankie remains entranced by the mysterious blackness she associates with Berenice. When Berenice's son, Honey, and her suitor, T.T., interrupt a discussion between Frankie and Berenice one evening, Honey perplexes Frankie. "'That sure is a cute suit you got on, Honey,'" Berenice says. "'Where'd you get it?'" Honey's response initially troubles Frankie: "Honey could talk like a white school-teacher; his lavender lips could move as quick and light as butterflies. But he only answered with a colored word, a dark sound from the throat that can mean anything. 'Ahhnnh,' he said" (36). Already forbidden and unknown, blackness becomes more fascinating to Frankie as it becomes less articulate.

Honey's contradictions attract Frankie, for he is, like herself and like Berenice, caught between a white world and a black one. Frankie feels a strong communion with Berenice and the two men: when the three patiently wait for Frankie to leave so that they can drink whiskey, "[s]he stood in the door and looked at them. She did not want to go away" (36). And yet once Frankie leaves, she suspects Berenice will betray her plan to join the wedding party. "She closed the door, but behind her she could hear their voices. With her head against the kitchen door she could hear the murmuring dark sounds that rose and fell in a gentle way. Ayee—ayee" (36). McCullers emphasizes Frankie's curiosity with black dialect and black culture while further establishing the maternal bond between Frankie and Berenice. The words of the three—"murmuring dark sounds"—nurture rather than threaten Frankie as she eavesdrops. The marginal identity they share provides Frankie what sense of self she has, and if she aspires to join the white world symbolized by the wedding, she nevertheless takes comfort in the black one she has discovered in the kitchen. The nurturing Frankie receives is of course limited: she hears the sounds as she does only because she is eavesdropping. When Honey asks Berenice what she and Frankie had been discussing, to Frankie's surprise Berenice does not betray the girl's confidence: "'Just foolishness,'" she says (36).

Frankie's awareness of Berenice's othered status throughout the novel draws her to the older woman: she thinks that "nobody human" (3) would ever know why Berenice chooses to have a blue glass eye, and yet as "a member of nothing in the world" and "an unjoined person" (1), Frankie identifies with precisely this sense of alienation; ultimately, it is Berenice's blackness with which Frankie claims empathy. The black world to which Berenice is a kind of envoy offers Frankie a definition of her present self, since, like her, it is incomplete and abstract; by contrast, the white world, associated strongly with the wedding, gives her hope for future wholeness.

Later in the novel, Berenice attempts to ease Frankie's distress by pointing to the similarities between them: "'We all of us somehow caught.

We born this way or that way and we don't know why. But we caught anyhow'" (113). But Berenice refuses to allow Frankie, who has adopted the name "F. Jasmine," to yoke their troubles too closely, asserting,

> "I'm caught worse than you is.... Because I am colored. Everybody is caught one way or another. But they done drawn completely extra bounds around all colored people. They done squeezed us off in one corner by ourselves. So we caught that first-way I was telling, as all human beings is caught. And we caught as colored people also. Sometimes a boy like Honey feel like he just can't breathe no more. He feel like he got to break something or break himself. Sometimes it just about more than we can stand." (113–14)

McCullers thus engages the nation's anxieties over race, explicitly referencing the Jim Crow era, allowing Berenice a critical voice free of irony that contrasts sharply with Frankie's juvenile longings. Frankie expresses a desire "to break something, too," so as to share in Berenice's sense of being cast out despite Berenice's attempts to isolate the black experience (114). Yet Berenice's assertion that "'they done squeezed us off in one corner'" only draws Frankie closer, for she herself has a "squeezed heart" (4). In delineating the terms of her own life, Frankie appropriates Berenice's blackness, attempting to explain her alienation from white society through Berenice's explanation of racial oppression.

Berenice rejects any such yoking: though willing to act as a maternal figure to both Frankie and John Henry, she will not allow either of them authority over her own experience: "'I am black . . . I am colored'" (113). Later, Berenice observes Frankie's inability to "pass" as black, ironically proposing a reversal of racial identity as Frankie attempts to understand why she cannot change her name as she sees fit. "'Why is it against the law to change your name?'" Frankie asks. Berenice responds with pointed mockery: "'Suppose I would suddenly up and call myself Mrs. Eleanor Roosevelt. And you would begin naming yourself Joe Louis. And John Henry would try to pass off as Henry Ford. Now what kind of confusion do you think that would cause?'" (107). Berenice's levity is hardly innocent: Frankie's proposal of a shared racial identity threatens Berenice's authority over her own identity, so Berenice insists that no such exchange can take place. She claims her suffering—and her identity—as her own.

Despite Berenice's objections, Frankie persists in associating her own alienation with that of Berenice and so with the black community. And, having latched on to blackness as key to her own development, Frankie cannot now remove it from her understanding of herself, for all of Berenice's objections. We sense her alienation when later, left behind by Berenice, Frankie wanders to John Henry's house, where she tries to communicate with her cousin to no avail.[1] With dusk falling, she stands apart from John Henry, watching him as a blues horn—"the sad horn of some colored boy"— begins to play from "somewhere in the town" (41). Despite the fact that she does not know the player, Frankie immediately feels a kinship with him that she does not feel with her cousin: "Frankie stood stiff, her head bent and her eyes closed, listening. There was something about the tune that brought back to her all of the spring: flowers, the eyes of strangers, rain" (41). The horn player acts as muse to Frankie's alienation, his music reflecting the tangle of her consciousness and drawing her into herself even as she strains to hear. She believes the player, like Berenice, speaks to her in a fragmented form of communication her cousin cannot comprehend. Blackness thus becomes metaphor for Frankie's alienation. The expression that the "colored boy" gives to his blues brings Frankie to reminisce—her own blues—about the spring, a time before she felt cast out of childhood, a time before her present "long season of trouble" (41).

And yet, like Berenice, the horn player stops short of offering anything beyond mere association: "Just at the time when the tune should be laid, the music finished, the horn broke off" (41). Frankie awaits guidance that will not come, and in place of finding her own direction she mimics the black blues that she has heard: in her own blues, she "began to talk aloud" but pays no attention to her own words (42). Her improvisation leads her not toward the black world that inspired it but toward a white world in which blackness itself is suppressed:

> For it was just at that moment that Frankie understood. She knew who she was and how she was going into the world. Her squeezed heart suddenly opened and divided. Her heart divided like two wings. And when she spoke her voice was sure.
> "I know where I'm going," she said. (42)

Embrace and repulse, unite and betray. In the literary union of black and white, the one follows the other. Frankie decides to go to the wedding, toward what she believes will be an enveloping whiteness that will take her away from the ambivalence and frustration of Berenice's black world. Her evasion of darkness, of the place of blackness in her nascent identity, comes to constitute the major conflict in the novel, yet Frankie's resolution yields no definitive action. Because she has decided to set her sights on a white identity and to escape Berenice, her heart is no longer "squeezed," as it had been, but after her decision to become a member of the wedding, she momentarily retreats into childhood and her dependence upon Berenice. She ventures to the shores of a white world only to return to the comforting waters of a black one. In the end, however, what growth she does attain comes as a result of her rejection of any connection she might feel to a black identity.

Back in Berenice's kitchen, Frankie remains uncomfortable with the remnants of her participation in a black world and with the extent to which her desires and tastes are shaped by that world. Frankie questions Berenice about the name of her favorite food, hopping-john; she is reluctant to call it by its southern name now that she plans to join the white world that the wedding has come to represent. Southern food, of course, like southern identity, emerges out of the conflation of black and white cultures, and Frankie demonstrates deep discomfort with this multicultural reality.

> "Tell me. Is it just us who call this hopping-john? Or is it known by that name through all the country. It seems a strange name somehow."
>
> ". . . Well, I have heard it called peas and rice. Or rice and peas and pot-liquor. Or hopping-john. You can vary and take your pick."
>
> "But I'm not talking about this town," F. Jasmine said. "I mean in other places. I mean through all the world. I wonder what the French call it."
>
> "Oh," said Berenice. "Well, you ask me a question I cannot answer." (80–81)

Berenice, who knows a thing or two about signifiers, dismisses the importance of such transformations of language in much the same way that she has tried to dissuade Frankie from changing her name to F. Jasmine. Berenice dismisses Frankie's longing for a different name for hopping-john that is less southern, and less black, while Frankie ponders: "I wonder what the French call it.'" In slighting the name "hopping-john," Frankie symbolically rejects the black and southern experience of which Berenice is a constant reminder; likewise, she refuses to see the contributions of this racial blending to her own tastes and desires. Hopping-john is, after all, her preferred dish: "Now hopping-john was F. Jasmine's very favorite food. She had always warned them to wave a plate of rice and peas before her nose when she was in her coffin, to make certain there was no mistake" (76). Once again she aims to overcome her discomfort by embracing whiteness. "I know where I'm going,'" Frankie tells us, and her chosen destination is her brother's wedding, the refined ritual in which she finds a purity that contrasts with the mongrel identity she has taken on in Berenice's kitchen (42).

Frankie's distress at her present circumstance increases when Berenice tells her that her change of names is just as illogical as would be a change of race. Frankie reacts by circling the kitchen table with a knife in her hand, frustrated that she cannot bring herself to tell Berenice of her plans to go dancing, plans that also represent for her an escape from the black world of Berenice's kitchen. Berenice finally stops her: "'Set here in my lap . . . [a]nd rest a minute.'"

> F. Jasmine put the knife on the table and settled down on Berenice's lap. She leaned back and put her face against Berenice's neck; her face was sweaty and Berenice's neck was sweaty also, and they both smelled salty and sour and sharp. Her right leg was flung across Berenice's knee, and it was trembling—but when she steadied her toes on the floor, her leg did not tremble any more. . . .
>
> F. Jasmine rolled her head and rested her face against Berenice's shoulder. She could feel Berenice's soft big ninnas against her back, and her soft wide stomach, her warm solid legs. She had been breathing very fast, but after a minute her breath slowed down so that she breathed in time with Berenice; the two of them were close together as one body, and Berenice's stiffened hands were clasped around F. Jasmine's chest. (112–13)

The passage reveals the two embraced "as one body," a nurturing in which Frankie momentarily accepts Berenice as mother, something she has been reluctant to do throughout the novel. And for this one moment Berenice's compassion, even forgiveness, overcomes Frankie's ambivalence over her association with blackness. Frankie will turn yet again from Berenice, but she finds momentary solace amid the confusion of racial identity that confronts her just as she nears adolescence. While McCullers described John Henry as "Frankie's inverted double" (qtd. in Carr 235), we know, of course, that her true double, or "twin," to use Arnold Rampersad's term, is Berenice, and their bond encompasses all of the characteristics of these literary unions so unique to American culture: fraternity, maternity, sexuality. At the conclusion of the novel, once Frankie has found that she will not be accepted as a member of the wedding, she lashes out at Berenice, who sits next to her on the long bus ride home: "She was sitting next to Berenice, back with the colored people, and when she thought of it she used the mean word she had never used before, nigger—for now she hated everyone and wanted only to spite and shame" (135). Frankie, now sensing the power to form an identity through betrayal, recalls the stereotypes of her southern culture in order to end their relationship.

If Frankie's rejection of Berenice is purely symbolic, she soon achieves a final break from her mentor when she and her father move out of their house, leaving Berenice behind. For her part, Berenice "had given quit notice and said that she might as well marry T.T." The Addamses' decision to move to "the new suburb of town" anticipates the white flight that would change the racial dynamic of every southern town and city in the later years of the century and marks the beginning of Frankie's final break with Berenice (149). The two gather in the kitchen a final time (and "the first time in a long while"), and Frankie recognizes the transformation of their world and of their relationship: "It was not the same kitchen of the summer that now seemed so long ago. The pencil pictures had disappeared beneath a coat of calcimine, and new linoleum covered the splintery floor. Even the table had been moved, pushed back against the wall, since now there was nobody to take meals with Berenice" (149).

The alteration of the kitchen signals the loss of the black world that Frankie, now Frances, associates with her childhood: John Henry's manic pencil drawings are painted over, covered in white just as Frankie vehemently cuts off her own association with the black world those drawings represented. McCullers further emphasizes Frankie's symbolic rejection of Berenice as Frankie makes sandwiches (thus supplanting Berenice's role as sustenance provider) for Mary Littlejohn, a new friend who is coming to see her: "Frances glanced at Berenice, who was sitting idle in a chair, wearing an old raveled sweater, her limp arms hanging at her sides" (150). Berenice has served her purpose for Frankie, who at the conclusion of the narrative has made a final break from the black world she has alternately embraced and rejected.

Frankie's view of herself depends on the contribution of otherness to her identity, yet she finally represses that knowledge in a bitter recoiling. Berenice's arms hang limp at her sides, her authority in the kitchen having been usurped and, so, her connection to Frankie breached. The literary relationship between black and white can only be maintained when forces outside of it exert little pressure upon the white character: Huck views Jim as an individual only when they are on the river. In like manner, Frankie abandons Berenice—and blackness—upon finding her own Tom Sawyer in Mary. McCullers sets her black character apart from Twain's in that Berenice lacks Jim's remarkable patience. While Jim reacts with only mild displeasure as he watches Huck and Tom fritter away the possibility of easy escape, Berenice reacts with the vitriol of a spurned lover when Frankie announces that she and Mary Littlejohn will "travel around the world together" after she moves:

> "Mary Littlejohn," said Berenice, in a tinged voice. "Mary Littlejohn."
> Berenice could not appreciate Michelangelo or poetry, let alone Mary Littlejohn. There had at first been words between them on

the subject. Berenice had spoken of Mary as being lumpy and marshmallow-white, and Frances had defended fiercely. . . .

"There's no use our discussing a certain party. You could not possibly understand her. It's just not in you." She had said that once before to Berenice, and from the sudden faded stillness in her eye she knew that the words had hurt. (150–51)

For the first time in the novel, Frankie prepares her own food, and, not coincidentally, the meal is for her and Mary Littlejohn, who has supplanted Berenice. Mary's surname (perhaps Frankie has found her new name for hopping-john?) associates both girls at the end of the novel with whiteness, for it was little John Henry who, as we've seen, was associated throughout the text with white identity. Berenice's conspicuous dislike for Mary further underscores her distance from Frankie at the end of the novel.

In particular, it is Mary Littlejohn's whiteness that offends: Frankie "had defended [Mary] fiercely" against Berenice's assertion that Mary was "lumpy and marshmallow-white." Berenice seems to object to the rejection of the black world that Frankie's new friendship represents. Frankie's assertion that Berenice "could not possibly understand" Mary Littlejohn ironically symbolizes Frankie's growth in the course of the novel, a growth that will register only after she forsakes her relationship with Berenice.

The final lines of the novel reveal the extent to which Frankie's identity remains fragmented, yet she has redirected her search for wholeness to the white world exclusive of Berenice: "'I am simply mad about—' But the sentence was left unfinished for the hush was shattered when, with an instant shock of happiness, she heard the ringing of the bell" (153). Frankie no longer associates her fragmentation with Berenice; rather, at the conclusion of the novel she has rejected her union with her mammy in favor of a possible wholeness in her relationship with Mary Littlejohn. At the end, we find Berenice at the margins of Frankie's consciousness and, as ever, at the margins of southern society. No longer romanced by an exoticized black world, Frankie participates in Berenice's marginalization at the novel's conclusion and gains a white identity as a result. The process reflects the reality of southern childhood for middle- and upper-class whites through the end of Jim Crow who almost invariably grew up to leave black mammies behind, reflecting the reality of the larger American culture.

Double Lives

Like *The Member of the Wedding*, Harper Lee's *To Kill a Mockingbird* confronts the oppression of blacks in the modern South; with Spencer's *Voice* and Shirley Anne Grau's *The Keepers of the House*, it comments upon the civil rights movement from an ostensibly liberal position within southern society. Atticus Finch's legal defense of Tom Robinson, a local black man wrongly accused of raping a white woman, parallels his daughter Scout's growing understanding of their mysterious neighbor, Arthur Radley. The didactic imperatives of the novel emerge from the interworkings of the two narratives: Lee ties Scout's curiosity about Radley (whom Scout calls "Boo") to Atticus's defense of Robinson. Scout's moral development in the course of the novel comes largely from Atticus, whom Lee depicts as a modern and enlightened southern gentleman. Atticus instructs through his interactions with black culture and in particular through his pro bono defense of Robinson. Lee portrays Tom Robinson, the namesake of Harriet Beecher Stowe's Tom, as the maligned victim who can only be saved by Atticus, pater familias in this southern society.

While Scout initially assumes Boo to be a lascivious demon haunting her neighborhood, by the end of the novel she has removed him from this essentialized position and come to see him outside such confines. Just as the townspeople type Tom Robinson as a menace, Scout, her brother, Jem, and their friend Dill view Boo Radley as a bogeyman, at one point daring one another to go as close as possible to his house. In the end, Boo becomes an ironic metaphor for white understanding of blacks in the novel, given the whiteness with which he is so strongly associated.

The children initially understand Boo only through the stories they have been told: like Tom Robinson, Boo is suspected of aberrant sexual behavior and blamed for Maycomb's more bizarre crimes. When the citizens of the town begin to find their chickens and pets mutilated, they blame Boo, and though the actual culprit is later found, "people still looked at the Radley Place, unwilling to discard their initial suspicions" (9). Such suspicions, of course, mirror those whites have of the black community, and Lee demonstrates the ways in which Scout learns to overcome her baseless fears of Boo even as her father demonstrates Tom's innocence to all Maycomb.

Scout comes to understand blackness through her relationship with her black mammy, Calpurnia. Like Frankie Addams, Scout seeks solace and self-definition in her mammy, who, like Berenice, serves as a maternal figure in the absence of a biological mother. Black mammies fill the absences in their domestic spaces, but the protagonists come to associate blackness with a passivity that hardly threatens the stasis of the white domestic space. Calpurnia is moral guide for Scout, but her guidance largely reaffirms the white social order within which she is employed. When, for instance, Scout is rude to Walter Cunningham, a poor white boy whom she has invited to eat with the family, Calpurnia sets her charge straight: "'Yo' folks might be better'n the Cunninghams but it don't count for nothin' the way you're disgracin' 'em—if you can't act fit to eat at the table you can just set here and eat in the kitchen!'" (27). Calpurnia's sense of propriety falls safely within the parameters of patriarchal white culture; in this, she contrasts with McCullers's Berenice, whose matriarchal refuge offers an exotic model of feminine sexuality.

In Scout's superstitions, we find a movement toward a black world that Calpurnia would disallow. When, for example, Scout and Jem discuss the superstitions surrounding "Hot Steams," the warm spaces in the air that are reputed to be spirits who can't get to heaven, Scout remembers that Calpurnia dismissed the idea as "nigger-talk" (41). The idea appeals to the children nonetheless, just as blackness and the possibility of interracial union intrigues them. If we encounter Jem spending his days reading the speeches of Henry Grady, the New South he envisions will be rather different from that of the editor of the *Atlanta Constitution*: for Lee, as for McCullers, blackness emerges as the catalyst for the moral growth of a white protagonist. Lee, however, defines that identity within the narrow confines of white perception.

Still, the novel's multiple voices allow the reader to glimpse the broader possibilities. When Calpurnia takes Scout and Jem to her church, the narrative momentarily escapes a white perspective and the concomitant rejection of black identity. Because of the controversy surrounding Tom Robinson's arrest, some of the church members are reluctant to accept the white children:

> I felt Calpurnia's hand dig into my shoulder. "What you want, Lula?" she asked, in tones I had never heard her use. She spoke quietly, contemptuously.
>
> "I wants to know why you bringin' white chillun to nigger church."
>
> "They's my comp'ny," said Calpurnia. Again I thought her voice strange: she was talking like the rest of them.
>
> "Yeah, an' I reckon you's comp'ny at the Finch house durin' the week." (135)

Lula's challenge to the children and Calpurnia reflects black resentment of the white community in Maycomb and perhaps as well the condescension inherent in the role Atticus Finch has made for himself. Lula points to the inescapable fact that Calpurnia forgets: though Cal earlier calls Scout and Jem "my children," theirs is primarily an economic arrangement (134). Scout's surprise at Calpurnia's "strange" voice, now inflected with her African American dialect, represents her remove from this black world. The special welcome the children receive from the pastor only serves to isolate them further from the congregation.

Still, the children come to recognize the members of the black community as individuals outside of the essentializing gaze of whites. Scout and Jem express their surprise when the town garbage collector, Zeebo, leads the congregation in a hymn. For the Finch children, Zeebo thus emerges as an individual capable of a complexity they could not have imagined earlier. As they leave the church, Scout yearns to "stay and explore," her curiosity having been piqued by this encounter with blackness, but Calpurnia won't allow it (140). Scout remains entranced: "'Why do you talk nigger-talk to the—to your folks when you know it's not right?'" (143). Scout's curiosity and surprise at Calpurnia's "modest double life" leads her to desire a bond with Calpurnia outside the white world in which they have functioned previously, much like the bond she will ultimately form with Boo Radley (143). For Scout there is an enthralling mystery in blackness itself that she will return to throughout the novel, and the doubleness she now perceives is American life itself, always characterized by a multilayered racial identity, Calpurnia's denials notwithstanding.

Scout interrogates race as the novel unfolds, seeking to understand the mystery of the black world at the edges of Maycomb. As she becomes increasingly aware of her father's role in the mediation between black and white in Maycomb, she questions him in the language she has adopted from her schoolmates, asking: "'Do you defend niggers, Atticus?'" The explanation Atticus offers Scout for his decision to represent Tom Robinson reveals his role as white patriarch. "'Of course I do,'" he replies. "'Don't say nigger, Scout. That's common'" (85). Atticus's initial acceptance of the word points to the position he takes in regard to Tom, whereas his insistence that Scout not use the term because it is "common" demonstrates his link to the traditional southern fictional representations of race and class. He forbids Scout to use the word not because it is degrading to blacks but because it reflects poorly upon the Finch family, which Atticus holds up as a bastion of southern pride. While class is the primary motivating force for Atticus, race will remain Scout's obsession.

Lee relies heavily upon numerous conventions of southern literature that characterize the white South's confrontation with blackness. Repeatedly in these southern novels we encounter scenes of beset justice in which a white character rescues an unjustly accused black man from certain death at the hands of an angry mob. As we have seen, Elizabeth Spencer employs irony in just such a scene in *The Voice at the Back Door* to reveal the complexity of both her white and black characters as they resist the essentializing stereotypes that the culture forces upon them. Lee, on the other hand, delivers the scene straight to the reader, inflating the traditional clichés with pathos. Her approach anticipates the pattern we find in popular southern novels following her own.

After Atticus takes a defensive position in front of the Maycomb jail where Tom Robinson is being held, an angry mob confronts him, intending to lynch the prisoner. When the mob demands to know if Tom is in the jail, Atticus coolly responds that he is, "'and he's asleep. Don't wake him up'" (172). Not to be put off by this paternal warning, the mob presses on, but Scout ultimately thwarts their intentions when she quietly asks after the son of one member of the mob. Her innocence amidst this racially charged scene leads him to call the lynching off, yet Lee's heavy sentiment undermines the intended weight of the scene. After the mob has left, Tom calls to them on the street:

> "Mr. Finch?"
> A soft husky voice came from the darkness above: "They gone?"
> Atticus stepped back and looked up. "They've gone," he said. "Get some sleep, Tom. They won't bother you any more." (176)

Atticus maintains his willingness to sacrifice himself for Tom Robinson, yet he has plainly established a distance between himself and Tom which he makes no effort to bridge: "'Get some sleep, Tom,'" he says. And when Jem worries that the mob might easily have killed his father, Atticus responds in the manner of Twain's Colonel Sherburn: "'Every mob in every little Southern town is always made up of people you know—doesn't say much for them, does it?'" (180). The emotional distance that Atticus establishes through his condescension is precisely the same as that which Scout will establish between herself and Boo Radley at the end of the novel. Having taken her lesson from her father, Scout will speak to Boo, twenty years her senior, as if he were a child.

Tom's trial underscores the theme of interracial union even as it reasserts white hegemony in Maycomb. Secretly watching the proceedings from among the blacks sitting in the courtroom balcony, Jem and Scout have become like Mr. Dolphus Raymond, the white man who so fascinates Scout because he chooses to live among blacks. When Jem explains to Scout that Raymond's children are to be considered "Negroes" in the terms of their southern culture, Scout recognizes the absurdity of racial categories: "'Well how do you know we ain't Negroes?'" she asks (185). It is a question he can't conclusively answer, since race under such terms is inherently fluid. We will see Atticus's two children moving toward knowledge of the absurdity of racial terms as they witness their father's defense of Tom Robinson from the black gallery.

Scout evaluates Tom from her perch in the balcony: "He seemed to be a respectable Negro, and a respectable Negro would never go up into somebody's yard of his own volition," as Mayella Ewell has accused him of doing (220). And Scout likewise finds Tom attractive: "Tom was a black-velvet Negro, not shiny, but soft black velvet. . . . If he had been whole, he would have been a fine specimen of a man" (220). Lee conveys Scout's ability to see the human traits that Tom possesses, even as her language contradicts such a view: Tom is no man on equal footing with other men but rather a sort of laboratory animal, and a damaged one at that, given his limp arm. Even as her protagonist moves closer to a recognition of the place of blackness in the formation of her own identity, Lee removes her black characters from the realm of humanity. In the end, the marginal identity that so fascinates will remain only as a moral measure of the white characters of Maycomb.

Like Stowe's Tom, Tom Robinson reacts with indifference to the harsh treatment he receives. He is unable to speak out in the face of bitter injustice throughout the courtroom scenes, in which we discover him to have been utterly passive during the events that led to the crime of which he stands accused.[2]

Upon hearing Tom's description of the events, Scout decides that "in their own way, Tom Robinson's manners were as good as Atticus's," a sensible enough conclusion, for Tom Robinson is Atticus Finch's black ideal (222). Lame, docile, victimized, he represents the black man that white liberals prop up time and again in novels that ostensibly call for better treatment of African Americans: he is foil to the novel's central figure of masculinity, Atticus. For Atticus, a feminine or polite masculinity is an expression of his role in southern gentility; by contrast, these same characteristics in Tom demonstrate his passivity and his status as victim. "'Why were you scared?'" Atticus Finch asks after Tom has testified. "'Mr. Finch, if you was a nigger like me, you'd be scared, too'" (223). Tom, it seems, has fantasies of his own about white identity.

In his summation, Atticus Finch debunks Maycomb's essentialized perception of blacks, arguing that the state's testimony against Tom Robinson has been designed to play upon the white jury's stereotypes of black behavior "in the cynical confidence" that the jury would assume that "*all* Negroes lie, that *all* Negroes are basically immoral beings, that *all* Negro men are not to be trusted around our women" (233). Atticus associates such manipulation on the part of the state "with minds of their caliber," suggesting again that the likes of Bob Ewell are to blame for racism in the South (233).

Atticus reminds the jury that this stereotype of blacks is unfounded, "'a lie as black as Tom Robinson's skin, a lie I do not have to point out to you. You know the truth, and the truth is this: some Negroes lie, some Negroes are immoral, some Negro men are not to be trusted around women—black or white. But this is a truth that applies to the human race and to no particular race of men. There is not a person in this courtroom who has never told a lie, who has never done an immoral thing'" (233). The summation confirms Atticus as the white patriarch we have always suspected him to be; he attempts to develop and complicate the white community's view of African Americans by denying the predominant stereotype. Yet we see here the seeds of stereotype as well: Atticus asserts that the lie is "as black as Tom Robinson's skin," ironically linking Tom with the very stereotype from which he ostensibly attempts to free him. And though surely Atticus speaks for Lee, she creates in Tom Robinson an affable, compliant victim to symbolize the predicaments of southern blacks. Like both Stowe and Twain in the previous century, Lee creates a character who poses no threat to the dominant paradigm, allowing one stereotype to replace another.

The jury acts in a more straightforward manner. For all of Atticus's pleading, they find Tom guilty of rape. When the black community nevertheless reveres Atticus for his efforts to help Tom, we see the final valuation of white identity over black that the novel has been moving toward throughout. The contemporary reader may well share Scout's astonishment that the loss of Tom Robinson's case results not in black protest but in black adulation of the white lawyer. Sitting quietly in the balcony in the moments after the announcement of the verdict, Scout marvels when the African American men and women around her stand to honor her father as he leaves the courtroom: "I looked around. They were standing. All around us and in the balcony on the opposite wall, the Negroes were getting to their feet. Reverend Syke's voice was as distant as Judge Taylor's: 'Miss Jean Louise, stand up. Your father's passin'"" (242). Maycomb's black community shares Tom Robinson's docile nature as well as his reverence for white identity; we find that only rarely in the novel does a black character break free from the sort of essentialized view of race that Atticus so eloquently denounces. The courtroom scene is a white fantasy of black behavior, in which the black community pays homage to the failed but noble efforts of a liberal white southerner, much as generations of readers of *Huckleberry Finn* have paid homage to Huck in celebrating his decision to go to hell and overlooking his failure to take up residence there.

When, at the end of the novel, Scout's teacher announces a pageant for the schoolchildren, she chooses Scout to portray an exceedingly appropriate Maycomb County agricultural product: a ham. Lee is a bit of a ham, too, particularly in this final section, in which she completes the link between Boo Radley's plight and Tom Robinson's.

Bob Ewell emerges as a sort of white trash sacrifice for middle-class guilt. When Ewell attacks Jem and Scout on their way home from the pageant, Boo Radley comes upon the scene and kills him. Scout later sees her savior in detail, in contrast to the stereotypes she had assigned to him earlier in the novel.

Like Tom Robinson, Boo Radley is an outcast impaired: his "sickly white hands" (310) and the "delicate indentations at his temples" (311) distinguish him from the Finches, and these characteristics also lead Scout to take a benevolent and finally paternalistic attitude toward him. Scout's aversion to Boo's whiteness—his "sickly white hands" that "stood out garishly against the dull cream wall" (310) remind us of Pap's "fish-belly white"—reflects on her discomfort with her own white identity, given what she has witnessed in the course of the novel. But the condescension inherent in her paternal stance at the end of the novel belies any such anxiety. At the end, Scout has returned to a white world she could never fully escape. The control she assumes over Boo Radley parallels that which Atticus takes over Tom Robinson in court, and if both Atticus and Scout are protective of their charges, they also limit them with their condescension.

FIGURES IN BLACK

Carson McCullers and Harper Lee employ familiar parameters of the relationship between black and white in developing their white protagonists through relationships with African Americans. While McCullers portrays Berenice as an autonomous and complex figure, Lee portrays Calpurnia as a figure ever tied to the patriarchal world headed by Atticus Finch. Like Tom Robinson, Calpurnia merely reaffirms her charge's white identity, whereas Berenice endeavors in vain to encourage Frankie to confirm an identity within the black world.

In the contemporary period, the pattern has become commonplace, and we find it in the work of southern writers of nonfiction like Anne Moody (*Coming of Age in Mississippi*) and Erskine Caldwell (*In Search of Bisco*) as well as in the work of a wealth of southern novelists.

NOTES

1. Berenice's association of John Henry with Henry Ford subtly criticizes white identity as well: throughout the novel, John Henry acts as an agent provocateur for white identity, since he does not share Frankie's identification with blackness and is much closer in character to Frankie's father than to Berenice.

2. Tom Robinson is implausibly passive in his courtroom description of his fateful meeting with Mayella Ewell:

> The witness swallowed hard. "She reached up an' kissed me 'side of th' face. She says she never kissed a grown man before an' she might as well kiss a nigger. She says what her papa do to her don't count. She says, 'Kiss me back, nigger.' I say Miss Mayella lemme outa here an' tried to run but she got her back to the door an' I'da had to push her. I didn't wanta harm her, Mr. Finch,

an' I say lemme pass, but just when I say it Mr. Ewell yonder hollered through th' window."

"What did he say?"

Tom Robinson swallowed again, and his eyes widened. "Somethin' not fittin' to say—not fittin' for these folks'n chillun to hear—"

"What did he say, Tom? You must tell the jury what he said."

Tom Robinson shut his eyes tight. "He says you goddamn whore, I'll kill ya."

"Then what happened?"

"Mr. Finch, I was runnin' so fast I didn't know what happened." (222)

JENNIFER MURRAY

Approaching Community in Carson McCullers's The Heart Is a Lonely Hunter

*T*he Heart Is a Lonely Hunter gives us a day, a year, and a day in the lives of
five distinct characters: Singer, Mick, Brannon, Blount, and Dr. Copeland.
Their lives are shot through with frustration and discouragement and the
intense privacy of their inner lives gives the reader the impression that they
are isolated, lonely beings. However, the frustrations they experience are
most often a product of their very passionate attempts to follow their desires
or convictions. Moreover, McCullers employs several devices which work
against the sense of loneliness and which lend a tenuous sense of unity, an
echoing of sensibility, to the discrete voices of the characters.

The very real ambiguities which structure our perception of the
lives of the characters of *Lonely Hunter* have given rise to vastly differing
opinions on the novel's meaning and on Carson McCullers's conclusions
concerning human relationships: Oliver Evans, for example, suggests that
what "[McCullers] conceives to be the truth about human nature is a
melancholy truth: each man is surrounded by a 'zone of loneliness,' serving
a life sentence of solitary confinement" (Clark 126). L. D. Rubin, Jr. offers
the same view in the form of a complaint: "[One would think] that so rare
a talent for observing and understanding and feeling compassion for others
would produce something other than the anguished conviction of emptiness
and solitude" (Clark 117). At the same time, many readers of *Lonely Hunter*

From *Southern Quarterly* 42, no. 4 (Summer 2004): pp. 107–114. © 2004 by the University of
Southern Mississippi.

have expressed a sense of the beauty of the experience of reading the novel, a feeling which the trajectories of the characters, and the events of the story, cannot account for. Early reviewers such as Richard Wright wrote of the novel's "sheen of weird tenderness" (Clark 17), and stated that one puts the novel down "with a feeling of having been nourished by the truth" (Clark 20). Julian Symons offers the view that McCullers's "poetic vision" allows her to transform "our common loneliness into something rich and strange" (Clark 22).

The unifying elements of the novel which constitute this "poetic vision" do not, I would argue, exist at the level of individual characterization, but are deployed in terms of symbolic representation, structure, and narrative voice. They are disseminated, not within the diegesis, but within the narration taken as a whole, and they implicitly provide the reader with an imaginative space in which to conceive of a less compartmentalized existence than the depiction of any of the individual lives can offer.

The third-person narrating voice, which adopts the perspective of each character in turn, is one of the most effective unifying devices of the novel. While the point of view is internal and therefore personal, the third-person technique retains a slight distance, and develops an intermeshing of voices. One of the ways in which it does this is through a careful construction of the temporal dimension of the novel. Time in *Lonely Hunter* is seen either as unreal—a sort of fairytale "once upon a time" space (part 1, chapters 1 and 6)—or as belonging to the cycles of natural time, giving us characters who are shown in the space of a day (part 1, chapters 2–5), a year (part 2), and a day (part 3). Both of these modes of representing time suggest a temporal order which is more symbolic than historical and which is therefore more easily accessible to reader identification.

A language of the unspecific underscores this symbolic dimension; the first lines of the novel are: "In the town, there were two mutes, and they were always together. Early every morning they would come out from the house where they lived and walk arm in arm down the street to work." The presentation of place—"a town"—and of time—"every morning"—is such that they could be anywhere and in any period in history. The phrases "always together" and "arm in arm" suggest the closeness and harmony that reign between the two characters who are often referred to simply as "the mutes." They are characters who partake of Everyman, a duo of opposites whose relationship "parallels the macrocosmic structure of the novel and, simultaneously, [they represent] the personality of mythic 'modern man' caught up in that macrocosm" (Sherrill 14).

The fairy-tale quality of the opening section is reinforced even as the specific realistic aspects of the narration become denser. The domestic life of

Singer and Antonapoulos described in the following passage, for example, reminds us of the house of the "Three Bears":

> On the oil stove in the kitchen Antonapoulos cooked all of their meals. There were straight, plain kitchen chairs for Singer and an overstuffed sofa for Antonapoulos. The bedroom was furnished mainly with a large double bed covered with an eiderdown comforter for the big Greek and a narrow iron cot for Singer. (2–3)

Furthermore, the peaceful course of the lives of Singer and Antonapoulos will meet with disruption. It comes in the form of illness: "Then one day the Greek became ill" (4). The final blow is carried out by the wicked Greek uncle who sends Antonapoulos away to an asylum. The novel is not a fairy tale, but it leans on the language of the tale in its opening moments so as to take the meaning attributed to Singer and his story beyond the personal and into the symbolic.

Following on from the presentation of Singer, each of the characters is introduced in succession within the same day. In this way, they are linked together, for the perspective of each character must be presented in turn to complete the chosen cycle of time, which is exactly one day. This day, paradoxically, begins at midnight: "On a black, sultry night in early summer Biff Brannon stood behind the cash register of the New York Café. It was twelve o'clock" (10). Brannon is introduced in his role as observer of humanity, watching over the wretched souls of the night, the lost and desperate, offering his café as a rampart against the absolute solitude of the dark hours.

His introductory chapter ends as he falls asleep at dawn with "The hard yellow rays of the sun [coming] in through the window so that the room was hot and bright" (27). The sun provides the transition to the next character's story which begins "The sun woke Mick early" (27). The penetrating and somewhat harsh rays of the sun provide the common element between one character finding sleep and another being roused from it.

Not light but sound provides the shift between Jake Blount's chapter to that of Dr. Copeland. On page 59, as early evening ends and Blount is settling to stay with Singer for a few days, we read, "From afar off there was the soft, silver ring of church bells." The same bells fade out of hearing several lines later: "Far from the main street, in one of the Negro sections of the town, Doctor Benedict Mady Copeland sat in his dark kitchen alone. It was past nine o'clock and the Sunday bells were silent now" (60).

No time is left unaccounted for as the narrator blends together images and sounds from the close of one character's environment to the opening of the next, so that even as the lonely image of Dr. Copeland in his kitchen marks the reader, there is an attenuation of the negative impact of this image through the linking of their worlds.[1] Dr. Copeland, we feel, is not entirely alone, because the bells he hears are heard by others, and the sun which shines on Brannon shines also on Mick. The characters' unawareness of the synchronicity of other happenings in the town does not prevent the readers' (unconscious) perception of it, and it is the reader who then begins to see connections and to project a form of community onto these characters' lives.

The novel's second part covers just a year in time and thereby allows for the exploration of the characters in their hopes and aspirations over a significant period. Similar transition techniques to those described earlier are used, but the effects are, at times, more extensive. At the start of February, we are in the presence of Dr. Copeland, and the narrator gives us a description of a change in the weather:

> Then after a few days *winter was upon* the town again. The mild *skies darkened.* A chill *rain fell* and the air *turned dank* and bitterly cold. In the town the Negroes suffered badly. Supplies of fuel had been exhausted and there was a struggle everywhere for warmth. An epidemic of pneumonia raged through the wet, narrow streets, and for a week Doctor Copeland slept at odd hours, fully clothed. Still no word came from William. (215, emphasis added)

Here, the voice of the narrator gives us changes in the weather which are presented, not from the point of view of any of the characters in particular, but as general truths in which the winter, the skies, the rain, and the air are in the subject position of the phrases. Similar to fairy tale description, the presentation of the weather suggests that its effects will be general and undiscriminating within the black community which is the focus of the narrator's discourse at this point. While the reader remains aware that the suffering of the black community is largely a result of the poverty and the misery of their living conditions, there is nonetheless a sense of shared struggle which informs the description.

Time advances, and weeks later, Dr. Copeland's daughter Portia brings news of Willie. She resituates the news so that the reader understands that it refers back to the onset of the winter weather:

> "It were about six weeks ago," Portia said. "You remember that cold spell then. They put Willie and them boys in this room like ice . . . and their feets swolled up and they lay there and struggle on the floor and holler out. And nobody come. They hollered there for three days and three nights and nobody come." (217)

The result is that Willie's feet freeze and are amputated. The suffering endured by the poor, black community during the cold winter months is amplified in its symbolic scope when it becomes the ally of a greater cruelty: the torture of a human being. The blanket of cold over the town becomes the cohering factor against which the community of the oppressed must struggle, but also, a catalyst for the reader's feelings of empathy. Whereas a general situation appeals to our sense of humanity on an intellectual level, a particular example, through the one-to-one identification which it provokes, makes a more emotional appeal to our sensitivity.

This dialogue between the general and the particular is an important structuring force in the characterization in the novel. One might reasonably suggest that McCullers's choice of her five main characters is an attempt to represent human society. This representation is partial and biased, with an overwhelming presence of middle-aged male figures, but it is nonetheless wide-ranging. The opposites of youth and age are represented by Mick and Dr. Copeland; female and male by Mick and the four others, as well as forms of androgyny represented by Mick and Brannon[2]; working-class and small businessman in Blount and Brannon; black and white in Dr. Copeland and the four others.[3] On one level, therefore, the characters are representative of various social, sexual, and racial positions, and the failure of their individual quests for meaning suggests that the causes of disillusionment cannot be restricted to any given position, since all experience discouragement and disillusion.

Yet McCullers does not reduce everything to one and the same; where the choice of characters, through its partial representation offers the framework of the 'general,' the individuality of the characterization gives voice to the specificity of human lives. Jake Blount, for instance, believes in the ideals of communism and strives to raise the consciousness of the workers of the town. Similarly, Dr. Copeland desires for his fellow members of the black community to recognize the oppression to which they are subjected and to fight against it. Their goals are similar in structure and are related, but the different focuses of their struggles—economic and racial—are important, as are their professed means of achieving their goals. Blount advocates worker solidarity and social struggle, whereas Copeland is convinced that salvation lies essentially in the education and formation of future generations. Together, they offer the reader the possibility of identifying with the desire for social advancement and commitment to the "common good." Paradoxically, the novel also exonerates the reader from any real engagement of this nature since all the efforts of these two men come to nothing concrete.

Mick's driving desires are more personal, as are Brannon's. These characters represent the need for personal fulfillment: Mick through artistic endeavors, and music in particular. When Mick sits listening to music by

Beethoven, she feels that it encompasses everything and abolishes time: "The whole world was this music and she could not listen hard enough! . . . This music did not take a long time or a short time. It did not have anything to do with time going by at all" (100). Through a pleasure savored alone, Mick feels transported beyond the limits of her objective self: "It was like she could knock down all the walls of the house and then march through the street big as a giant" (214). Mick's young age gives her an intensity of expression which is far more attenuated in Brannon. Yet he, too, savors individual pleasures, fantasy worlds and questioning:

> Along with the Agua Florida he found in the closet a bottle of lemon rinse Alice had always used for her hair. One day he tried it on himself. The lemon made his dark, white-streaked hair seem fluffy and thick. He liked it. . . . Certain whims that he had ridiculed in Alice were now his own. Why? (192–93)

Through these two characters, the novel addresses the secret desires of the reader, those desires which fall outside of the demands of society and are nurtured in solitude.

Desire, however, is not necessarily love, and contrary to what the title of the novel might suggest, what the "lonely hearts" of the story are looking for is not primarily romantic love. For most of them, it is quite plainly a non-question. This is not the case, however, for Singer whose deep love and attachment to a specific person is his one sustaining desire. All else is "killing time." Gayatri Chakravorty Spivak describes the relationship between them as "a human relationship of love and sexuality at furthest remove from so-called 'normal' relationships. . . . It is an unconsummated and, indeed, sexually unacknowledged relationship between two deaf-mute male homosexuals of completely incompatible personalities" (133). Singer's love for Antonapoulos is specific, absolute, non-transferable and beyond explanation: "Sometimes he thought of Antonapoulos with awe and self-abasement, sometimes with pride—always with love unchecked by criticism, freed of will. When he dreamed at night the face of his friend was always before him, massive and gentle. And in his waking thoughts they were eternally united" (276). When Antonapoulos dies, Singer is unable to invest his love/desire elsewhere (his brief contact with other deaf-mutes after Antonapoulos's death leaves him feeling terribly isolated [279]) and he chooses death.

The reader wonders what the effect of Singer's death will be on those who have come to depend on him, for he is their "sort of home-made God," according to Brannon (198). There is, however, a fundamental difference between Singer and the others: whereas Singer's whole being is invested in his imaginary construction of a perfect Antonapoulos, whose happiness is

Singer's principal source of satisfaction, the others are not really concerned with Singer's happiness. Their relationship to him is more akin to that of the patient and the psychiatrist, a site of projection and transfer, where inner conflicts may be aired and worked on. In losing Singer, they are (only) losing a careful listener, not the receptacle of all of their love and personal investment.

Covering just a day—a day in which Singer is no more—the final chapters of the novel attest to the resilience of the characters' personalities. Their lives are not any simpler, and, certainly, one could easily build a case showing that their spirits have been beaten. Klaus Lubbers, for example, chooses to quote that Dr. Copeland leaves town "exhausted and sick in spirit" and that Jake will forever be "a stranger in a strange land" (192). But McCullers also offers forms of optimism which suggest an alternative reading: Blount will go off to another town in search of new workers to preach to, for "[there] was hope in him, and soon perhaps the outline of his journey would take form" (299). In spite of his failing health and regular discouragement, Dr. Copeland has not lost the desire to fight for black equality: "The words in his heart grew big and they would not be silent" (287). Mick is resigned to a job as a cashier, but her youth and enthusiasm, expressed in her final words—"All right! O.K.! Some good" (302)—allow the reader to suppose that she will find new desires, new journeys of her own.

Finally, Brannon, who never stops questioning life ("Why? The question flowed through Biff always, unnoticed, like the blood in his veins" [190]) comes to a tentative feeling of having gained some sudden sense of understanding: "For in a swift radiance of illumination he saw a glimpse of human struggle and of valor. Of the endless fluid passage of humanity through endless time. And of those who labor and of those who—one word—love. His soul expanded" (306). However, Brannon's final thoughts also have their darker side, for along with this glimpse of love comes terror, a terror which "throttles" and deforms him: "Sweat glistened on his temples and his face was contorted" (306). Even as Brannon's intellect seizes upon some new, more enriching way of being, his emotional defenses are already expressing their resistance to transformation.

There is hope in *The Heart Is a Lonely Hunter*, but most of all, there is ambivalence in the endings of these characters' personal voyages. The novel may be read as desperately pessimistic or faintly hopeful, as a parable on the inevitable frustrations of human hope and desire, or as a tentative tribute to the resistance of the human spirit. No certainties about Brannon's future or the future of any of the other characters are offered. Indeed, even considered in its positive elements, Biff Brannon's moment of revelation at the novel's close is rather puzzling. It may suggest that there is a form of love to be reached for which lies beyond the social and the personal. The register of feeling expressed in Brannon's perception of "the endless fluid passage of humanity through endless time" (306) would be coherent with the "oceanic" feeling described by Freud in *Civilisation and Its Discontents*.[4] Freud describes this feeling as an impression of "limitlessness and of a bond with the universe," in which the individual's perception of the boundaries between self and other might be temporarily effaced, leaving them with a sudden sense of being at one with the world. If this "oceanic feeling" were indeed the content of the awkwardly stated "one word—love" of McCullers's text, it would be hard to understand what could be frightening about it, since by definition, it is outside political and individual action, closer in its structure to an all-embracing Christian attitude of "brotherly love."

It may be worth looking back to Singer to understand Brannon's moment of illumination—perhaps the image of Singer patiently listening to the frustrations of his friends might awake in Brannon a greater awareness of the interconnectedness of human lives. Yet, if Singer witnesses, he does not bear witness, nor does he transmit anything to anyone else, apart from Antonapoulos who seems either unable to understand what he is being told, or is completely indifferent to it. Concerning his relationship with Blount and Copeland, Singer feels that "what they wanted him to sanction he did not know" and, thinking of Mick, Singer reflects that "she said a good deal that he did not understand in the least" (275). Moreover, before taking his life, Singer is not shown to give a thought to any of those who have come to depend on his friendship. If Brannon's revelation of love is based on Singer's feelings towards the townspeople, there is something ironic being suggested.

The undeniable strength of the novel is not, I believe, to be found in the lives of any of the characters in particular. There is no "key" perspective or philosophy to be discovered in any of their separate paths or choices. Rather, the novel's force is in the overall movement of empathy with suffering, hardship, and failure, but also with love, companionship, and desire that it provokes in the reader. McCullers's narrator offers no transcendental values against which to evaluate the characters, no judgment of their choices. We are given only the unapologetic exposure of their strengths and weaknesses and are thereby placed in a position of understanding towards them. We identify with them not because of their age, sex, color, or politics, but because, together, they create the overall impression of a community of rich, complex creatures, and we recognize the desires that animate them: "without her dream, which she clings to so stubbornly . . . Mick would lack the interest that she has for us, and certainly the same is true of Doctor Copeland." (Evans, *Carson McCullers* 48).

This tentative sense of community is supported by the array of undeclared textual strategies which I have underlined throughout this essay and which give the reader an alternative, more positive, perception of the story told. The result is a fictional world into which we, not unlike the characters in their subjective constructions of Singer, might project our own hesitations, frustrations, and aspirations, and feel that our sensibility therein finds its echo. Like the various characters who people the night café, we feel (momentarily) reconciled to the space we share with a world of diverse others.

NOTES

1. These devices also include the repetition of alliterated sounds such as "From afar off," a chiastic repetition of "Far from" (59–60).

2. The androgynous aspects of the characters Mick and Brannon are the central concern of Taetzsch's article.

3. Moreover, secondary characters, such as Portia (adult woman), Bubber, Ralph, and Baby (children), Harry (Jewish), Simms (religious fanatic), add to this sense of a representative group.

4. A feeling which was recounted to Freud by "a friend" and suggested as the origin of religious feeling.

WORKS CITED

Clark, Beverly Lyon, and Melvin J. Friedman. *Critical Essays on Carson McCullers*. New York: Hall, 1996.

Evans, Oliver. *Carson McCullers: Her Life and Work*. London: Peter Owen, 1965.

————."The Case of Carson McCullers." Clark 124–28.

Freud, Sigmund. *Civilisation and Its Discontents*. 1929. Ed. James Strachey. Trans. Joan Rivière. London: Hogarth P, 1973.

Lubbers, Klaus. "The Necessary Order: A Study of Theme and Structure in Carson McCullers' Fiction." *Jahrbuch für Amerikastudien* 8 (1963): 187–200.

Ruben, L. D., Jr. "Carson McCullers: the Aesthetics of Pain." Clark 111–23.

McCullers, Carson. *The Heart is a Lonely Hunter*. 1940. New York: Bantam, 1953.

Sherill, Rowland. "McCullers' *The Heart is a Lonely Hunter*: The Missing Ego and the Problem of the Norm." *Kentucky Review* 2.1 (1968): 5–17.

Spivak, Gayatri Chakravorty. "[A Feminist Reading: McCullers' *Heart is a Lonely Hunter*]." Clark 129–42.

Symons, Julian. "The Lonely Heart." Clark 22–25.

Wright, Richard. "Inner Landscape." Clark 17–18.

NAOMI MORGENSTERN

The Afterlife of Coverture: Contract and Gift in "The Ballad of the Sad Café"

The sturdy figure of the "worker," the artisan, in clean overalls, with a bag of tools and lunch-box, is always accompanied by the ghostly figure of his wife.

—Pateman 131

Isn't that the ultimate homeland security—standing up and defending marriage?

—Senator Rick Santorum (R-Pa.), "Chairman"

American literature is replete with examples of women trying to negotiate alternative relationships to the marriage contract. From Hannah Foster's *The Coquette* (1797), in which Eliza Wharton pays with her life for imagining that she and her male friends can enter into contracts *other* than the marriage contract, to Hester Prynne's imagining of a new sexual contract in Hawthorne's *The Scarlet Letter* (1850) ("As a first step, the whole system of society is to be torn down" [113]), to Isabel Archer's tragic attempt to "marry herself" in James's *The Portrait of a Lady* (1881), American fiction has repeatedly exposed the paradox at the heart of the "genderless" contract. In narratives by Harriet Jacobs, Hannah Crafts, Kate Chopin, William Dean Howells, and Edith Wharton, the depiction of woman's paradoxical relationship to contract ideology urges us, indeed, to reconsider the crucial though often

From *Differences: A Journal of Feminist Cultural Studies* 16, no. 1 (Spring 2005): pp. 103–25. © 2005 by Brown University and *Differences*.

overlooked opposition between contracts and gifts. In this paper, I will argue
that women's equivocal relationship to contract—a relationship sustained by
what I call the afterlife of coverture—has everything to do with a pervasive
desire to keep contract and gift apart. To that end, I will turn to a mid-
twentieth-century novella, Carson McCullers's "The Ballad of the Sad Café,"
which mourns for an experience of incalculable giving even as it confronts
questions of sexual and explicitly marital violence with unusual force and
economy.

"The Ballad of the Sad Café" tells the story of a "queer marriage" that
takes place nowhere *and* in an isolated Southern mill town in the middle of the
twentieth century. It is the marriage of Miss Amelia Evans to Marvin Macy,
and it was "unlike any other marriage ever contracted [. . .], it was a strange
and dangerous marriage lasting only for ten days, [it] left the whole town
wondering and shocked" (4–5). McCullers's story of the marriage contract's
"sorry bargain" transforms the ballad's conventional preoccupation with
coherent social ordering (the ballad is a collective form)[1] into something of a
feminist critique of marriage. Illuminating the paradox of a patriarchal logic
whereby the woman appears as both the subject and object of contractual
exchange, McCullers's "strange and dangerous marriage" also reminds us that
marriage marks the site of a founding violence (marriage, as we are regularly
reminded, is essential to the state—"the last barrier of civilization").[2]

But as a ballad, McCullers's novella also demonstrates a preoccupation
with tragic love, a preoccupation that risks frustrating straightforward
feminist critiques of the institution of marriage. "The Ballad of the Sad
Café's" tragic lover does not simply suffer from the absence of full politico-
legal enfranchisement. She also suffers from the warring knot of desires that
circulate around the ambiguities of contract and gift. Outside of an economy
of exchange, even as it might be said to haunt its origins, the gift signals an
originary loss at work in any system of circulation. Refusing all reciprocity,
the gift also maintains an uneasy relationship with the violence that founds
a new legal or contractual order. Miss Amelia's excruciatingly ambivalent
relationship to the gifts of love, as I hope to show, rehearses the perversity
and the violence of contract ideology even as it effects her eventual isolation.
Hence, to contemplate the relationship between gifts and contracts—is the
gift a "primitive" form of the contract, or is the gift the sublime and elusive
other of contract, that which contract can only ever defile?—is simultaneously
to trace "The Ballad of the Sad Café's" complex transformation of a store
into a café and a café into a tomb. Is it Miss Amelia's furious resistance
to the gift or her peculiar understanding of its impossibility that explains
her displacement from the center of exchange to the collapsing interior of a
ghost house?[3] Indeed, it is only by considering the novella's fascination with
gifts (gifts that demand; gifts that poison; gifts of lack) that we can begin

to appreciate Miss Amelia's enigmatic relationship to marriage and to the circuit of exchange. The marriage contract, as McCullers's novella continues to inform us sixty years after its publication, marks the site of an engagement with contracts and gifts, violence and the ethical, that persistently refuses to come out even.[4]

CONTRACT AND VIOLENCE

The marriage contract's exemplary political status has long been familiar to American historians. "As an intentional and harmonious juncture of individuals for mutual protection, economic advantage, and common interest," writes historian Nancy Cott, "the marriage bond resembled the social contract that produced government. As a freely chosen structure of authority and obligation it was an irresistible model" (16). Historians of marriage in the nineteenth and early twentieth century were also quick to reinforce the relationship between contract and marriage. George Eliot Howard, author of *A History of Matrimonial Institutions* (1904), triumphantly asserts, "Whether regarded historically or biologically, monogamy and self–betrothal [i.e., contract] appear simply as two aspects of the same institution; they are connected by a psychic bond, and together they constitute the highest type of marriage and the family" (222–23).

At the same time, however, nineteenth-century American law articulated uncertainty about the extent to which marriage should conform to the general privileging of contractual relations established between free individuals unbeholden to public notions of equity. Hence, "the varied but determined resistance to voluntary divorce," notes Michael Grossberg, "and [the] repeated assertions of state nuptial responsibility [that] acted as constant reminders of the limits of matrimonial contractualism. [. . .] Marriage remained simply too important," Grossberg continues, "to be left entirely to the invisible hand of the nuptial marketplace" (21). Finally, Linda Kerber has shown most persuasively that despite being well aware of the discourse on equal rights for women, the American founders chose to maintain English law concerning marriage, thus extending coverture into the democratic era. Not until 1992, Kerber points out, with the Supreme Court's decision in *Planned Parenthood of Pennsylvania v. Casey*, did the Court specifically announce that it would no longer recognize the power of husbands over the bodies of their wives. "That is the moment," writes Kerber, "when coverture, as a living legal principle, died" (307). In other words, something analogous to a "conjugal kingdom" continued to function within the democratic state long after the American Revolution. The 1907 Expatriation Act is only one of the examples we might look at in this respect. Under this legislation, American women were compelled to follow the citizenship of their husbands: an American man could make his foreign-born wife into a citizen, but an American woman would lose her citizenship upon marrying a foreign man.[5] Marriage, then, could be said to maintain, like sedimentary layers, relationships to various forms of political organization: the hierarchizations of feudalism, as well as the social contractualism of the Enlightenment and the aggressive individualism of market contractualism.

But marriage is also, as Carole Pateman has shown, an exemplary instance of the specifically fraternal violence of contract ideology. In *The Sexual Contract*, Pateman returns to the foundational myth of modern civil society (the story of an original contract establishing "free social relations" between "individuals") and asks what the "freedom" of the original contract is free from and what it has power or right over. The answer is clear. Despite the rhetoric of gender-neutral individuality associated with the Enlightenment break from patriarchal feudalism, the individual of democratic contract ideology is a man: post-feudal political power is *fraternally* democratic.[6] "Odd things happen to women," Pateman concludes, "when the assumption is made that the only alternative to the patriarchal construction of sexual difference is the ostensibly sex-neutral 'individual'" (187).

In Pateman's version of things, the individual of contract theory is a man with impermeable boundaries, a man who can own things, a man who is never compromised by his relationship to another. At the same time, what Pateman calls "fraternal patriarchy" has insisted that the sexual contract and the social contract are separable entities and that the sexual contract merely concerns the private sphere. Hence, contracts function paradoxically when it comes to women. And we see this clearly in the case of marriage, since it is here that civil society's insistence on the separation of private and public spheres comes up against contract theory's invocation of "free social relations" between individuals. The marriage contract requires that women, those creatures classically considered incapable of full participation in the public sphere, also be entirely competent individuals who can enter into contractual relationships.

As Pateman reminds us, moreover, there are two moments to the marriage contract: the speech act ("I do") and the sex act (the consummation). While the distinction between the verbal and the bodily is certainly a highly relevant one, I would like to suggest instead a destabilizing supplementary reading: for the first act (the speech act) is also the one that temporarily *grants* the woman status as "individual," while the second act (the sex act) is the act that *revokes* precisely that status (as one feminist critic writes, "[W]hen a woman says 'I do,' she gives up her right to say 'I won't'" [qtd. in Russell x]). In other words, Pateman's paradox of the marriage contract is narratable. It manifests itself as two chronologically ordered moments. And, I will suggest, it is specifically the second act that subordinates. To appreciate this we only have to remind ourselves that rape within marriage was not legally recognized in most of the United States until the 1970s—regardless of how violent or apparently consensual the particular act of consummation. In 1975 Susan Brownmiller could write, "Rape, as the current law defines it, is the forcible perpetration of an act of sexual intercourse on the body of a woman not one's wife" (380). The incoherence of marital rape throughout most of the twentieth century is surely the most tangible sign of the afterlife of coverture in the United States, where it was not until 1978 that a husband was charged with raping his wife. Rape is not merely an event that may or may not happen; rather, it is (or was) part of the structure that gives (social) meaning to marriage.[7] To contemplate a rape that is not a crime is to contemplate an example of foundational violence—perhaps we should say *the* foundational violence: the violence of a political primal scene that makes an apparently nonviolent contractual order possible. Rape within marriage (rape that does not count as rape) restages not only the irreducible violence of any revolutionary founding but also the specifically gendered violence that ushers in a fraternal political order under the discursive cloak of contractual equality.

The political philosophers of contractual social relations have not, it should be added, entirely ignored the problem of a founding violence. Indeed, one could show that Hobbes and Rousseau, to take only two examples, are obsessed with trying to manage the place of violence in any founding contractual moment. "Before the names of Just and Unjust can have place," writes Hobbes, "there must be some coercive power, to compel men equally to the performance of their covenants, by the terrour of some punishment, greater than the benefit they expect by the breach of their Covenant" (202). The burden of Hobbes's political philosophy is to negate the violence of this coercive supplement by reminding his readers (with what often sound like tautological formulations) that what is gained through contract cancels out the excess of this necessary terror. Similarly, Rousseau manages to argue that even death cannot be considered too high a price to pay in return for what the contract gives. If the state says to one of its citizens, " 'It is in the state's interest that you should die,' " writes Rousseau, "he must die, because it is only on this condition that he has hitherto lived in safety, his life being no longer only a benefit due to nature, but a conditional gift of the state" (71). Surely it is only political philosophy's sleight of hand that is able to make the giving of one's own life into a good deal.[8]

From a feminist perspective, one of the most persistent displacements of contractualism's founding violence takes place whenever the marriage contract effects the subordination of women to men. Thus for Carole Pateman the social contract's relationship to a violent sexual contract undermines, or ought to undermine, every attempt to combat sexual injustice simply by fully opening up the social contract to women. "When feminism uncritically occupies the same terrain as contract," she writes, "a response to patriarchy that appears to confront the subjection of women head-on also serves to consolidate the peculiarly modern form of patriarchal right" (17). A feminist engagement with the politics of contractual relations, in other words, cannot proceed without deconstructing the opposition between contract and its difficult others: violence and the gift.

A SORRY BARGAIN

The protagonist of "The Ballad of the Sad Café" is a large, rich, and powerful woman who lives alone. Miss Amelia Evans is "solitary" as her father was before her—and regulates most of the exchanges in her community: "She would have been as rich as a congressman, if it were not for her one great failing, and that was her passion for lawsuits and the courts [. . .]. It was said that if Miss Amelia so much as stumbled over a rock in the road she would glance around instinctively as though looking for something to sue about it" (5). In addition to being voraciously litigious, Miss Amelia owns and runs the town's store and the town's still, and she is the local doctor. Miss Amelia is consumed with the work of calculation, with weighing and measuring: everything should come out even. There is nothing sorrier, she believes, than a "sorry bargain" (36). She goes so far as to display her own kidney stones, removed from her in a "terrible" operation, in a big glass-doored cabinet. To admit that these stones are anything less than treasures would be to admit that she had gotten the short end of the stick. "With all things which could be made by the hands Miss Amelia prospered." She only fails when it comes to personal dealings with human beings. For "people unless they are nilly-willy or very sick cannot be taken into the hands and changed overnight to something more worthwhile and profitable" (5).

When Marvin Macy, an "evil character" and the most handsome man in the region, falls in love with Miss Amelia, "that solitary-gangling queer-eyed girl," he reverses character and begins to court her (27, 28). She, however, resists any such transformation. Macy comes to Miss Amelia's house with "a bunch of swamp flowers, a sack of chitterlins, and a silver ring" (30), and Miss Amelia appears to accept these gifts and the accompanying proposal of marriage. A wedding takes place: Amelia wears her mother's wedding gown, at least twelve inches too short for her, and gropes in an "impatient, bored and exasperated" manner for the pocket of her overalls. But once married, she refuses to live up to her end of the deal. She refuses to go to bed with her husband; she spends their wedding night smoking, drinking coffee, reading the Farmer's Almanac, and learning to use her new typewriter. She is more than happy to treat her "groom" like a "customer," this being the only model of human relationships that she is willing to entertain; anything more or else is out of the question.

One of the appealing characteristics of McCullers's heroine is that Miss Amelia is simultaneously an exceptional woman, coded, in fact, as an "invert" (with her short haircut, her overalls, her muscular biceps and big hairy thighs—"in youth she had grown to be six feet two inches tall which in itself is not natural for a woman" 14), and at the "very center" of things. She is not "abjected." While signifiers of "inversion" suggest lesbianism, crucially and characteristically this is *not* in any simple way the story of a woman's love for another woman. McCullers's investment is in the "queer" as opposed to the "homosexual." Her interest is in what exceeds or challenges the laws of gender and sexual normativity. The townspeople hope the marriage to Marvin Macy will "put a bit of bride-fat on [Miss Amelia]" and "change her at last into a calculable woman" (31). But Miss Amelia "fails" to be feminized, fails to do what women do, to look the way women look. She resists marriage and in the end she is doomed for it. Betrayed and abandoned, the ghost in her own haunted house, she is ultimately associated with "sexless[ness]" (3). "[T]he great muscles of her body shrank until she was thin as old maids are thin when they go crazy" (70). To exceed the laws of sex and gender, in McCullers's world, is to be associated with sadness and defeat. We learn in *The Member of the Wedding* that "freaks" never get married or even go to weddings (271–72). It is precisely this sense of doom, or the pre-scripted, I would add, that makes McCullers's story both appealing and difficult for feminist critics.[9]

Recent criticism of "The Ballad of the Sad Café" claims that McCullers's novella is a feminist text that critiques the forced social process of gendering. Such criticism wants to assume that the novella is about gender configurations that in all their pathos could and should be different. Gilbert and Gubar, for example, argue that "The Ballad of the Sad Café" reveals "the culturally determined psychic logic that condemns the autonomous woman as a freak who must necessarily be sentenced to the defeat that is femininity" (104–05).[10] Indeed, McCullers is perhaps best known for her more "realistic" portraits of female adolescents, of girls who are reluctant to give in to feminization—what Gayle Rubin refers to as "signing the social contract" (196). However, it is noteworthy that sexual initiation in McCullers's texts is frequently allegorized, or doubled, by a violence done to another body. In *The Heart Is a Lonely Hunter*, for example, Mick's sexual initiation makes her feel as if "her head was broke off from her body and thrown away" (235). This feeling and figure is doubled when Willie Copeland, who is being held under cruel conditions in a labor camp, loses his feet to gangrene (217–18). In *The Member of the Wedding* the rupture of Frankie's dream of a "we of me," of getting married along with the bride and groom—a fantasy so "queer" that it is "straight"—is followed shortly thereafter by her childhood companion's violent death from meningitis.

Yet, despite this violent pattern in McCullers's work, we might still expect Miss Amelia to be at ease with marriage. A woman with her good business sense might be expected to see and accept the institution of marriage precisely for its institutionality, for its embeddedness in legal and economic codes. Why refuse to enter into an exchange with the groom, husband-as-customer, unless Miss Amelia has a different sense of this situation altogether? Miss Amelia's enigmatic response to marriage with Marvin Macy ("Within half an hour Miss Amelia had stomped down the stairs in breeches and a khaki jacket. Her face had darkened so that it looked quite black" 31) is, however, entirely in keeping with the peculiar status of women in civil society: she is both that which is exchanged and that which enters into the act of exchanging. Marriage turns those who would like to be "individuals" (see the repeated emphasis on Miss Amelia's "solitary" nature—she is nothing if not the proud owner, the contractual subject, who meticulously separates out her private life from her public one) into husbands and wives, and these terms have legal bearing and historical weight. However sacrificing that hang-dog Marvin Macy might appear to be, the law and history are on his side. His role is prescripted: "A groom is in a sorry fix when he is unable to bring his well-beloved bride to bed with him, and the whole town knows it" (31).[11]

But what gives McCullers's story greater depth, and at the same time, perhaps, allows it to fulfill the ballad's function as a story of doomed and tragic love, is its preoccupation with the logic and illogic of the gift. Gifts punctuate and drive the narrative of McCullers's story: from the gifts Marvin Macy brings to Miss Amelia, to the gifts she gives to Cousin Lymon and hence to the townspeople (culminating in the gift of the Café itself). This is not to mention the poison that Macy and Miss Amelia attempt to give to each other and that bears a significant etymological relationship to the gift ("the etymology of *gift*, translation of the Latin *dosis*, itself a transcription of the Greek *dosis*, dose, dose of poison" [Derrida 36]).[12]

THE GIFT OF LACK

If we try to give a name to what might be contract's other, or to what haunts, troubles, disrupts contract even as it seems indissociable from contract whenever it comes into view, it is hard to avoid language that seems more at home in literary representation, psychoanalytic theory, and deconstructive philosophy than in political philosophy, yet this "other" was already available to Thomas Hobbes in 1651:

The mutuall transferring of right is that which men call contract
[...]. When the transferring of right is not mutuall; but one of
the parties transfereth, in hope to gain thereby friendship, or
service from another, or from his friends; or in hope to gain the
reputation of charity, or magnanimity; or to deliver his mind
from the pain of compassion; or in hope of reward in heaven; this
is not contract, but GIFT, FREE-GIFT, GRACE; which words
signifie one and the same thing. (192–93)

Hobbes's formulation here might seem to reverse certain familiar versions
of the gift. Giftness, for Hobbes, involves the sanguine calculation of a
profitable return, while contract, by its very mutuality, seems to cancel out
any hope of extra contractual gain. This sense of nothing being lost with
the social contract's original renunciation of freedom recurs in Rousseau's
famous account of one hundred years later. "Each in giving himself to all
gives himself to none," writes Rousseau; "[A]nd since there are no associates
over whom he does not acquire the same rights as he cedes, he gains the
equivalent of all that he loses [...]" (55). From the perspective of this
political philosophy, as from that of Miss Amelia, a gift—a giving up without
certainty of equal or, ideally, greater return—would represent a sorry bargain.
The problem, of course, is how to keep contract and gift from appearing to
contaminate each other. How can one be persuaded to renounce something
before the fruits of that renunciation have come to pass? After all, giving up
without return is the very definition of madness: "To say that a man gives
himself for nothing," writes Rousseau, "is an absurd and incomprehensible
statement; such an action is illegitimate and void, simply because anyone
who does it is not in his right mind. To say the same about an entire people
is to imagine a nation of madmen, and madness does not make rights" (50).
The gift, we might say, is as troubling from the perspective of Enlightenment
political founding as tyrannical violence only insofar as it imagines that it has
transcended the madness of both founding violence and the gift does the
modern social contract convinces itself that it has inaugurated a new era.

The "Ballad of the Sad Café" has its own tyrant: Marvin Macy, who
has distinguished himself by severing others' body parts (be they squirrels'
tails or human ears), tempting the despondent towards death and shaming
young girls. But Macy is also the story's first and most insistent gift-giver (he
first comes to Miss Amelia's house, we recall, offering "a bunch of swamp
flowers, a sack of chitterlins, and a silver ring" [30]). When it becomes clear
that Miss Amelia's willingness to marry him does not mean that she will let
him into her bedroom, Macy responds by buying her more gifts (which she
promptly resells as merchandise in her store, acting as if she owes nothing in
return—as if the gifts were not, in fact, contractual). This pattern of giving

and of refusing to recognize any debt escalates until "on the fourth day [Marvin Macy] does an extremely simple-minded thing" (32). He brings in a lawyer to help him legally sign over all of his possessions to Miss Amelia. She agrees and files away the legal document, but she is on her guard. When a drunken Marvin Macy approaches his "bride" with wet wide eyes and places a hand on her shoulder ("He was trying to tell her something" [32]), she punches him in the face. In fact, Miss Amelia meets all her bridegroom's further efforts with blows until he leaves town. "So," remarks the narrator, "all he [Marvin Macy] had ever done was to make [Miss Amelia] richer and bring her love. But, strange to say, she never spoke of him but with a terrible and spiteful bitterness" (33).[13]

Marvin Macy's gifts make Miss Amelia furious, then, and it is as if what makes her furious is her very sense that there is no gift, that even as a gift is given—indeed, even if "all" is given—something is expected in exchange. The problem with gifts is that they do not require consent. If gifts can be seen to be above and beyond the marketplace, they are also before it. It could even be said that there is a primitive violence to the gift: one is bound whether one likes it or not, says the gift! If a gift is when someone gives something to another, this giving also never takes place ("A subject," writes Derrida, "will never give an object to another subject [. . .]" [24]). It is as if Miss Amelia agreed to receive but not to receive the excess-as-obligation, the presence-as-lack that the gift (which is therefore in some crucial sense not a gift) implies. Macy's gifts demand that she acquiesce in the "excess as obligation" of the marriage bed. It is the "gift" of unrestricted sexual access (the structured repetition of a founding primal rape) that Miss Amelia eventually recognizes and despises in Marvin Macy's gifts. "The Ballad of the Sad Café," in other words, implicitly registers an unbearable intimacy between gifts and the fraternal violence preserved in the legal invisibility of marital rape. Macy's gifts figure and demand the "gift of rape" that both founds and remains forever outside of the marriage contract. It is this "gift" that helps to maintain fraternal contract ideology's promise of individual completeness. It is fraternalism's secret gift to itself.

"The Ballad of the Sad Café" is doubly ambivalent when it comes to the gift, however, because it acknowledges that the gift bears not only a relationship to the gendered violence of the fraternal marriage contract but also to desire. And as I have already suggested, the story refuses to reveal definitively whether Miss Amelia is the subject tragically incapable of recognizing desire or tragically bound to understand desire better than anyone else in town. For if there is something impossible about gifts—the gift ruptures economy, reciprocity, and temporality—it is also hard to imagine love and desire without giving.[14] The gift, I would assert, and particularly the lover's gift, is always asking for *more* than a fair return. My gift is a demand that you give me precisely what I do not deserve: your love. My gift is a token of my lack; it is because I have nothing of value to give that I can give endlessly. "It is for this reason," McCullers's narrator suggests, "that most of us would rather love than be loved. Almost everyone wants to be the lover. And the curt truth is that, in a deep secret way, the state of being loved is intolerable to many" (27). Such is what Lacan calls "the radical form of the gift," to give what one does not have (286). "[This] is called love, but it is also hatred and ignorance" (263). "The Ballad of the Sad Café" poses a riddle the answer to which is the kernel of wisdom that the storyteller wants to pass on: *When is giving really taking? When the gift is the gift of the lover's lack.* The very thought of the gift disrupts both political and marital investments in the autonomous individual, whether that individual is one person (the citizen) or one people unified in the body that is the political or marital state.

And, of course, Marvin Macy is not the only gift-giver in "The Ballad of the Sad Café." Everything we know about Miss Amelia would lead us to believe that the café of the novella's title (like her marriage) should be an impossibility. The café begins to take shape when Miss Amelia stops, when she is given pause and suspends her calculations: she gives the tearful stranger who has appeared out of nowhere to "claim kin" (he is her "cousin" Lymon) a free swallow of her whiskey. In a gesture that recalls Marvin Macy placing his hand on Miss Amelia's shoulder, she first reaches out and "touches the hump on his back":

> Then Miss Amelia did a rare thing; she pulled out a bottle from her hip pocket and after polishing off the top with the palm of her hand she handed it to the hunchback to drink. Miss Amelia could seldom be persuaded to sell her liquor on credit, and for her to give so much as a drop away free was almost unknown. "Drink," she said. "It will liven your gizzard." (9)

Why does Amelia give to Lymon? Lymon introduces himself by producing an enigmatic photo that in the shadowiest of ways connects the two misfits through their mothers. The very insubstantiality of the evidence Lymon offers seems very much to the point here. Miss Amelia falls for the something and someone that links her to her mother, something that promises the return of an impossible relationship with an original and always lost object.[15] In addition, in his very undecidability (Lymon is not man, not woman, not child) he is the ideal love object; in loving him one gives up nothing.[16] For these reasons, Lymon encourages Miss Amelia to give where she had never given before. In other words, while love for Lymon is irreducibly enigmatic, it is also overdetermined: he is a "queer" love object, representing the instability of the law of sexual difference (in choosing Lymon, one need not make a singular choice); he appears to offer the return of an impossible lost love object; and he demands "all"—the rejection of a contractual relation is his sum and substance. Lymon, that is to say, is the uncanny embodiment of desire.

Once Miss Amelia starts giving gifts to Lymon, she never seems to stop. The swallow of whiskey is followed by a good meal, a warm bed, and ultimately by the café itself. On Saturday nights the townspeople gather at Miss Amelia's store to buy their liquor. There has never before been any "feeling of joy in [this] transaction," but on this occasion Miss Amelia breaks her own "rule" and allows people to open and drink their liquor sociably, right on her "premises." She even goes so far as to "hospitably" open and offer some "free" crackers.[17] "This was the beginning of the café," the narrator tells us, "It was as simple as that" (21–22).

A café exceeds a store by what may only be a modicum of desire (Miss Amelia's initial mouthful of liquor, her free crackers, her simple gesture), but the difference is also enormous. The near-utopian café that brings everyone into the circuit of exchange is founded upon something that exceeds "joyless transaction." While the contractual relations of a store regulate competition, a café produces intimate relations of exchange in the form of a community. But if a gift can turn a store into a café, it can also be the beginning of trouble. Miss Amelia can fight off the fraternal violence of the marriage contract, but she cannot successfully do battle with her own desire.

THE ALLEGORY OF GENDER

In McCullers's novella, everyone occupies the position of the lover and the beloved in turn, and thus, with a melancholic inevitability, Cousin Lymon falls for Marvin Macy: ("'Oh, Marvin Macy,' groaned the hunchback, and the sound of his name was enough to upset the rhythm of his sobs so that he hiccuped. 'He has been to Atlanta.' [. . .] 'He has been to the penitentiary.'" [53]); Lymon smiles at Marvin Macy "with an entreaty that was near to desperation" (49), and Miss Amelia, betrayed by her beloved, could be said to relose her lack (she reloses the lost love object that Lymon appeared to recover).[18] This betrayal culminates in a bloody fight between Marvin Macy and Miss Amelia that memorably figures what Carole Pateman calls "the true origin of political right," that which has been overlooked by contract theorists from the seventeenth century to the present.[19] In McCullers's rendering, however, this primal political scene becomes a battle that Miss Amelia should have won:

> For a while the fighters grappled muscle to muscle, their hip-
> bones braced against each other. Backward and forward, from

side to side, they swayed in this way. [...] At last she had him down, and straddled; her strong big hands were on his throat [...] Yet at the instant Miss Amelia grasped the throat of Marvin Macy the hunchback sprang forward and sailed through the air as though he had grown hawk wings. He landed on the broad strong back of Miss Amelia and clutched at her neck with his clawed little fingers. The rest is confusion. Miss Amelia was beaten before the crowd could come to their senses. Because of the hunchback the fight was won by Marvin Macy, and at the end Miss Amelia lay sprawled on the floor, her arms flung outward and motionless [...]. (67–68)

Such an ending for the novella would seem to have it both ways. Miss Amelia is defeated (this is the story of sexual difference as sexual hierarchy), yet it is an unjust defeat: if it had been a fair fight, she would have emerged victorious. But if "The Ballad of the Sad Café" is sad about the gender hierarchy that the fight imposes, it is also, surely, sad about the love object, Cousin Lymon, that Miss Amelia simultaneously loses. Miss Amelia, in other words, is not only the victim of a politico-legal injustice; she is also haunted by a loss that leaves her longing for completeness. If the fight approximates a contractual agreement (it is meant to be fair; the terms have been agreed to in advance), it is thrown by a gift—by the incalculable intervention of the character who precipitates Miss Amelia's relationship to the gift and to desire. Lymon's excessive intervention, it is worth noting, is the only wholly fantastic event in the story: "[W]hat took place," we are told "has been a mystery ever since" (68). As contract has no place for desirousness, I would assert, so Miss Amelia, the ultimate contractual subject, cannot survive her desire. Miss Amelia's loss at the hands of Marvin Macy and Cousin Lymon not only rehearses the gendered discrepancies of Enlightenment contract ideology; it also exposes the structure of a political violence that displaces the self-disrupting force of desire onto women, or femininity.[20] Marriage, as I have suggested, is one of the privileged sites for the operation of this displacement in the fraternal contractual order (it is where, to recall the townsfolk's words, someone like Amelia can be turned into a "calculable woman"). With its reworked primal scene Carson McCullers's text could be said to at once cite, resist, and unsuccessfully mourn the (un)decidability of the law of sexual difference and its psychical and political legacy.

"However," as the novella insists, "here in this very town there was once a café" (4), a café that, with its founding relation to the gift and its achievement of community, is surely Miss Amelia's (and the novella's) doomed alternative to marriage. As such, the café can also be read to figure all attempts to found an economy of desire outside of the fraternal allegory of gender. But if conventional marriage protects the male subject from the self-disruptions of desire (by deploying the woman's paradoxical relationship to contract: she is the fantastic figure who can autonomously contract herself out of politico-legal existence), Miss Amelia's café, lacking such easy displacements, exposes itself to all of desire's risks and vulnerabilities. The café, born of Cousin Lymon and Miss Amelia's less than perfect union, is at once the novella's inscription of a feminist (and queer) alternative to marriage under patriarchal or fraternal hegemony *and* its depiction of the cost of refusing to give up on giving up.

Those who speak out in support of what has been legislatively referred to as the "Defense of Marriage" frequently suggest that "traditional marriage" is an essential feature of "civilized" social organization ("something that every civilized society in five thousand years of recorded history has recognized" as one Senator put it ["Senate Debate" 231]).[21] Those same defenders of marriage clearly relish their invocation of the catastrophic social collapse that would result from any attempt to challenge traditional marriage (same-sex marriage, says one, is a "revolution [. . .] that seeks to break down the most basic building block of our society").[22] "The Ballad of the Sad Café" begins and ends with the depiction of a society that seems to have broken down ("Nothing moves—there are no children's voices [. . .]. The peach trees seem to grow more crooked every summer [. . .]" [70]), and we might be tempted to read this collapse as the novella's (conservative) judgment on any attempt to offer an alternative to the logic of the marriage contract. Instead, I would suggest that this desolation inscribes the very force of fraternal political power, on the one hand, and the self-disruptive force of that which threatens contract ideology's ideal subject on the other. Indeed, the insistence of the apocalyptic motif in conservative defense-of-marriage rhetoric ("woe betide the society that fails to honor that heritage" ["Senate Debate" 235–36]) testifies, in its own "queer" way, to the uncanny appeal of a catastrophic self-undoing.

"The Ballad of the Sad Café" gives us, finally, a remarkable theorization of the relationship between contract and gift, exchange and desire. The novella tries to maintain an investment in a character who is both female and central to an economy of exchange until it cannot, somehow, sustain this doubleness any further. "The Ballad of the Sad Café" insists that Amelia is defeated both from outside (she is punished as the transgressive woman who will not submit to the sorry bargain that is matrimony) and from within (she is defeated by the irreducible loss of her own desire). But to rid oneself of this loss is, precisely, to conjure up the disembodied, prepsychical, contract-making "individual" of patriarchal fantasy. In 1972 the Supreme Court declared (in *Eisenstadt v. Baird*):

The marital couple is not an independent entity with a mind and heart of its own, but an association of two individuals, each with a separate emotional and intellectual makeup. If the right of privacy means anything, it is the right of the individual, married or single, to be free from unwanted governmental intrusion [. . .]. (qtd. in Witte 210)

Our only choice, it would seem, is between one autonomous subject of the social contract and two autonomous subjects of the same social contract. If we need something other than a choice between a naturalized account of sexual difference and gender neutrality, then, we also need new ways of counting. While straight marriage notoriously results in problems with calculation (does one plus one equal one or two?), queer marriage, in "The Ballad of the Sad Café," questions the idea that any "one" is (ever) a whole number.

NOTES

1. "The singer [of a ballad] does not forget his or her position as the representative of the public voice. Bias there is in ballads, of course, but it is the bias of a party, community, or nation, not an individual's subjective point of view" (Preminger et al. 116).

2. This particular version of a familiar phrase is taken from Nick Carraway's ironic description of Tom Buchanan's defense of marriage at the end of Fitzgerald's *The Great Gatsby* (124).

3. In his 1915 study of exchange among Trobriand Islanders, anthropologist Bronislaw Malinowski attempted to categorize gifts according to their degree of "purity" and concluded that the one pure gift was the gift that the husband gives to the wife! Taking issue with Malinowski's understanding of the gift, Marcel Mauss, in his classic anthropological study of the gift (1925), begins by suggesting that gifts, as we tend to think of them, are impossible, and proceeds to argue for the ways in which gifts represent a primitive form of contract *and* an ethical beyond towards which "we" in the capitalist West should aspire. In *Given Time*, on the other hand, Jacques Derrida is intrigued by the impossibility—the space that is not a space—of Mauss's rejected gift. See also Hyde, who acknowledges that there are both "good" and "bad" forms of the gift, but who chooses only to contemplate the desirable presents, or goods, as if they could easily be sorted out into respective categories.

4. If feminist philosopher Claudia Card reminds us of the intimate and ongoing relationship between marriage and physical violence ("Legal marriage thus enlists state support for conditions conducive to murder and mayhem" [8]), Deborah Bergoffen argues that marriage must be reclaimed from right-wing fundamentalist thinkers: "Marriage lies on the cusp of the ethical and the political," she writes. "Marriage is a promise—an impossible promise insofar as it promises to sustain what cannot be sustained, the erotic-ethical event—whose effect is to recognize and acknowledge our sustained desire for the other [. . .]. As erotic, the body takes up the risk of violation for the sake of the gift" (27).

5. See Kerber 41. "Women have been citizens of the United States as long as the republic has existed," writes Kerber.

Passports were issued to them. They could be naturalized; they could claim
the protection of the courts. They were subject to the laws and were obliged
to pay taxes. But from the beginning American women's relationship to the
state has been different in substantial and important respects from that of men
[. . .]. The assumption that married women owe their primary civic obligation
to their husbands persisted long after the Revolution. It continued to define
relationships among men, women, and the state. It lurks behind what many
people take to be the common sense of the matter in our own time. (xx–xxi,
xxiii)

Kerber's work is very useful for understanding what I am referring to as the afterlife of
coverture.
    6. Pateman writes: "Patriarchy ceased to be paternal long ago. Modern civil society
is not structured by kinship and the power of fathers; in the modern world, women are
subordinated to men *as men*, or to men as a fraternity. The original contract takes place
after the political defeat of the father and creates modern *fraternal patriarchy*" (3). See also
MacCannell on what she calls "the regime of the brother."
    7. While in July of 1980 only eight states had passed laws criminalizing rape in
marriage, by 1989 forty-two states had passed such laws. Still, Russell comments, it is
"easier" to make rape in marriage illegal than it is to "exorcise" pervasive misogyny. Now
that many of the laws are in place, she argues, there is significantly less interest in "wife
rape." Russell recounts a face-off with a divorce lawyer who noisily opposed the idea of rape
in marriage. "'The specter of the women's liberation movement,' he warned, 'is now in your
bedroom'" (x). Of particular note here is how opponents of the idea that there can be rape
in marriage become panicked about contracts. Surely, they argue, not every sex act must be
negotiated.
    8. We might consider, in this regard, the analogy between the soldier/husband/citizen
who must patriotically give his life to the state in times of war and the bride given to the
state of marriage. The concept of a renunciation of rights that simultaneously confirms the
individual's participation in a contractual order also calls to mind the status of a prisoner.
"The Ballad of the Sad Café" is framed, somewhat enigmatically, by a chain gang working—
and singing—on the edge of town: "Just twelve mortal men, seven of them black and five
of them white boys from this county. Just twelve mortal men who are together" (72). Miss
Amelia, it should be recalled, has a black servant, a man without the rights and privileges
that would disrupt her relationship to the contractual order (31, 34), and Marvin Macy,
we are briefly informed, is also the owner of a Klansman's robe (33). While race is literally
marginalized in "The Ballad of the Sad Café," race and identity formation are central and
explicit concerns in McCullers's *The Member of the Wedding* (see Davis).
    9. McCullers has been quoted as saying, "I was born a man" (see Carr). While no appeal
to the biographical is necessary to establish McCullers's investment in the transgression
of gendered norms, there are several fascinating (because distorted) autobiographical
traces in her works. In 1943 she certainly knew a thing or two about marriage and its
disappointments. She had been married to and had divorced Reeves McCullers ("Ballad"
was completed months after the divorce). Reeves had betrayed Carson in numerous ways,
but the one unforgivable act, as far as she was concerned, was the emptying of her bank
account (McCullers, *Illuminations* 30–31). Reeves, then, is a kind of anti-Marvin Macy
figure. As opposed to giving all, he takes all. And, in accordance with the logic of the gift in
this story, the two are psychically equivalent. While recent work on McCullers has chosen
to emphasize her love for women, and particularly for Annemarie Clarac-Schwartzenbach,

one should not forget her "queer" relationship to Reeves McCullers, whom she remarried in 1945. McCullers certainly had weddings on her mind: she wrote "The Ballad of the Sad Café" while taking time off from her major project, *The Member of the Wedding*.

10. For other feminist readings of "The Ballad of the Sad Café," see Broughton; Carlton; Portada; Sosnoski; Westling. McCullers's work has most often been characterized as "female gothic" (see Kahane; Moers). For discontent with this classification see Evans and McCullers herself in "The Russian Realists." Charles Hannon argues that missing the novella's original publication date (1943 not 1951 as many critics have assumed) results in erasing the crucial wartime context. His work justifies or fills out gothic readings by suggesting that "Amelia's resistance to the 'normalization' of labor, gender, and sexuality after her husband's return makes her a freakish, 'grotesque' character, a frightening prophecy for readers unwilling to cooperate with the return to a masculinist economy after the war" (97). For all his emphasis on historical and cultural specificity, Hannon is finally interested in the ways in which "The Ballad of the Sad Café" (in the person of Miss Amelia) *resists* its own historical moment.

11. Miss Amelia can be associated with a series of heroines who are either canny or woefully ignorant about gender and exchange (the "traffic in women," identified by Lévi-Strauss as the very essence of culture). Jane Eyre knows to be wary of Rochester's premarital gifts (which are not "gifts" at all), gifts that will ultimately serve to place her all the more securely in his power. In McCullers's gothic tale, Amelia is both Jane Eyre and Bertha Mason: she is her own madwoman in the attic. She knows to be suspicious of the gift, but she is also the one who suffers the cost of refusing to give in. See also Lily Bart's ultimate refusal to enter into "a plain business arrangement, such as one man would make with another" (Wharton, *The House of Mirth*, 233). The knowledge of the impossibility of making such an agreement is the fruit of her tragic education. For another "southern gothic" portrait of the refusal of debt and melancholic femininity, see Faulkner's "A Rose for Emily."

12. The OED records the earliest sense of gift, in Old English, as being used to mean "payment for a wife" and, in the plural, with the sense "wedding," which, the OED continues, corresponds to the Dutch word for poison.

13. One way to read Miss Amelia's refusal is to read her as an "apparitional lesbian" in Terry Castle's sense of the term. But one should not fall into the trap of offering "lesbian" as the only answer. For positing an identity or an identity category as if it were distinctive, singular, and self-explanatory would be to miss precisely what this text has to say about subjectivity and its ghosts. For recent work on McCullers and lesbianism see Kenschaft. For a recent essay on McCullers's investment in the queer see Adams.

14. For a compelling attempt to describe the essence of the gift see Hyde's discussion of the literature on kidney donation. Hyde argues that the donors are donors because they do not calculate: "The choice is instantaneous; there is no time delay, no period of deliberation. Moreover, the donors themselves do not regard their choice as a decision at all!" (65). Note the magic or impossibility here: making a choice without making a decision. If there were a moment of decision, of calculation (which of course there must be), there would be no gift.

15. "Everything in the sphere of this first attachment to the mother," writes Freud, "seemed to me so difficult to grasp in analysis—so grey with age and shadowy and almost impossible to revivify" ("Female Sexuality" 226). The missing mother is the lost object who casts a shadow over McCullers's fiction. Frankie's mother in *The Member of the Wedding* dies when she is born and is only a photograph in her father's drawer. Mick's mother in *The Heart Is a Lonely Hunter* is almost absent. Sherman Pew dreams that his mother, a woman he knows nothing about, is the glorious diva, Marian Anderson (*Clock*

without Hands). The mother in "A Domestic Dilemma" is dangerous and absent in her very presence. And then there is the riddle of maternity posed by "Madame Zilensky and the King of Finland": Madame Zilensky's three sons have three different fathers, yet they all look alike and look nothing like her. What is this enigma if not one of lost origin? In "The Haunted Boy," the protagonist must relive the threat of losing his suicidal mother in order to refind her, a process that also marks his passage out of childhood. If mothers are missing in her fiction, Carson McCullers's mother was, until her own death, quite present in her daughter's life. Since for much of her adult life McCullers was ill and disabled, her mother continued to care for her daughter in a particularly maternal way. It is as if McCullers left the most psychosexually significant of bonds out of her fiction. Or, like a good dreamer/fiction writer, only represented those bonds in a distorted or negated form.

16. In this Lymon recalls *A Portrait of a Lady*'s Gilbert Osmond. If Isabel chooses nobody, Miss Amelia chooses all.

17. The connection between the gift and nourishment is not an incidental one. The love relationship in which gifts are given uncannily repeats an earlier bond in which desire and hunger were even more difficult to tell apart. See also Freud's "Negation" on the function of judgment and eating versus spitting out. When Marvin Macy visits the café, Miss Amelia tries to poison him and ends up almost poisoning herself (57). Later, before leaving town, Macy and Lymon "fix [. . .] a dish of Miss Amelia's favorite food [. . .] seasoned [. . .] with enough poison to kill off the country" (69).

18. When Cousin Lymon and Marvin Macy first encounter one another, they exchange a "peculiar stare [. . .] like the look of two criminals who recognize each other" (47). Cousin Lymon and Marvin Macy, that is to say, recall Miss Amelia's "crossed" eyes—"eyes which are turned inward so sharply that they seem to be exchanging with each other one long and secret gaze of grief" (3–4). Taken together, I would suggest, these two sets of eyes figure the novella's attempt to deconstruct the opposition between inter- and intrasubjectivity. Miss Amelia's eyes, moreover, call to mind those of Berenice Sadie Brown, the African-American housekeeper and surrogate mother in *The Member of the Wedding*. She has a "dark and sad" right eye and a "bright blue glass" left eye: "It stared out fixed and wild from her quiet, colored face, and why she had wanted a blue eye nobody human would ever know" (259).

19. Paulson reads this scene of male violence and defeat of the "mother" as "ganging up" (187).

20. "The allegory of gender [difference]," as Michael Warner has written, "protects against a recognition of the role of the imaginary in the formation of the erotic. [. . .] It provides reassurance that imaginary intersubjectivity has been transcended." Moreover, this allegory produces a particular role for the queer subject: "[T]o the extent that our culture relies on the allegorization of gender to disguise from itself its own ego erotics, it will recognize those ego erotics only in the person of the homosexual, apparently bereft of the master trope of difference" (202). McCullers's fiction, I would argue, theorizes "ego erotics," or the extent to which desire does not depart from various projects of self-differing (identification, narcissism, melancholia). Heterosexuality, or fraternal patriarchy, in this reading, is the fiction used to compensate for the fact that we never leave home.

21. The Defense of Marriage Act was passed by overwhelming margins in both the House and the Senate and was signed into law by President Clinton in September 1996 in the middle of the night (!).

22. Albert Mohler, President of the Southern Baptist Theological Seminary speaking on CNN's *Larry King Live*, March 2000. ("Should Same Sex Couples Have the Right to Marry?" <www.cnn.com/TRANSCRIPTS/0003/09/lkl.oo.html>).

WORKS CITED

Adams, Rachel. "'A Mixture of Delicious and Freak': The Queer Fiction of Carson McCullers." *American Literature* 71 (1999): 551–83.

Bergoffen, Debra B. "Marriage, Autonomy, and the Feminine Protest." *Hypatia: A Journal of Feminist Philosophy* 14.4 (1999): 18–35.

Brontë, Charlotte. *Jane Eyre*. 1847. New York: Norton, 1987.

Broughton, Panthea Reid. "Rejection of the Feminine in Carson McCullers' 'The Ballad of the Sad Café.'" *Twentieth-Century Literature* 20 (1974): 34–43.

Brownmiller, Susan. *Against Our Will: Men, Women, and Rape*. New York: Simon and Schuster, 1975.

Card, Claudia. "Against Marriage and Motherhood." *Hypatia: A Journal of Feminist Philosophy* 11.3 (1996): 1–23.

Carlton, Ann. "Beyond Gothic and Grotesque: A Feminist View of Three Female Characters of Carson McCullers." *Pembroke Magazine* 20 (1988): 54–62.

Carr, Virginia Spencer. *The Lonely Hunter: A Biography of Carson McCullers*. Garden City: Doubleday, 1975.

Castle, Terry. *The Apparitional Lesbian: Female Homosexuality and Modern Culture*. New York: Columbia UP, 1993.

"Chairman Santorum Marriage Remarks on Senate Floor." 14 July 2004. <http://www.senate.gov/src/agenda/index.cfm?fuseaction=ViewArticle&articleid=318>.

Clark, Beverly Lyon, and Melvin J. Friedman, eds. *Critical Essays on Carson McCullers*. New York: G. K. Hall, 1996.

Davis, Thadious. "Erasing the 'We of Me' and Rewriting the Racial Script: Carson McCullers's *Two Member[s] of the Wedding*." Clark and Friedman 206–20.

Derrida, Jacques. *Given Time: I. Counterfeit Money*. Trans. Peggy Kamuf. Chicago: U of Chicago P, 1992.

Evans, Oliver. *Carson McCullers: Her Life and Work*. London: Peter Owen, 1965.

Faulkner, William. "A Rose for Emily." *The Faulkner Reader*. New York: Random, 1977. 489–98.

Fitzgerald, F. Scott. *The Great Gatsby*. 1926. New York: Penguin, 1950.

Foster, Hannah Webster. *The Coquette*. 1797. In *The Power of Sympathy and the Coquette*. Ed. Carla Mulford. New York: Penguin, 1996.

Freud, Sigmund. "Female Sexuality." 1931. *The Standard Edition of the Complete Psychological Works of Sigmund Freud*. Trans. and ed. James Strachey. Vol. 21. London: Hogarth, 1955. 225–43. 24 vols. 1953–74.

———. "Negation." 1925. *The Standard Edition*. Vol. 19. 235–39.

"Gift." *The Oxford English Dictionary*. 2nd ed. 1989.

Gilbert, Sandra M., and Susan Gubar. *No Man's Land: The Place of the Woman Writer in the Twentieth Century*. New Haven: Yale UP, 1989.

Grossberg, Michael. *Governing the Hearth: Law and Family in Nineteenth-Century America*. Chapel Hill: U of North Carolina P, 1985.

Hannon, Charles. "'The Ballad of the Sad Café' and Other Stories of Women's Wartime Labor." *Genders* 23. Ed. Thomas Foster, Carol Siegel, and Ellen E. Berry. New York: New York UP, 1996. 97–119.

Hawthorne, Nathaniel. *The Scarlet Letter*. 1850. New York: Norton, 1988.

Hobbes, Thomas. *Leviathan*. 1651. New York: Penguin, 1982.

Howard, George Eliot. *A History of Matrimonial Institutions: Chiefly in England and the United States with an Introductory Analysis of the Literature and the Theories of Primitive Marriage and the Family*. Chicago: U of Chicago P, 1904. 2 Vols.

Hyde, Lewis. *The Gift: Imagination and the Erotic Life of Property*. New York: Vintage, 1979.

James, Henry. *The Portrait of a Lady*. 1908. New York: Penguin, 1984.

Kahane, Claire. "The Gothic Mirror." *The (M)other Tongue: Essays in Feminist Psychoanalytic Interpretation*. Ed. Shirley Nelson Garner et al. Ithaca: Cornell UP, 1985. 334–51.

Kenschaft, Lori J. "Homoerotics and Human Connections: Reading Carson McCullers 'As a Lesbian.'" Clark and Friedman 220–33.

Kerber, Linda K. *No Constitutional Right to Be Ladies: Women and the Obligations of Citizenship*. New York: Hill, 1988.

Lacan, Jacques. *Écrits: A Selection*. Trans. Alan Sheridan. New York: Norton, 1977.

MacCannell, Juliet Flower. *The Regime of the Brother: After the Patriarchy*. New York: Routledge, 1991.

Malinowski, Bronislaw. *The Sexual Life of Savages in North-Western Melanesia: An Ethnographic Account of Courtship, Marriage, and Family Life among the Natives of the Trobriand Islands, British New Guinea*. 1915. London: Routledge, 1932.

Mauss, Marcel. *The Gift: The Form and Reason for Exchange in Archaic Societies*. 1925. New York: Norton, 2000.

McCullers, Carson. "The Ballad of the Sad Café." 1943. *The Ballad of the Sad Café and Other Stories*. New York: Bantam, 1971. 3–72.

———. *Clock without Hands*. Boston: Houghton, 1961.

———. *Collected Stories of Carson McCullers*. Boston: Houghton, 1987.

———. "A Domestic Dilemma." 1951. *Collected Stories* 148–57.

———. "The Haunted Boy." 1952. *Collected Stories* 158–70.

———. *The Heart Is a Lonely Hunter*. 1940. New York: Bantam, 1953

———. *Illuminations and Night Glare: The Unfinished Autobiography of Carson McCullers*. Ed. Carlos L. Dews. Madison: U of Wisconsin P, 1999

———. "Madame Zilensky and the King of Finland." 1941. *Collected Stories* 110–18.

———. *The Member of the Wedding*. 1946. *Collected Stories* 255–392.

———. *Reflections in a Golden Eye*. 1941. New York: Bantam, 1950.

———. "The Russian Realists and Southern Literature." *Decision: A Review of Free Culture* 2.1 (July 1941): 15–19.

Moers, Ellen. "Female Gothic." *Literary Women*. New York: Doubleday, 1976. 90–110.

Pateman, Carole. *The Sexual Contract*. Stanford: Stanford UP, 1988.

Paulson, Suzanne Morrow. "Carson McCullers' 'The Ballad of the Sad Café': A Song Half Sung, Misogyny, and 'Ganging Up.'" Clark and Friedman 187–205.

Portada, Arleen. "The Sex Role Rebellion and the Failure of Marriage in the Fiction of Carson McCullers." *Pembroke Magazine* 20 (1988): 63–71.

Preminger, Alex, and T. V. F. Brogan et al., eds. *The New Princeton Encyclopedia of Poetry and Poetics*. Princeton: Princeton UP, 1993.

Rousseau, Jean-Jacques. *The Social Contract*. 1762. Oxford: Oxford UP, 1999.

Russell, Diana. *Rape in Marriage*. Bloomington: Indiana UP, 1990.

Rubin, Gayle. "The Traffic in Women: Notes on the 'Political Economy' of Sex." *Literary Theory: An Anthology*. Ed. Julie Rivkin and Michael Ryan. Malden: Blackwell, 1998. 533–60.

"Senate Debate on the Defense of Marriage Act, October 9, 1996." *Same-Sex Marriage: Pro and Con*. Ed. Andrew Sullivan. New York: Random, 1997. 229–38.

Sosnoski, Karen. "Society's Freaks: The Effects of Sexual Stereotyping in Carson McCullers' Fiction." *Pembroke Magazine* 20 (1988): 82–88.

Warner, Michael. "Homo-Narcissism; or, Heterosexuality." *Engendering Men: The Question of Male Feminist Criticism.* Ed. Joseph A. Boone and Michael Cadden. New York: Routledge, 1990. 190–206.

Westling, Louise. *Sacred Groves and Ravaged Gardens: The Fictions of Eudora Welty, Carson McCullers, and Flannery O'Connor.* Athens: U of Georgia P, 1985.

Wharton, Edith. *The House of Mirth.* 1905. New York: Norton, 1990.

Witte, Jr., John. *From Sacrament to Contract: Marriage, Religion, and Law in the Western Tradition.* Louisville: Westminster John Knox, 1997.

ELLEN MATLOK-ZIEMANN

Ambiguity—the Ideal Way of Having the World

Despite the bleak ending of *The Member of the Wedding*, McCullers offers here a vision that briefly allows a harmonious way of being. In the depiction of an adolescent girl suspended between childhood and adulthood, she reveals both the tensions and possibilities of instability, of "becoming." *The Ballad of the Sad Café* portrays a woman who, in many ways, resembles Mick and Frankie. Miss Amelia is, as Westling describes her, "a grown-up tomboy" ("Carson McCullers's Amazon Nightmare" 109) who, despite her age—she is thirty years old—apparently has not yet learned to accept her role as a woman. McCullers's choice of a "*grown-up* tomboy" (emphasis mine) as the main protagonist suggests the importance of the state of suspension, instability, as it provides ample ground for the process of "becoming." But she more than stresses the potentials of an unfixed state; since in patriarchal society such a state can be tolerated only for adolescents, the drastic extension of Miss Amelia's adolescence is thus a critique of society's inability or refusal to make possible "being-in-the-world."

In *The Ballad of the Sad Café*, McCullers creates a woman who is strong, fearless, and independent. A "dark, tall woman with bones and muscles like a man" (BSC 8), she is, in fact, *stronger* than any man in town, behaving in a decidedly masculine manner and possessing even magical powers when concocting potions to heal her patients. Such a woman must appear like a figure

From *Tomboys, Belles, and Other Ladies: The Female Body-Subject in Selected Works by Katherine Anne Porter and Carson McCullers*, pp. 138–57. © 2005 by Ellen Matlok-Ziemann.

from a fairy tale, since she actually insists on, and sustains her independence in a society characterized by rigid norms, regarding race, class, and gender. Indeed, . . . in this ballad McCullers ridicules the myth of the Southern lady, in challenging gender boundaries and norms of heterosexuality by creating the giant Amazon Miss Amelia who is not restricted by "real" norms to the extent of Mick and Frankie.[49] If one disregards the fact that *The Member of the Wedding* was written several years after the publication of *The Ballad of the Sad Café*, one could actually argue that McCullers combines and amplifies Mick's and Frankie's tomboy qualities in Miss Amelia to expose in an intriguing and more radical manner gender constraints in patriarchal society and to explore ways of "being-in-the-world." Clearly, the narrative form of a ballad offers McCullers the possibility both to create this extraordinary woman with supernatural powers, using the ballad's characteristics to enhance an "unreal" magical atmosphere, and to sharpen her critique. In fact, McCullers employs the same means that Katherine Anne Porter applied to "The Princess." Porter, too, realized the potentials of the fairy tale and was thus able to explore more radically a woman's possibilities to develop an independent self. While in the more conventional narrative "Pale Horse, Pale Rider," Miranda is constrained by a more "real" situation and fights desperately and in vain for control, in the fairy tale "The Princess," which permits magic, charms, and spells, Porter is free to investigate unexpected, unfamiliar, and thought-provoking means of resistance against patriarchal society.[50]

Everything about Amelia seems out of proportion. Although there are many similarities between her and Mick and Frankie, Miss Amelia's features, her (bodily) power, her generous love, her struggle, and her defeat, are immensely exaggerated. Like Mick and Frankie, this "manly giantess," as Millichap describes Miss Amelia (329), cannot be miniaturized. But whereas the "ordinary" tomboys are merely on the verge of "outgrowing" gender boundaries, posing a *potential* threat to images of the delicate, petite lady, Miss Amelia actually is a threat. McCullers creates a giant woman whose "unnatural" height causes a very strong unease in the inhabitants. While Mick's and Frankie's suspension of boundaries is transitional, McCullers here insists on a permanent suspension and makes visible how such an insistence challenges patriarchal society. Although Miss Amelia should have conformed to the prescribed boundaries long ago, defeated by society and incapable of sustaining this period of transition, she refuses to do so. This tension is further increased with Miss Amelia's name that is not ambiguous as Mick's and Frankie's but clearly indicates her femaleness and her failure of, or rather resistance to, marriage.[51] McCullers thus emphasizes the discrepancy between a name which evokes expectations of a "proper" woman and Amelia's masculine body. As the meaning of her name also suggests, Amelia is "laborious" (Online Etymology Dictionary), indicating that her insistence on a suspension of gender boundaries is troublesome to patriarchal society and, as we will see, that her femaleness is laborious to her.[52] But even the sustaining of this suspension requires an immense effort on the part of Miss Amelia.

In the main part of the novel, she is the only woman[53] who can sustain this suspension for many years and who is able to resist gender constraints. McCullers seems to suggest that if only the period of instability, adolescence, can be prolonged, the result can produce a perpetual suspension of gender boundaries that makes possible "being-in-the-world." Indeed, despite the harsh violation of her boundaries, Miss Amelia is exceedingly successful, being not only the richest woman in town, but also a skilled carpenter, a hard-working entrepreneur, producer of whiskey which possesses magical qualities, and seller of chitterlings and sausages. But although she has embodied this powerful "tomboy" for many years, she is not punished for her "masculine" appearance and behavior. On the contrary, she is feared and respected in town and there are men who would actually have courted her had she taken any interest in them (BSC 9).[54] She seems at ease with both her environment and her self, possessing apparently a habitual body that allows her to have the world (Merleau-Ponty 162), and assumes subjectivity through the power she has over others. Her power is so great that the inhabitants trust her judgment of the weather and follow her decision to slaughter a hog after the first cold spell (BSC 55). In contrast to Mick and Frankie who have to struggle with "real" expectations, codes, gender norms, and cannot achieve autonomy to the extent Miss Amelia is able to, she is in control of her self, others, and, to some extent, even nature.

Although there are strong indications that Miss Amelia has achieved a harmonious way of being by extending her tomboyishness, the depiction of her face suggests that she is not part of "being-in-the-world." That her face possesses a "tense, haggard quality" (BSC 8), almost to the point of becoming "pathological," reveals the strenuous nature of sustaining the transitional period of suspension; it is "laborious." The fact that she is slightly cross-eyed also visualizes the pressure under which she is placed.[55] Further, the interaction with her environment is not reciprocal in a Beauvoirian sense. She feels at ease, harmonious, only with matter and human beings she can manipulate and control; by treating everyone as an other, she objectifies and denies them subjectivity. In contrast to Mick and Frankie, whose desire to participate in "becoming" is characterized by a reciprocal interaction with others, having "thousands of thousands and thousands of friends" (MW 139), Miss Amelia is not at all interested in such an interaction as it does not serve her business interests. She avoids contact even with relatives. When she happens to meet her cousin, both show their contempt by spitting on the side of the road (BSC 12).

McCullers exaggerates Miss Amelia's business interests and her desire for control to make visible the mechanisms in patriarchal society that seek to destroy the other. The many instances of her frequent involvement in "long and bitter litigation over just a trifle" (BSC 9) are aimed at increasing her power over others; since she is part of a *male* world, she does not value, as Beauvoir would have it, the freedom of others (*Ethics* 49, 60). It is thus not very surprising that she is "a solitary person" (BSC 9), who not only rejects "the love of men" but all those who are not controllable, not "willy-nilly or very sick." McCullers clearly overemphasizes Miss Amelia's imitation of man, has her possess physical and economic powers no other man has, and actually exaggerates "normal" male behavior by having her perform an overly zealous businessman. While one could consider and thus ridicule Miss Amelia's involvement in trifles and her performance of "man" as being inadequate, McCullers actually expresses her critique of typically male (capitalist) practices.[56] McCullers has, then, Miss Amelia impersonate and mock "man" like a drag king. Whereas in *The Member of the Wedding*, McCullers's focus lies on the construction of "woman," in this novel Miss Amelia's parody[57] also exposes the construction of "man."[58]

McCullers also reveals the underlying fear that undermines Miss Amelia's sense of self, her ability to control. She is a highly esteemed healer, taking great pains to find the right cure for various symptoms, thereby assuming control of the malfunctioning body, of nature. No treatment is too dangerous or extraordinary to make her hesitate; neither is there a disease "so terrible but what she would undertake to cure it" (BSC 23). She is, however, powerless when it comes to dealing with "a female complaint":

> If a patient came with a female complaint she could do nothing. Indeed at the mere mention of the words her face would slowly darken with shame, and she would stand there craning her neck against the collar of her shirt, or rubbing her swamp boots together, for all the world like a great, shamed dumb-tongued child. (BSC 23)

Although it is true that Miss Amelia is part of a predominantly male culture, raised as a motherless child by her father, one cannot assume, as does Carlton (61), that her lack of knowledge of anything other than male culture contributes to her confusion and embarrassment when confronted with female complaints. Rather, these feelings reveal her effort to reject, expel, that which threatens her self: femaleness. She distinctly senses how femaleness invades—like the shame that slowly darkens her face—her self. Yet, although she seeks to assert that she is part of the male world by touching the texture of her "masculine" apparel, craning her neck against her shirt or rubbing her rough swamp boots together, as if to convince herself that femaleness does not exist, she fails. Losing her voice, her subjectivity, she becomes, in fact, a "shamed dumb-tongued child."

The same dis-ease can be discerned in the scene when Miss Amelia wears her mother's wedding-dress. That Miss Amelia looks ridiculous in gowns, this one especially, since it is "at least twelve inches too short for her" (BSC 37), contributes to the failure of her performance of the "proper" woman. While McCullers's use of Miss Amelia as a drag king earlier made visible the construction of "man," Miss Amelia's failed attempt at performing a bride, her mimicry, now illustrates the construction of the other gender.[59] As Miss Amelia dons this bridal gown, she reveals with her body the artificiality of femininity and is utterly alienated by it. She keeps making an "odd gesture," and as she tries to reach "for the pocket of her overalls, and [is] unable" to find it her face [becomes] impatient, bored, and exasperated" (BSC 37–38). A situation clearly never encountered before, the wedding ceremony thus conflicts with her "habitual [masculine] body." At the same time, however, Miss Amelia expresses more than dis-ease with donned femininity. She rejects her own performance of gender, since, like female complaints, it threatens to invade her self. Almost as if trying to escape the constraints of femininity, she hurries "out of the church, not taking the arm of her husband, but walking at least two paces ahead of him" (BSC 38). On their way home she talks about work and treats her husband like a customer, a behavior that suggests her desire to "undo" the wedding ceremony, refusing to let this incidence become an experience that might eventually constitute a sediment of her past.[60]

Not only do female complaints become the abject; McCullers has Miss Amelia connect embarrassing and shameful female cycles with the cycles of nature.[61] Miss Amelia thus conceives of the nature she cannot control as equally frightening as the female complaints which must be rejected, repelled, at all costs in order to sustain her subjectivity.[62] As it, for instance, snows for the first time in many years, this unusual natural event prompts the inhabitants to react in various ways. Miss Amelia's reaction is most interesting. Unable to "form an immediate opinion of this new event" (BSC 69), she simply ignores it by drawing the shutters and locking all windows in her house. Although the narrator claims that she is not afraid of snow, that it is merely something she does not know, her shutting out nature suggests more than a momentary lack of knowledge. Indeed, the narrator continues, if Miss Amelia "*admitted* this snowfall she would have to come to a decision" (emphasis mine). This decision would force her to accept an inability to sustain her subjectivity through control only, as she would have to admit that she cannot deny part of her "natural" self, her body. By shutting out nature, she refuses to accept that she, a body-subject, is both transcendent and immanent. Clearly, her body is a way of having the world, and it thus enables her as a body-subject to project herself to others, to transcend. At the same time, however, the body sets limits as well, is immanent. By shutting out nature "until every [snow] flake ha[s] melted" (BSC 72), Miss Amelia denies the immanent aspect of her body and seeks, like Mick, to transcend through pure will in a Cartesian manner.[63]

In another passage McCullers discloses not only Miss Amelia's fear and rejection of femaleness and nature but also her fascination with it. In a glass-doored cabinet, the most important piece of furniture in her house, she keeps her treasures, two of which are especially significant. One is a large acorn she found when her father died, a symbol, according to Paulson, of her father's procreative powers, and the other is a "little velvet box holding two small greyish stones" (BSC 44). In particular, the grey stones draw her attention; when she has "nothing to do, Miss Amelia [takes] out this velvet box and stand[s] by the window with the stones in the palm of her hand, looking down at them, with a mixture of fascination, dubious respect, and fear" (BSC 44). Expressing simultaneously fear of—horror—and fascination with the kidney stones removed under surgery, she is clearly drawn to a power that weakens and endangers her subjectivity. She is, as Kristeva would put it, "under the sway of a power as securing as it is stifling" (13). These stones, causing unbearable pain, render her powerless and subject her to her sick body, to immanent "nature." As her body makes it impossible to sustain her subjectivity, reducing her "willy-nilly" to a weak patient and confining her to a hospital, she experiences this incident "from the first minute to the last" as terrifying (BSC 44). Removed from her body, these stones come to represent excrement, expelled as the abject in an effort to secure her sense of self. The fact that Miss Amelia keeps them as treasures and views them with "fascination, dubious respect, and fear," reveals that she will not be able to free her self from dangerous (female) nature; the abject will continuously besiege her and threaten to invade her self.

Interestingly, Miss Amelia's sick body becomes "pathological" in a double sense. Both Merleau-Ponty and Beauvoir point out that, in case of sickness, a body-subject's way of having the world is, sometimes severely, disturbed. Physical movements can be difficult, or, as Miss Amelia experiences it, pain can cause such terror that it prevents her from interacting "properly." To her, however, the effect of kidney stones is not just a normal process of a disease that cannot be entirely controlled. Rather than being part of the "basic process of living" (Heinämaa, *Toward a Phenomenology of Sexual Difference* 110) to Miss Amelia, like any natural phenomenon threatening her autonomy, disease connotes dangerous, shameful femaleness. Suffering, then, from kidney stones is no longer an "ordinary" disease but one which, in effect, threatens her sense of self and forces her to admit her loss of power, control. For a brief period she must experience her self as weak, a characteristic ascribed to "real" women. The fact that her "pathology" carries a doubleness can be clearly discerned in her refusal to let this "terrible experience" become sediment of her habitual body and in her insistence on keeping the kidney stones as a treasure, as fascinating and fearsome excrement. It is this other "pathology" that reveals gender technologies.

Miss Amelia's sense of self rejects the conventional patriarchal concept of a weak woman, since she feels that her compliance with it would entail the loss of her autonomy. A "normal" heterosexual relationship, transforming her "into a calculable woman" (BSC 38), is thus out of the question. McCullers makes this very clear by pairing Miss Amelia off with Marvin Macy, who, almost as tall as she, not only possesses an "evil character" (BSC 35) but has raped and shamed several "gentle young girls." Although his love for her radically alters his "evil" personality, it does not change the fact that heterosexuality in patriarchal society strips women of their autonomy. Consequently, since McCullers insists on "becoming" through the suspension of gender boundaries, and since any "normal" man like Marvin Macy would contribute to a stabilization of gender, Miss Amelia's marriage to him cannot last for more than ten days; it ends with the humiliation of his masculine pride (his sexual advances are firmly and violently rejected). In fact, Miss Amelia's violent rejection of her husband can be compared to the behavior of Porter's princess who, not permitting bodily touch, protected her self with the impenetrable masks and shifts that eventually killed her. Yet, while the princess's violence is ultimately aimed at herself, Miss Amelia successfully uses brute physical force against her (potential) oppressor Marvin Macy. McCullers is thus able to voice her critique without victimizing women.

In patriarchal society, McCullers suggests, a long-lasting intimate (sexual) relationship between a woman and a man, in which both partners can sustain their autonomy, is only possible if man's power is diminished. To achieve "being-in-the-world," McCullers thus physically and mentally miniaturizes Miss Amelia's second partner, Cousin Lymon. This miniature of a man combines the qualities of Bubber in *The Heart Is a Lonely Hunter* and of John Henry in *The Member of the Wedding*. He is weak, mischievous, and apparently easily manipulated. The depiction of him illuminates his childlike powerlessness. As he approaches Miss Amelia's premises in the dark, his figure does not even seem human, more like "a calf" (BSC 10). Coming closer, he looks more like a child, "somebody's youngun" (BSC 11) than an adult. As McCullers dwarfs him to merely four feet with a childlike face that is "both soft and sassy," she constructs, on the one hand, a man whose feminine appearance[64] meets the requirements of a lady—petite and naive like a child—and who, "sickly at night" (BSC 32) with a terribly twisted body, suffers the consequences of conforming to gender constraints. On the other hand, this dwarf puts Miss Amelia at ease since he cannot possibly pose a threat to her sense of self.

But not only his physique is "unmanly." His hands tremble and he starts crying, a behavior that is regarded as a "regular Morris Finestein" (BSC 13), a severe reproach of "unmanliness." Whenever a man behaves in a "prissy" manner or cries, he is harshly reprimanded with this epithet which refers to a Jew who once lived there and always cried when someone called him a "Christ-killer" (BSC 14). By having men belittle and ridicule Cousin Lymon's (and Morris Finestein's) "feminine" behavior, McCullers discloses and criticizes rigid norms of masculinity.[65] But Cousin Lymon's deviation from "proper" masculinity does not only question existing concepts of gender. By having Miss Amelia actually offer him to drink from her whiskey bottle and invite him into her house to eat supper, accepting him, McCullers also emphasizes the importance of the blurring of gender boundaries that such a deviation provides.

Cousin Lymon often appears like a mere child, neatly licking "his tears from around his mouth" and doing as he is told (BSC 14). Instead of taking regular "proper snuff" like the other men in town, he prefers a mixture of sugar and cocoa (BSC 25). Yet, despite his childish manners and the difficulty of determining his age,[66] there are tensions that leave him, too, suspended between the boundaries of childhood and male adulthood. When he, for instance, reappears for the second time, his manner neither resembles that of an adult nor is it distinctly childish. Standing in the center of the group of men who entered Miss Amelia's store, he examines each man's lower region with "shrewd deliberation" (BSC 24). One could explain this odd behavior by his height, that it requires too much effort for a small person to look up, but he *deliberately* views them in this manner. The impression he gets after viewing their "lower regions" also indicates that McCullers uses his ambiguous behavior to mock ordinary, heterosexual men. Taking in their view from "the waist to the sole of the shoe," he then closes "his eyes for a moment and [shakes] his head, as though in his opinion what he had seen did not amount to much." In fact, the upper parts of their bodies and their faces do not in any way alter or influence his earlier judgment. ". . . Only to confirm himself, he tilt[s] back his head and [takes] in the halo of faces around him with one long, circling stare" (BSC 24–25).

The fact that Cousin Lymon is neither child nor "ordinary" man is further illustrated by his behavior towards others. He is a person who, once settled, immediately casts himself into the world by establishing relations with Miss Amelia's customers. His interest in other people creates an atmosphere of "illicit gladness" and an "air of freedom" (BSC 27), hardly an achievement made possible by a child. Not familiar with "fellowship" (BSC 29), however, everyone present is tense and senses "the oddity of the situation" (BSC

27). By this establishing of "immediate contact" that sets him apart from other "and more ordinary people," McCullers suggests on the one hand that "ordinary people" do not interact and are not part of "being-in-the-world." Only small children, not constrained by patriarchal norms, possess such "an instinct." But they are not able to reflect on their past, present, and future and thus are not—yet—body-subjects in a Beauvoirian sense. On the other hand, McCullers underlines the importance and potential of a suspension of gender boundaries, because the tension and "the oddity of the situation" promises "becoming."

In this relationship no one is reduced to an other. Since both Miss Amelia and Cousin Lymon not only challenge existing concepts of gender but also open up the possibility of achieving "being-in-the-world," their relationship is marked by a lack of struggle in which each partner seeks to sustain his or her autonomy, differing entirely from Miss Amelia's short marriage. From the first night the giantess and the dwarf are together, McCullers clearly emphasizes their harmonious interaction. At the same time, however, their union is rendered grotesque, distorted, in a manner that brings to mind Porter's treatment of femininity in "The Princess." As we remember, the princess's excessive use of feminine clothing and ornaments constitutes a severe deviation from the norms in her kingdom. Porter thus achieves an effect that lets femininity appear in a different—unfamiliar—light; that which is actually very familiar to us, "normal," seems suddenly alien. Femininity becomes grotesque. Similarly, McCullers alienates us from the normalcy of heterosexuality by indicating the possibility of sex between a giant and a dwarf.[67] That the strange relationship between Miss Amelia and Cousin Lymon also includes the possibility of a sexual union is suggested by their going upstairs to Miss Amelia's private rooms. Indeed, as she walks up slowly, "the hunchback hover[s] so close behind her that the great swinging light ma[kes] on the staircase wall *one great, twisted shadow* of the two of them" (BSC 17, emphasis mine). But, although they become one, the distortion of their shadow reflects the inhabitants' disapproval of the otherwise considered "holy" heterosexual activities in town. Not surprisingly, Mrs MacPhail, "a warty-nosed old busybody," soon claims that Miss Amelia and Cousin Lymon are "living in sin" (BSC 32).[68]

Miss Amelia's and Cousin Lymon's union is thus initially regarded with bewilderment, confusion, and disapproval, indicating the inability of patriarchal society to conceive of the potentials of the blurring of gender boundaries. In fact, the town clearly expresses not only disapproval but also hostility towards Miss Amelia and accuses her of having murdered Cousin Lymon, when he has not been seen for several days. They are unable to imagine a relationship in a Beauvoirian sense, since no one has experienced reciprocal relations in which each individual is at once subject and object.

"Fellowship, the satisfactions of the belly, and a certain gaiety and grace of behavior" are qualities that are denied people of this town (BSC 29). That Miss Amelia would not dispose of someone not useful to her is thus unthinkable. Such a society makes subjectivity impossible, turning almost the entire town into a passive mass, lacking agency. Twice people seem to be driven to action by some unknown force. The first time a group of men, certain that something terrible has happened to Cousin Lymon, gathers in front of Miss Amelia's store waiting. What they are waiting for they do not know. "[T]hey will act in unison, not from thought or from the will of any one man, but as though their instincts had merged together so that the decision belongs to no single one of them, but to the group as a whole . . . And whether the joint action will result in ransacking, violence, and crime, depends on destiny" (BSC 21). Although, at first sight, it might appear that these men represent an ideal form of "fluid identities" since their instincts have merged, they actually cease to be individuals and appear like puppets moved by "destiny." As Beauvoir would argue, they live in "bad faith," as they are denied the possibility of projecting themselves towards the world.[69]

But McCullers elucidates not only how a suspension of boundaries threatens and exposes rigid patriarchal society. By depicting a very different Miss Amelia and the effect of her change on the entire town, McCullers actually explores an ideal "being-in-the-world." Hostility and the ignorance of "fellowship" miraculously cease, as Miss Amelia unexpectedly inquires whether the many customers in her store want "waiting on" (BSC 27). Earlier, they felt that their lives were "not worth much" (BSC 66) and were used to being treated disrespectfully, not only when buying whiskey. Never before did they experience pleasure, dignity, or pride. Yet, Miss Amelia's breach of her own rule and her sudden hospitality contribute to a radical change of their attitude. Now all feel an atmosphere of community that does not give rise to any "rambunctiousness, indecent giggles, or misbehavior whatsoever" (BSC 29) but instead encourages a sharing among friends and a certain gaiety. But it is not simply Miss Amelia's altered behavior towards her customers that enables a reciprocal relationship but her personal change. Although "outwardly" she appears as before Cousin Lymon's arrival (BSC 29), there are features that indicate a softening of her otherwise tense and "haggard" face (BSC 8), which now expresses a "certain joy" (BSC 30). She swallows often, her hands sweat, her skin is paler, and her lips are "not so firmly set as usual" (BSC 30). Not threatened by an "ordinary" heterosexual man like Marvin Macy, the strenuous—"laborious"—effort of sustaining her grown-up tomboyishness, entailing a denial of feelings such as uncertainty, joy, and softness, is no longer necessary. For the first time in her life, her body is not a tool for securing her independence, is not simply, as Beauvoir would put it, "brute fact" (*Ethics* 41); her self and body become one, a body-subject.

Indeed, McCullers's "being-in-the-world" has no boundaries and allows each individual to develop continuously. Many changes take place in the following six years. Not only do Miss Amelia's facial features soften but also her manners, as she is no longer quick to "cheat her fellow man and to exact cruel payments" (BSC 31). Her abilities to cure improve as her whiskey becomes "even finer than before" (BSC 31).[70] Through her love, Miss Amelia has turned the miserable, fearful dwarf into a sociable being, who, although he often initiates fights among others and is inclined to nose "around everywhere," to know "everybody's business," and to trespass "every waking hour" (BSC 49), makes the newly-established café so popular. As soon as he enters the room, there is "always a quick feeling of *tension*" (emphasis mine), leaving everyone in the café in suspense. As Miss Amelia's interaction with him allows him to grow—"become"—she, in fact, has realized what Beauvoir finds necessary for the assuming of subjectivity. Such a realization entails the recognition of subjectivity as a transcendence towards others which does not entrap but instead allows the other her or his freedom.[71] The positive effect of Miss Amelia's change is also clearly discernable in how her customers show consideration and respect toward each other. Her café is thus the only place in the area that makes warmth and dignity possible.[72]

Miss Amelia's and Cousin Lymon's harmonious union and the question of a possible sexual relationship have puzzled many critics. Some have discussed Miss Amelia's tomboyishness as a rejection of femininity in general and criticized, in particular, her "failure" to accept heterosexuality.[73] As Miss Amelia is obviously not interested in this form of sexuality, one could draw the conclusion that she is not interested in *any* form of sexuality. Both Fowler and Gleeson-White, too, consider Miss Amelia, and, to some extent, Cousin Lymon, sexually disinterested (Gleeson-White, 101). Whatling, on the other hand, drawing on theories of performativity, argues that the masculine Miss Amelia and the feminized Cousin Lymon are not only a parody of heterosexuality but "a parody of a parody," engaging in a lesbian butch-femme role play in which Miss Amelia impersonates a butch and Cousin Lymon a femme (246). Whatling finds that Miss Amelia woos Cousin Lymon, and is positioned "in the role of the courtly lover, obedient, idealising, courteous and ultimately abject" (245).[74] Cousin Lymon, on the other hand, performs a Southern belle as he, for instance, descends the staircase with the "proudness of one who owns every plank of the floor beneath his feet" (BSC 24). Considering the fact that in *The Heart Is a Lonely Hunter* and *The Member of the Wedding*, McCullers explores possible sexual relationships between tomboys and feminized younger boys, Whatling's suggestion of a butch-femme role play of a grown-up tomboy and a miniaturized man seems plausible, as it also includes the possibility of sexuality. The exclusion of sexuality would entail a denial of the body which makes impossible an ideal "being-in-the-world."

Yet, despite the fact that a butch-femme role play certainly mocks the norm of heterosexuality, I would rather avoid constricting definitions of Miss Amelia's and Cousin Lymon's sexual preferences, be they heterosexual, lesbian, or homosexual,[75] and keep this issue unresolved, suspended. The failure to codify Miss Amelia's sexual (or any) behavior is potentially more disturbing and challenging than even considering her a butch. McCullers confuses and teases the reader by *not* making clear whether or not they "live in sin" (BSC 32). Mrs MacPhail and "her cronies" do not doubt that this "unnatural" giant woman and the weakly dwarf engage in "unholy" sex. On the other hand, all "sensible people [agree] in their opinion about this conjecture—their answer [is] a plain, flat *no*" (BSC 32–33). Yet, "good people," who are unable to exclude a possible sexual relationship, regard this question as a matter concerning only Miss Amelia, Cousin Lymon, and God. Not only are Miss Amelia's sexual preferences suspended, but also her and Cousin Lymon's family connection remains unclear. "If they were related, they were only a cross between first and second cousins, and even that could *in no way* be proved" (BSC 32, emphasis mine). McCullers abstains from providing any clues that would enable an unequivocal reading of her text.[76] Rather, she uses this uncertainty, suspension, to open up possibilities of "becoming."

It is significant that in this tale McCullers is able to sustain such a suspension, "being-in-the-world," for six years; it is an astonishingly long timespan often overlooked.[77] In the more "real" world of *The Member of the Wedding*, Frankie cannot keep alive a mere vision for longer than a day. But even in a narrative containing elements of a proper ballad that make "becoming" possible through the enhancement of a magical, unreal atmosphere, it seems that the blurring and suspension of boundaries must come to an end. With the return of Marvin Macy, the "he-man" (Gilbert and Gubar, "Fighting for Life" 149), from prison, McCullers illustrates the destructiveness of the restoration of the earlier and "ordinary" patriarchal situation, one which ultimately defeats Miss Amelia.

As soon as the news of Marvin Macy's release is heard, a different kind of tension emerges. While the tension created by Cousin Lymon caused a sense of community, an "outburst of talking and a drawing of corks" (BSC 49), this piece of news brings back Miss Amelia's strained efforts to remain autonomous. Her face darkens and hardens, becomes tense, and despite the warmth of the evening she starts shivering (BSC 52). When Marvin actually arrives in town, trespassing on Miss Amelia's premises, thus revoking her order from years ago not to set foot on her property and re-claiming his rights as a husband, her "special and bitter hate" erupts and clearly announces the end of "being-in-the-world" (BSC 59). His return, however, does more than destroy Miss Amelia's harmonious way of being. It also renders her helpless. As Miss Amelia merely watches Marvin Macy setting his "split hoof" on her premises (BSC 53) but does not turn him away, she seems powerless. Fearing to lose Cousin Lymon, who, attracted to Marvin Macy, follows him wherever he goes, she is unable to drive Marvin Macy away. Since Cousin Lymon enabled her to be part of "being-in-the-world," she cannot simply give him up, or, as the narrator proposes, make "the issue clear once and for all, and tell the hunchback that if he had dealings with Marvin Macy she would turn him off her premises" (BSC 64). Although she hates Marvin Macy bitterly, she cannot entirely fall back on her earlier manners and treat Cousin Lymon as she would a matter of business.

But despite the very difficult situation in which Miss Amelia finds herself, McCullers has her not only tease and mock her former husband but actually embody the suspension of gender in a most provoking manner. Already during the six years living with Cousin Lymon, she has behaved provokingly. While she usually wears her boots and overalls, on Sundays she puts on "a dark red dress that [hangs] on her in a most peculiar fashion" (BSC 31), mocking proper heterosexuality sanctioned by the Church with a dress whose color connotes danger, female blood, and sexual lewdness.[78] McCullers further emphasizes Miss Amelia's outrageous behavior in order to mock her husband's masculine pride. When Marvin Macy begins to visit her café regularly, she puts "aside her overalls and [wears] *always* the red dress" (BSC 64, emphasis mine). She also adds to the intended aggravation by decorating her café in red. She has red curtains for the windows and buys paper roses that look real. As if to underline the red interior of the café, her great iron stove, roaring with fire, turns red too (BSC 65). The wearing of a red dress and decorating of the café in red are thus not Miss Amelia's desperate attempt to attract Cousin Lymon with "feminine weakness," as Paulson argues (194). Rather, it constitutes a deliberate use of femininity to aggravate her husband.[79] As Westling and Gleeson-White have pointed out, Miss Amelia's behavior, indeed, the ballad as a whole, discloses "McCullers's complete rejection of heterosexual union" (Westling, *Sacred Groves* 125, Gleeson-White 76). No matter how feminine and sexually appealing her dress is, she will never be within reach for him. Almost as if to irritate him further, she gives "him free drinks and [smiles] at him in a wild crooked way" (BSC 64). Miss Amelia, then, does not, like young Mick and Frankie, unconsciously fall back to the power that threatens her self, femininity.

As McCullers has Miss Amelia perform woman again, this performance is not something that alienates her from her self and increases her dis-ease as her appearance of a bride did. Again, the artificiality of the construction of woman becomes as visible as during the wedding ceremony, as she clenches her fists and wears "her peculiar red dress hanging awkwardly around her bony knees" (BSC 68). In this scene, however, she does not make any odd gestures, nor does she express impatience or fury. She appears to be at ease with her ambiguous behavior, embodying a masculine woman trying to perform both a "proper" woman, thus exposing norms of patriarchy through mimicry, and a "proper" man through a drag king act which mocks the construction of man. In fact, it is not even clear whether she is a biological woman or man. In another passage, McCullers indicates this uncertainty particularly well. Hovering over the stove, Miss Amelia does not "warm her backside modestly. . . . Now as she [stands] warming herself, her red dress was pulled up quite high in the back so that a piece of her strong, hairy thigh could be seen by anyone who cared to look at it" (BSC 71). Her "hairy thigh" may indicate that Miss Amelia is actually a man performing woman. But McCullers does not confirm such a suggestion and leaves this matter unresolved.[80]

Miss Amelia is used as a hybrid not only, as Gleeson-White argues, to create "unsustainable *dis-ease*" (117, my emphasis), but also to emphasize that "becoming" relies on a going beyond existing gender norms. Miss Amelia's *ease* of embodying both woman and man and her relationship with a similarly ambiguous man/child/lady figure, her actual lack of showing a "pathology," suggests this very strongly. To McCullers, ambiguity provides the ideal "way of having the world." In order to heighten further the potential of ambiguity and its importance she uses its contrast, certainty and clear boundaries, to illustrate the devastating effect on "being-in-the-world" not merely for Miss Amelia but for everybody. Marvin Macy's return functions as such a contrast. His relation to Cousin Lymon (and to others) recalls Mick's nightmare in which she had swum through a crowd of people who severely injured her. In this dream, relations between human beings precluded individual freedom but sought their destruction. Similarly, Marvin Macy treats Cousin Lymon as if to destroy him, calling him a "runt" (BSC 60), "Brokeback" (BSC 61), and cuffing him so hard that he falls. Most devastating, however, is Miss Amelia's bitter fight with Marvin Macy which she, despite her refusal to become a victim of patriarchy, must lose, since Cousin Lymon aligns himself with the "he-man."

The gender battle between Miss Amelia and Marvin Macy undoubtedly constitutes the climax of the ballad. Again, McCullers creates almost unbearable tension as both Miss Amelia and the "loomfixer" (BSC 41) prepare themselves for the fight.[81] Since the battle will settle the question of the sustainability of "becoming" once and for all, she no longer wears the red dress to irritate her husband but changes into her old overalls. For a long time during the fight both opponents seem equally strong, and then Miss Amelia's victory seems in sight, but she is ultimately defeated by Cousin

Lymon's alliance with her enemy. Seeing Marvin Macy lying helplessly on the ground, he sails "through the air as though he had grown hawk wings. He land[s] on the broad back of Miss Amelia and clutches at her neck with his clawed little fingers" (BSC 80).[82] Yet, according to Gilbert and Gubar, McCullers depicts not only a struggle, in which Miss Amelia actually carries out and receives blows better than any man, but a fight that can be likened to heterosexual intercourse. Indeed, as Miss Amelia and Marvin Macy are locked together, "grappled muscle to muscle, their hipbones braced against each other," they sway "backward and forward, from side to side" (BSC 80), as if engaging in a sexual act. Gilbert's and Gubar's reading seems plausible when one takes into account the threat that heterosexual intercourse and its effects pose to Mick's and Frankie's sense of self. This is specifically obvious in Mick's case. Her sexual encounter with Harry has such a destructive impact on her creativity, her yearning to be part of "becoming," that she gives up all her hopes and plans and accepts initiation into "proper" womanhood. Miss Amelia's defeat, then, resembles the fate of Mick and Frankie and forces, finally, an acceptance of the boundaries of gender.

Her physical change after the fight seems to corroborate that heterosexuality forces women to accept "womanhood." After the fight she lies "sprawled on the floor, her arms flung outward and motionless" (BSC 80). Her voice changes and becomes as powerless as her hand that opens "feebly and [lies] palm upward and still" (BSC 81). Yet, not only gestures express her powerlessness. She lets her hair "grow ragged" which, as it turns grey, emphasizes her weakness (BSC 82). Even her body shrinks, becomes miniaturized as her face lengthens, "and the great muscles of her body [shrink] until she [is] thin as old maids when they go crazy" (BSC 82–3). Her healing powers are diminished and the recommended cures are now so "far-fetched and agonizing that no one in his right mind would consider them for a moment" (BSC 82).[83]

Her defeat, however, appears much more devastating than either Mick's or Frankie's. While the younger tomboys, transformed into "proper" girls, participate in "normal" life, either working at Woolworth's or "growing down" into a child behavior, Miss Amelia is utterly isolated. In the beginning of the ballad she is described as a woman whose face is "sexless and white," looking down on the town from one of the windows of the formerly so popular café now boarded up completely and leaning "so far right that it seems bound to collapse" (BSC 7). But the astonishing fact is that it was not the inhabitants[84] who forced her into this isolation; they would actually have liked to help although they did not know how. "Several housewives" indicate, too, their willingness to include Miss Amelia in their community as they nose "around with brooms and [offer] to clear up the wreck" (BSC 82). Miss Amelia, however, rejects their help. Having once experienced "being-in-the-world" through ambiguity but now being denied it, Miss Amelia cannot face the ordinariness of patriarchal society with its rigid gender norms, and therefore refuses to become part of such a society.

McCullers's explorations of the possibilities of "becoming" are, indeed, quite bleak. But despite Miss Amelia's "self-imposed isolation" and the loss of all her powers, McCullers has not abandoned the idea of a suspension of gender boundaries. While Gleeson-White finds "a remnant of power" in the image of Miss Amelia looking *down* on the town (77),[85] I understand Miss Amelia's rejection of the housewives as an insistence on the blurring of gender boundaries: that she, despite the terrible outcome of the fight, refuses to become an "ordinary" woman. Although she now takes on such a woman's proportions, shrinks in size, and loses her voice and power, she is nonetheless suspended between "proper" femininity and masculinity. A remnant of her disturbing power is thus not her superior position but rather the continuous suspension which McCullers indicates by depicting Miss Amelia's face as "*sexless* and white" (BSC 7, emphasis mine); she is neither woman nor man. Again, the failure to codify her produces a strong feeling of unease. The narrator, too, is affected by this: "sometimes in the late afternoon when the heat is at its worst a hand will slowly open the shutter and a face will look down on the town. It is a face like the *terrible dim faces known in dreams*—sexless and white" (emphasis mine). The dimness of her face contributes to an uneasy uncertainty, almost rendering her a figure from a nightmare that recalls either the failed opportunity of sustaining "being-in-the-world" or the threat she once posed to rigid patriarchal society. Appearing at a time when the heat is unbearable only underscores her disturbing power.

Admittedly, this disturbing power is now quite limited. Although McCullers is able to sustain an unsettling instability throughout the ballad, one should not belittle the extreme violence with which Miss Amelia is confronted. As Paulson points out (187), women in this town are either absent or silenced. The fight thus constitutes the most terrifying means of silencing women. Its extreme brutality makes visible the extent to which women, who demand a voice, a subjectivity, are subjected to men's violence. The fact that McCullers frames her ballad with the depiction of a chain-gang emphasizes only too clearly this violent aspect. Immediately after the description of Miss Amelia's face, in the beginning of the text, the narrator gives the advice that since there "is absolutely nothing to do," to go down to "the Forks Falls Road and listen to the chain gang" (BSC 8), thus connecting her "lingering face" and the desolation of the town with the chain-gang.

Gilbert and Gubar argue that McCullers uses the chain-gang to emphasize Miss Amelia's utter isolation. While she is lonely, a "prisoner of sex" (153), the prisoners of the chain-gang are at least together in their misery and are "sustained by their own community."[86] As McCullers provides a more detailed description of the chain-gang at the end of the ballad, one cannot assert that prisoners of a chain-gang are better off than Miss Amelia.[87] The prisoners appear to be identity-less men, chained together at their ankles,[88] wearing all the same prison suits. Even their guard is dehumanized, his eyes reduced to "red slits" (BSC 84). As the prisoners and the guard have lost their individuality, they are also denied subjectivity. The fact that they sing together, create beautiful music, "both sombre and joyful," does not diminish the cruelty of their punishment. Although McCullers has one voice after another join in the singing, she also underlines the loneliness that each prisoner must suffer. The music sinks "down until at last there remains one lonely voice, then a great hoarse breath, the sun, the sound of the picks in the silence" (BSC 85).

In fact, the depiction of the chain-gang re-tells in a condensed form Miss Amelia's story. Like the music that "causes the heart to broaden and the listener to grow cold with ecstacy and fright," Miss Amelia's insistence on suspension and uncertainty broadened not only her self, but Cousin Lymon, and the entire town for six years. However, "becoming" also challenged, exposed, and ridiculed patriarchal society in frightening ways which could not be tolerated. Miss Amelia is thus punished and left with a voice as hoarse as a prisoner's, and is finally silenced.

NOTES

49. As Joseph R. Millichap points out, *The Ballad of the Sad Café* contains many characteristics of a proper ballad, such as the concentration on a certain-crucial-situation (the strange love triangle of Miss Amelia, Cousin Lymon, and Marvin Macy) and the unfolding of the action by itself. Further, McCullers's ballad possesses "a magical atmosphere" (333).

50. In *Reflections in a Golden Eye* (RE), a novel which McCullers herself considered a fairy tale, she depicts two women whose possibility to assume subjectivity is denied in a similarly exaggerated manner as Miss Amelia. Captain Penderton's wife Leonora embodies—not quite—the perfect Southern lady. She is regarded as a "good hostess, an excellent sportswoman, and even as a great lady" (RE 21). Yet, McCullers ridicules the myth of the lady by exaggerating Leonora's lack of intelligence and her interest in food and sex. Major Langdon's wife Alison could represent another Miss Amelia as she, too, has a companion who in appearance is similar to Cousin Lymon. His figure is rather small and feminine. But, in contrast to Miss Amelia, Alison can only protest against patriarchal society by mutilating herself (she cuts off her nipples with garden shears); she is too weak to offer resistance in the manner Miss Amelia does. Towards the end of this novel, she is actually removed from this society and dies.

51. Miss Amelia does marry once but never changes her name. Furthermore, her marriage lasts only ten days.

52. Amelia is also a medical term for a specific kind of birth defect, namely the complete absence of an infant's limb (National Library of Medicine). However, although

this term appears in the revised edition of *The American Illustrated Medical Dictionary* from 1929, I do not know whether McCullers was familiar with this term and named her heroine Amelia to emphasize her lack of normalcy.

53. In fact, in this ballad women are rarely mentioned. See Suzanne Morrow Paulson 187.

54. Of course, it is somewhat easier for Miss Amelia than for any other woman in town to entertain habits of life that are "too peculiar ever to reason about" (BSC 20), because she inherited her father's wealth and position.

55. Significantly, towards the end of the ballad and after her fight with Marvin Macy, a deterioration of her esotropia can be discerned. "[S]lowly day by day they [are] more crossed, and it [is] as though they [seek] each other out to exchange a little glance of grief and lonely recognition" (BSC 83). As Miss Amelia becomes a recluse, boarded up in the upper level of her café, her eyes "are turned inward so sharply that they seem to be exchanging with each other one long and secret gaze of grief" (BSC 7–8).

56. Similarly, Charles Hannon connects *The Ballad of the Sad Café* with the historical context when the novel was written (it was first published in 1943) and finds that Miss Amelia represents one of the many women who were forced to take over their men's or father's businesses and became increasingly independent while husbands, fathers fought in World War II. Marvin Macy's return, then, resembles the soldiers' return who could not accept the changed position of women in society.

57. Judith Halberstam, answering the question of what a Drag King is, writes that a "Drag King assumes masculinity as an act. S/he understands herself to be engaged in some kind of parody of men" (36). For a more detailed discussion, see Judith "Jack" Halberstam's and Del LaGrace Volcano's *The Drag King Book*.

58. In another passage McCullers has Miss Amelia flex her supple muscles after supper, showing off her "masculinity" (BSC 17). In *The Heart Is a Lonely Hunter*, McCullers also overemphasizes masculinity by depicting Blount's raw strength (See also Gleeson-White 82). She does, however, not make use of a drag king to mock the construction of "man." Porter, too, discloses the construction of "man" in an intriguing manner. Gabriel's effort to masquerade as a shepherd, a "proper man," at the Mardi Gras ball fails miserably. See chapter two, section 2.3.

59. The fact that McCullers chooses a wedding for Miss Amelia's enforced performance is significant. As Gleeson-White points out, the "wedding represents (as all weddings in fact do) the domestication and heterosexualization of social relations" (92).

60. Interestingly, the people of the town accept her strange behavior as decent enough. Yet, her refusal to consummate her marriage is considered "unholy" (BSC 38), indicating the extent to which such a refusal threatens the norm of "holy" heterosexuality.

61. Suzanne Morrow Paulson also argues that Miss Amelia's "refusal to heal female ailments is her denial of her own gender, her own vulnerability to natural cycles" (198).

62. McCullers thus follows a long tradition of connecting nature with femaleness. Beauvoir also discusses woman's alleged closeness to nature. She argues that woman "is the wished-for intermediary between nature, the stranger to man, and the fellow being who is too closely identical" (*The Second Sex* 172).

63. Beauvoir writes that although men and women are body-subjects, characterized by the ambiguity of transcendence and immanence, in patriarchal society women are reduced to immanence because of their supposed closeness to nature. Miss Amelia's rejection of femininity mirrors precisely the issue addressed by Beauvoir.

64. Gleeson-White (63–66) and Whatling (245) draw attention to the feminine appearance of Cousin Lymon.

65. In "Rejection of the Feminine in Carson McCullers' *The Ballad of the Sad Café*," Panthea Reid Broughton considers the reference to Morris Finestein important since it reveals "the town's concept of sexual roles" (38).

66. Many critics see a child in Lymon and thus consider Miss Amelia's relationship with him a mother–child relationship. Doreen Fowler regards Lymon's later alliance with Marvin as an attempt at gaining independence from an overpowering mother, Miss Amelia. Gleeson-White argues that Miss Amelia's relationship with Cousin Lymon "is asexual, resembling that of mother and child" (73).

67. Whatling argues that the pairing of the masculine Miss Amelia and the feminized Cousin Lymon is "a deformation of the heterosexual norm into a grotesque parody of itself" (246).

68. Since Miss Amelia and Cousin Lymon might be related, McCullers also challenges the taboo of incest.

69. The second time, after the end of Miss Amelia's harmonious way of being, they gather to witness the fight between Miss Amelia and Marvin Macy. Even three young boys from Society City who "could always be seen at cockfights and camp meetings" are drawn to Miss Amelia's premises (BSC 77). That the fight will take place on that day at seven o'clock is known "to everyone, not by announcement or words, but understood in the unquestioning way that rain is understood, or an evil odour from the swamp."

70. Clearly, Miss Amelia's whiskey possesses magical qualities. It brings out in every man an awareness and an understanding of things "that have gone unnoticed, thoughts that have been harboured far back in the dark mind" (BSC 15). Miss Amelia's whiskey warms a man's "soul" and makes him see "the message hidden there." In . . . two [other] novels McCullers emphasizes the more destructive effects of alcohol. In *The Heart Is a Lonely Hunter*, Mick drinks beer which creates a greater distance to her "inside room" and in *The Member of the Wedding*, a drunk soldier almost rapes Frankie.

71. Beauvoir writes that only "the freedom of others keeps each one of us from hardening in the absurdity of facticity" (*Ethics* 71).

72. Kenneth D. Chamlee, examining the cafés in *The Heart Is a Lonely Hunter*, *The Member of the Wedding*, and *The Ballad of the Sad Café*, draws attention to the unique positive quality of Miss Amelia's café. Whereas Biff's restaurant is a rather dreary place and "The Blue Moon Café" a hotel for soldiers and prostitutes, Miss Amelia's café allows the people to become human beings.

73. See James and Gleeson-White.

74. Miss Amelia also spoils "him to a point beyond reason" and even carries him on her back when wading through a bog (BSC 31).

75. Whatling further discusses the possibilities of a homosexual relationship between Cousin Lymon and Marvin Macy (246). She also argues that Miss Amelia's and Cousin Lymon's relationship could be both lesbian and homosexual, since just as "Amelia is a woman performing masculinity to Lymon's male femme, so Lymon is a man performing femininity to Amelia's butch" (246).

76. McCullers's refusal to resolve this uncertainty has contributed to a variety of diverging readings of her texts. See Evans, Fowler, Taetzsch, Kenschaft, Gleeson-White, and Whatling.

77. For instance, in "Themes of Eros and Agape in the Major Fiction of Carson McCullers," Donna Bauerly claims that Miss Amelia is only "momentarily capable of sharing her love with the whole town" (74).

78. Again, it is not clear whether Amelia is merely a masculine woman, trying to perform proper femininity, or whether she is a butch, or even asexual.

79. Westling and Gleeson-White also consider Miss Amelia's behavior an act meant to infuriate her husband.

80. Gleeson-White considers Miss Amelia a hybrid which "so points to the failure or impossibility of any stable identity" (117).

81. Its outcome is foreshadowed by a "hawk with a bloody breast" flying over town and circling "twice around Miss Amelia's property" (BSC 75). The "bloody breast," like the dark red feathers that decorated the wedding dress of Porter's Amy, indicates female blood and suggests that Miss Amelia will become a "proper" woman.

82. See also Paulson's discussion of homosocial bonds and love triangles in McCullers's text (196).

83. Although Miss Amelia is clearly denied subjectivity, her physical and mental defeat illustrates that body and self cannot be separated.

84. Marvin Macy and Cousin Lymon left town after having demolished the café.

85. The fact that Miss Amelia is confined to the upper level of her house does not necessarily entail a superior, more powerful, position. Rather, as her eyes are "turned inward so sharply that they seem exchanging with each other one long and secret gaze of grief" (BSC 7–8), she comes close to being what Gilbert and Gubar call in their analysis of Charlotte Brontë's *Jane Eyre* "the madwoman in the attic" (336–71). See also their discussion of Miss Amelia in "Fighting for Life," where they claim that Miss Amelia has "been metamorphosed from a woman warrior to a helpless madwoman" (153).

86. Paulson regards the chain-gang as "homosocial togetherness" (200) while Kenschaft sees it as "a note of optimism," since "*any* two people can make music together, no matter how unlikely other people find the match" (231).

87. See also Margaret Whitt's discussion of the brutality of chain-gangs.

88. One could also argue that the chain-gang symbolizes Miss Amelia's, Cousin Lymon's, and Marvin Macy's relationship with each other, that they are chained together. Many critics have focused on this love–hate relationship, using McCullers's definition of love in *The Ballad of the Sad Café* to explain the failure of achieving a reciprocal love relationship. See also Millichap who advocates a move away from this theme.

BIBLIOGRAPHY

Primary Sources

McCullers, Carson. [1940] *The Heart Is a Lonely Hunter*. London: Penguin Books, 1961.

———. [1941] *Reflections in a Golden Eye*. London: Penguin Books, 1942.

———. [1943] *The Ballad of the Sad Café*. London: Penguin Books, 1951.

———. [1946] *The Member of the Wedding*. London: Penguin Books, 1962.

———. *The Mortgaged Heart*. Ed. Margarita G. Smith. London: Barrie & Jenkins, 1972.

———. *Illumination & Night Glare*. Ed. Carlos L. Dews. Madison, Wisconsin: U of Wisconsin P, 1999.

Porter, Katherine Anne. "The Circus." *The Collected Stories of Katherine Anne Porter*. A Harvest Book. San Diego, New York, London: Harcourt Brace & Company, 1979.

———. "The Fig Tree." *The Collected Stories of Katherine Anne Porter*. A Harvest Book. San Diego, New York, London: Harcourt Brace & Company, 1979.

———. "The Grave." *The Collected Stories of Katherine Anne Porter*. A Harvest Book. San Diego, New York, London: Harcourt Brace & Company, 1979.

———. "The Journey." *The Collected Stories of Katherine Anne Porter*. A Harvest Book. San Diego, New York, London: Harcourt Brace & Company, 1979.

————. "Old Mortality." *The Collected Stories of Katherine Anne Porter*. A Harvest Book. San Diego, New York, London: Harcourt Brace & Company, 1979,

————. "Pale Horse, Pale Rider." *The Collected Stories of Katherine Anne Porter*. A Harvest Book. San Diego, New York, London: Harcourt Brace & Company, 1979.

————. "The Source." *The Collected Stories of Katherine Anne Porter*. A Harvest Book. San Diego, New York, London: Harcourt Brace & Company, 1979.

————. "The Princess." *Uncollected Early Prose of Katherine Anne Porter*. Eds. Ruth M. Alvarez and Thomas F. Walsh. Austin: U of Texas P, 1993.

Secondary Sources

Adams, Rachel. "'A Mixture of Delicious and Freak': The Queer Fiction of Carson McCullers." *American Literature* 71: 3 (September 1999): 551–583.

American Heritage Dictionary. Fourth Edition. Boston: Houghton Mifflin Company, 2000.

The American Illustrated Medical Dictionary. Fifteenth Edition. Philadelphia and London: W. B. Saunders Company, 1929.

Arp, Kristina. "Beauvoir's Concept of Bodily Alienation." *Feminist Interpretations of Simone De Beauvoir*. Ed. Margaret A. Simmons. University Park: The Pennsylvania State UP, 1995.

Bauerly, Donna. "Themes of Eros and Agape in the Major Fiction of Carson McCullers." *Pembroke Magazine* (1988): 72–76.

Beauvoir, Simone de. [1943] *She Came to Stay*. London: Flamingo, 1989.

————. [1946] *All Men Are Mortal*. London: Virgo P, 1995.

————. [1948] *The Ethics of Ambiguity*. New York: Citadel P, 1976.

————. [1949] *The Second Sex*. London: Vintage, 1997.

Bell, Barbara Currier. "Non-Identical Twins: Nature in 'The Garden Party' and 'The Grave'." *The Comparatist* 12 (May 1988): 58–66.

Bigwood, Carol. "Renaturalizing the Body (with the Help of Merleau-Ponty)." *Body and Flesh: A Philosophical Reader*. Ed. Donn Welton. Oxford: Blackwell Publishers, 1998.

Bolsterli, Margaret. "'Bound' Characters in Porter, Welty, McCullers: The Prerevolutionary Status of Women in American Fiction." *The Bucknell Review* 24:1 (1978): 95–105.

Bordo, Susan. *Unbearable Weight: Feminism, Western Culture, and the Body*. Berkeley: U of California P, 1995.

Box, Patricia. "Androgyny and the Musical Vision: A Study of Two Novels by Carson McCullers." *The Southern Quarterly* 16:2 (January 1978): 117–123.

Bradshaw, Charles. "Language and Responsibility: The Failure of Discourse in Carson McCullers's *The Heart Is a Lonely Hunter*." *The Southern Quarterly* 37:2 (Winter 1999): 118–26.

Brook, Barbara. *Feminist Perspectives on the Body*. London and New York: Longman, 1999.

Brooks, Cleanth. "On 'The Grave'." *Critical Essays on Katherine Anne Porter*. Ed. Darlene Harbour Unrue. New York: G. K. Hall & Co., 1997.

Broughton, Panthea Reid. "Rejection of the Feminine in Carson McCullers' *The Ballad of the Sad Café*." *Twentieth Century Literature* 20 (1974): 34–43.

Butler, Judith. "Sexual Ideology and Phenomenological Description: A Feminist Critique of Merleau-Ponty's *Phenomenology of Perception*." *The Thinking Muse: Feminism and Modern French Philosophy*. Eds. Jeffner Allen and Iris Marion Young. Bloomington: Indiana UP, 1989.

————. "Imitation and Gender Insubordination." *The Second Wave: A Reader in Feminist Theory*. Ed. Linda Nicholson. New York, London: Routledge, 1997.

———. *Gender Trouble: Feminism and the Subversion of Identity.* [1990] New York, London: Routledge, 1999.

Carby, Hazel. *Reconstructing Womanhood: The Emergence of the Afro-American Woman Novelist.* Oxford: Oxford UP, 1987.

Carlton, Anne. "Beyond Gothic and Grotesque: A Feminist View of Three Female Characters of Carson McCullers." *Pembroke Magazine* 20 (1988): 54–62.

Carr, Victoria Spencer. *The Lonely Hunter: A Biography of Carson McCullers.* New York: Archer Press/Doubleday, 1976.

Cash, W. J. *The Mind Of The South.* New York: Alfred A. Knopf, Inc., 1946.

Cashin, Joan E. "According to His Wish and Desire: Female Kin and Female Slavery in Planter Wills." *Women of the American South: A Multicultural Reader.* Ed. Christie Anne Farnham. New York: UP, 1997.

Chamlee, Kenneth D. "Cafés and Community in Three Carson McCullers Novels." *Studies in American Fiction* 18:2 (1990): 233–40.

Cheatham, George. "Fall and Redemption in *Pale Horse, Pale Rider.*" *Renascence* 39:3 (Spring 1987): 396–405.

———. "Death and Repetition in Porter's Miranda Stories." *Critical Essays on Katherine Anne Porter.* Ed. Darlene Harbour Unrue. New York: G. K. Hall & Co., 1997.

Ciuba, Gary M. "One Singer Left to Mourn: Death and Discourse in Porter's 'Pale Horse, Pale Rider'." *South Atlantic Review* 61:1 (Winter 1996): 55–76.

Clinton, Catherine. *The Plantation Mistress: Woman's World in the Old South.* New York: Pantheon Books, 1982.

———, ed. *Half Sisters of History: Southern Women and the American Past.* Durham: Duke UP, 1994.

Cohn, Deborah. "Paradise Lost and Regained: The Old Order and Memory in Katherine Anne Porter's Miranda Stories and Juan Rulfo's *Pedro Páramo.*" *Hispanófila* 124 (Sept. 1988): 65–86.

Damasio, Antonio R. *Descartes' Error: Emotion, Reason, and the Human Brain.* New York: HarperCollins Publishers, 1994.

Descartes, Rene. [1641] *Meditationen über die Erste Philosophie.* [*Meditations on First Philosophy.*] Stuttgart: Philipp Reclam jun., 1978.

DeMouy, Jane Krause. *Katherine Anne Porter's Women: The Eye of Her Fiction.* Austin: U of Texas P, 1983.

DiCicco, Lorraine. "The Dis-ease of Katherine Anne Porter's Greensick Girls in 'Old Mortality'." *The Southern Literary Journal.* 33:2 (Spring 2001): 80–99. September 2003. http://webl.infotrac.galegroup.com/itw/infomark.

Erdim, Esim. "The Ring or the Dove: The New Woman in Katherine Anne Porter's Fiction." *Women and War: Changing Status of American Women from the 1930s to the 1950s.* Ed. Maria Diedrich, New York: Berg, 1990.

Evans, Oliver. *Carson McCullers: Her Life and Work.* London: Peter Owen, 1965.

Farnham, Christie Anne, ed. *Women of the American South: A Multicultural Reader.* New York: UP, 1997.

Fiedler, Leslie A. *Love and Death in the American Novel.* Normal: Dalkey Archive P, 1966.

Fine, Laura. "Gender Conflicts and Their Dark Projections in Coming of Age White Female Southern Novels." *The Southern Quarterly* 36:4 (Summer 1998): 121–29.

Flanders, Jane. "Katherine Anne Porter and the Ordeal of Southern Womanhood." *The Southern Literary Journal* 9:1 (1976): 47–60.

Fornatoro-Neil, M. K. "Constructed Narratives and Writing Identity in the Fiction of Katherine Anne Porter." *Twentieth Century Literature* 44:3 (Fall 1998): 349–61. September, 2003. http://webl.infotrac.galegroup.com/itw/infomark.

Fowler, Doreen. "Carson McCullers's Primal Scenes: *The Ballad of the Sad Café*. *Studies in Contemporary Fiction* 43 (Spring 2002): 260–70. September 15, 2003. http://webl. infotrac.galegroup.com/itw/infomark/945.

Fullbrook, Edward and Kate Fullbrook. *Simone de Beauvoir: A Critical Introduction*. Cambridge: Polity P, 1998.

Fuller, Janice. "The Conventions of Counterpoint and Fugue in *The Heart Is a Lonely Hunter*." *The Mississippi Quarterly* 26:3 (Spring 1988): 55–67.

Gardiner, Judith Kegan. "'The Grave,' 'On Not Shooting Sitting Birds,' and the Female Esthetic." *Studies in Short Fiction* 20:4 (Fall 1983): 265–270.

Gatens, Moira. "Modern Rationalism." *A Companion to Feminist Philosophy*. Eds. Alison M. Jaggar and Iris Marion Young. Oxford: Blackwell Publishers, 2000.

Gibbons, Kaye. "Planes of Language and Time: The Surfaces of the Miranda Stories." *The Kenyon Review* 10:1 (Winter 1988): 74–79.

Gilbert, Sandra M. and Susan Gubar. *The Madwoman in the Attic: The Woman Writer and the Nineteenth-Century Literary Imagination*. London: Yale UP, 1984.

———. "Fighting for Life." *Critical Essays on Carson McCullers*. Eds. Beverly Lyon Clark and Melvin J. Friedman. New York: G. K. Hall & Co, 1996. 147–54.

Gleeson-White, Sarah. "Revisiting the Southern Grotesque: Mikhail Bakhtin and the Case of Carson McCullers." *The Southern Literary Journal* 33.2 (2001): 108–23.

———. *Strange Bodies: Gender and Identity in the Novels of Carson McCullers*. Tuscaloosa, Alabama: U of Alabama P, 2003.

Graver, Lawrence. *Carson McCullers*. Pamphlets on American Writers 84. Minneapolis: U of Minnesota P, 1969.

Grosz, Elizabeth. *Volatile Bodies: Toward a Corporeal Feminism*. Bloomington: Indiana UP, 1994.

Gutting, Gary. *French Philosophy in the Twentieth Century*. Cambridge: Cambridge UP, 2001.

Hait, Christine H. "Gender and Creativity in Katherine Anne Porter's 'The Princess'." *From Texas to the World and Back: Essays on the Journeys of Katherine Anne Porter*. Eds. Mark Busby and Dick Heaberlin. Fort Worth, Tx: TCU, 2001.

Halberstam, Judith and Del LaGrace Volcano. *The Drag King Book*. London: Serpent's Tail, 1999.

Hannon, Charles. "*The Ballad of the Sad Café* and Other Stories of Women's Wartime Labor." *Bodies of Writing, Bodies in Performance*. Eds. Thomas Foster, Carol Siegel, Ellen E. Berry. New York: New York UP, 1996.

Harding, Sandra. "Who Knows? Identities and Feminist Epistemology." *(En)gendering Knowledge: Feminists in Academe*. Eds. Joan E. Hartman and Ellen Messer-Davidow. Knoxville: U of Tennessee P, 1991.

Heath, Stephen. "Joan Riviere and the Masquerade." *Formations of Fantasy*. Eds. Victor Burgin, James Donald and Cora Kaplan. New York: Methuen & Co., 1986.

Heinämaa, Sara. "What Is a Woman? Butler and Beauvoir on the Foundations of Sexual Difference." *Hypatia* 12:1 (Winter 1997): 20–39.

———. *Toward a Phenomenology of Sexual Difference: Husserl, Merleau-Ponty, Beauvoir*. Oxford: Bowman & Littlefield Publishers, 2003.

Hendrick, George. *Katherine Anne Porter*. New York: Twayne Publishers, 1965.

Hennessy, Rosemary. "Katherine Anne Porter's Model for Heroines." *Colorado Quarterly* 25 (1977): 301–15.

The Internet Encyclopedia of Philosophy. *Maurice Merleau-Ponty (1908–1961)*. April 11, 2003. http://www.utm.edu/research/iep/m/merleau.html.

The Internet Encyclopedia of Philosophy (a). *René Descartes (1596–1650)*. April 11, 2003. http://www.utm.edu/research/iep/d/descarte.html.

Irigaray, Luce. *This Sex Which Is Not One*. Ithaca, N.Y.: Cornell UP, 1985.

James, Judith Giblin. *Wunderkind: The Reputation of Carson McCullers, 1940–1990*. Columbia, SC: Camden House, 1995.

Jones, Anne Goodwyn. *Tomorrow Is Another Day: The Woman Writer in the South, 1859–1936*. Baton Rouge and London: Louisiana State UP, 1981.

———. "Gender and the Great War: The Case of Faulkner and Porter." *Women's Studies* 13:1–2 (1986): 135–48.

——— and Susan V. Donaldson, eds. *Haunted Bodies: Gender and Southern Texts*. Charlottesville: UP of Virginia, 1997.

Kenschaft, Lori J. "Homoerotics and Human Connections: Reading Carson McCullers 'As a Lesbian'." *Critical Essays on Carson McCullers*. Eds. Beverly Lyon Clark and Melvin J. Friedman. New York: G. K. Hall & Co, 1996. 220–233.

Kittel, Charles. *Einführung in die Festkörperphysik*. München: R. Oldenbourg Verlag, 1980.

Klein, Renate. "(Dead) Bodies Floating in Cyberspace: Post-modernism and the Dismemberment of Women." *Radically Speaking: Feminism Reclaimed*. Eds. Diane Bell and Renate Klein. London: Zed Books, 1996.

Kristeva, Julia. *The Powers of Horror*. New York: Columbia UP, 1982.

Kruks, Sonia. "Existentialism and Phenomenology." *A Companion to Feminist Philosophy*. Eds. Alison M. Jaggar and Iris Marion Young. Oxford: Blackwell Publishers, 1998.

———. *Retrieving Experience: Subjectivity and Recognition in Feminist Politics*. Ithaca and London: Cornell UP, 2001.

Langer, Monika M. *Merleau-Ponty's Phenomenology of Perception: A Guide and Commentary*. London: MacMillan P, 1989.

Laqueur, Thomas. *Making Sex: Body and Gender from the Greeks to Freud*. Cambridge: Harvard UP, 1990.

Leder, Drew. "A Tale of Two Bodies: The Cartesian Corpse and the Lived Body." *Body and Flesh: A Philosophical Reader*. Ed. Donn Welton. Oxford: Blackwell Publishers, 1998.

Lee, Janet and Jennifer Sasser-Coen. *Blood Stories: Menarche and the Politics of the Female Body in Contemporary U.S. Society*. New York: Routledge, 1996.

Longman Dictionary of Contemporary English. Harlow: Pearson Education Limited, 2003.

Lubbers, Klaus. "The Necessary Order." *Carson McCullers*. Ed. Harold Bloom. New York: Chelsea House Publishers, 1986.

Lundgren, Eva. *Ekte Kvinne? Identitet på kryss og tvers. [A Natural Woman? Identity Crosswise. My translation]* Oslo: Pax Forlag A/S, 2001.

Marsden, Malcolm M. "Love as Threat in Katherine Anne Porter's Fiction." *Twentieth Century Literature* 13 (1967): 29–38.

Merleau-Ponty, Maurice. [1945] *Phenomenology of Perception*. London & New York: Routledge, 2002.

Millichap, Joseph R. "Carson McCullers' Literary Ballad." *The Georgia Review* 27 (Fall 1973): 329–39.

Moi, Toril. *What Is a Woman? And Other Essays*. Oxford: Oxford UP, 1999.

Mooney, Harry John. [1957] *The Fiction and Criticism of Katherine Anne Porter*. Pittsburgh: U of Pittsburgh P, 1962.

Morgan, Kathryn Pauly. "Woman and the Knife: Cosmetic Surgery and the Colonization of Women's Bodies." *Hypatia* 6:3 (Fall 1991): 25–53.

Nance, William L. *Katherine Anne Porter & the Art of Rejection*. Chapel Hill: The U of North Carolina P, 1963.

National Library of Medicine. November 17, 2004. http://www.ncbi.nlm.nih.gov/entrez/query.fcgi?cmd.

Newsletter of the Katherine Anne Society. 10 (May 2003). January 19, 2005. http://www.lib.umd.edu/Guests/KAP/10/KAPbib2003.html.

Nussbaum, Martha. "The Professor of Parody." *The New Republic Online*. November, 2001. http://www.thenewrepublic.com/archive/0299/022299/nussbaum022299.html.

Online Etymology Dictionary. September 24, 2004. www.etymonline.com/fletym.htm.

Paulson, Suzanne Morrow. "Carson McCullers's *The Ballad of the Sad Café*: A Song Half Sung, Misogyny, and 'Ganging Up'." *Critical Essays on Carson McCullers*. Eds. Beverly Lyon Clark and Melvin J. Friedman. New York: G. K. Hall & Co, 1996. 187–205.

Pembroke Magazine 20 (1988).

Perry Constance M. "Carson McCullers and the Female *Wunderkind*." *The Southern Literary Journal* 19:1 (Fall 1986): 36–45.

Petry Alice Hall. "Baby Wilson Redux: McCullers' *The Heart Is a Lonely Hunter*." *Southern Studies* 25:2 (Summer 1986): 196–203.

Plewczyński, Dariusz. "Landau Theory of Social Clustering." *Physica A* 261 (1998): 608–617.

Portada, Arleen. "Sex-Role Rebellion and the Failure of Marriage in the Fiction of Carson McCullers." *Pembroke Magazine* 20 (1988): 63–71.

Pratt, Annis. *Archetypal Patterns in Women's Fiction*. (With Barbara White, Andrea Loewenstein, and Mary Wyer.) Brighton: The Harvester P, 1982.

Reichl, L. E. *A Modern Course in Statistical Physics*. Austin: U Texas P, 1987.

Riviere, Joan. "Womanliness as a Masquerade." *Formations of Fantasy*. Eds. Victor Burgin, James Donald and Cora Kaplan. New York: Methuen, 1986.

Rooke, Constance and Bruce Wallis. "Myth and Epiphany in Porter's 'The Grave'." *Studies in Short Fiction* 15 (1978): 269–75.

Russell, Bertrand. *History of Western Philosophy*. London: Unwin Paperbacks, 1979.

Schindl, K. "Space Charge." *Beam Measurement*. Eds. S-I. Kurokawa, S. Y. Lee, E. Perevedentsev, and S. Turner. London: World Scientific Publishing, 1999.

Schwartz, Edward G. "The Way of Dissent." *Katherine Anne Porter: A Critical Symposium*. Eds. Lodwick Hartley and George Core. Athens: U of Georgia P, 1969.

Scott, Anne Firor. *The Southern Lady: From Pedestal to Politics 1830–1930*. Chicago: UP of Chicago, 1970.

———. "After Suffrage: Southern Women in the Twenties." *Myth and Southern History. Vol. 2: The New South*. Eds. Patrick Gerster and Nicholas Cords. Second Edition. Urbana and New York: U of Illinois P, 1989.

Smith, Lillian. *Killers of the Dream*. New York: W. W. Norton & Company, 1994.

Smith, C. Michael. "'A Voice in a Fugue': Characters and Musical Structure in Carson McCullers' *The Heart Is a Lonely Hunter*." *Modern Fiction Studies* 2 (Summer 1979): 258–63.

Soper, Kate. *What Is Nature?* Oxford: Blackwell Publishers, 1995.

Sosnoski, Karen. "Society's Freaks: The Effects of Sexual Stereotyping in Carson McCullers' Fiction." *Pembroke Magazine* 20 (1988): 82–88.

Spivak, Gayatri Chakravorty. "A Feminist Reading: McCullers's *Heart Is a Lonely Hunter.*" *Critical Essays on Carson McCullers.* Eds. Beverly Lyon Clark and Melvin J. Friedman. New York: G. K. Hall & Co., 1996. 220–233.

Stout, Janis P. *Strategies of Reticence: Silence and Meaning in the Works of Jane Austen, Willa Cather, Katherine Anne Porter, and Joan Didion.* Charlottesville: UP of Virginia, 1990.

———. *A Sense of the Times.* Charlottesville: UP of Virginia, 1995.

———. "Katherine Anne Porter's "The Old Order": Writing in the Borderlands." *Studies in Short Fiction* 34 (1997): 493–505.

Taetzsch, L. "Crossing Trajectories in *The Heart Is a Lonely Hunter.*" *The New Orleans Review* 19:3–4 (Fall–Winter 1992): 192–99.

Theriot, Nancy M. *Mothers and Daughters in Nineteenth-Century America: The Biosocial Construction of Femininity.* Lexington: UP of Kentucky, 1996.

Tidd, Ursula. *Simone de Beauvoir.* London: Routledge, 2004.

Titus, Mary. "'Mingled Sweetness and Corruption': Katherine Anne Porter's 'The Fig Tree' and 'The Grave'." *South Atlantic Review* 53:2 (May 1988): 111–125.

———. "Katherine Anne Porter's Miranda: The Agrarian Myth and Southern Womanhood." *Redefining Autobiography in Twentieth-Century Women's Fiction: An Essay Collection.* Eds. Janice Morgan, Colette Hall, and Carol L. Snyder. New York: Garland, 1991.

Turner, Bryan S. *The Body and Society: Explorations in Social Theory.* Second Edition. London: Sage Publications, 1996.

Unrue, Darlene Harbour. *Truth and Vision in Katherine Anne Porter's Fiction.* Athens: U of Georgia P, 1985.

———, ed. *Critical Essays on Katherine Anne Porter.* New York: G. K. Hall & Co., 1997.

Vintges, Karen. "Simone de Beauvoir: A Feminist Thinker for our Times." *Hypatia* 14:4 (Fall 1999): 133–44.

Walsh, Thomas F. "The Dreams [Sic] Self in 'Pale Horse, Pale Rider'." *Wascana Review* 14:2 (Fall 1979): 61–79.

Warren, Colleen. "A Filament Spinning Outward: Female Identity Reconceptualization in Porter's Fiction." *Southern Studies* 4:4 (1993 Winter): 377–90.

Weischedel, Wilhelm. *Die philosophische Hintertreppe: Die grossen Philosophen in Alltag und Denken.* München: dtv, 1975.

Welton, Donn. "Introduction: Situating the Body." *Body and Flesh: A Philosophical Reader.* Ed. Donn Welton. Oxford: Blackwell Publishers, 1998.

Wescott, Glenway. "Katherine Anne Porter Personally." *Katherine Anne Porter: A Critical Symposium.* Eds. Lodwick Hartley and George Core. Athens: U of Georgia P, 1969.

West, Ray B. *Katherine Anne Porter.* Pamphlets on American Writers, Number 28. Minneapolis: U of Minnesota P, 1963.

Westling, Louise. *Sacred Groves and Ravaged Gardens: The Fiction of Eudora Welty, Carson McCullers, and Flannery O'Connor.* Athens: U of Georgia P, 1985.

———. "Carson McCullers's Amazon Nightmare." *Carson McCullers.* Ed. Harold Bloom. New York: Chelsea House Publishers, 1986.

———. "Tomboys and Revolting Femininity." *Critical Essays on Carson McCullers.* Eds. Beverly Lyon Clark and Melvin J. Friedman. New York: G. K. Hall & Co., 1996. 155–165.

Whatling, Clare. "Reading Miss Amelia: Critical Strategies in the Construction of Sex, Gender, Sexuality, the Gothic and the Grotesque." *Modernist Sexualities.* Eds. Hugh Stevens and Caroline Howlett. Manchester: Manchester UP, 2000.

White, Barbara A. "Loss of Self in *The Member of the Wedding.*" *Carson McCullers.* Ed. Harold Bloom. New York: Chelsea House Publishers, 1986.

Whitt, Margaret. "From Eros to Agape: Reconsidering the Chain Gang's Song in McCullers's *Ballad of the Sad Café.*" *Studies in Short Fiction* 33 (Winter 1996): 119–123.

Wimsatt, Mary Ann. "The Old Order Undermined: Daughters, Mothers, and Grandmothers in Katherine Anne Porter's Miranda Tales." *Southern Mothers: Facts and Fictions in Southern Women's Writing.* Eds. Nagueyalti Warren and Sally Wolff. Baton Rouge, LA: Louisiana State UP, 1999.

Wolf, Naomi. *The Beauty Myth: How Images of Beauty Are Used Against Women.* New York: Doubleday, 1991.

Wright, Richard. "Inner Landscape." *Critical Essays on Carson McCullers.* Eds. Beverly Lyon Clark and Melvin J. Friedman. New York: G. K. Hall & Co., 1996. 17–18.

Wu, Cynthia. "Expanding Southern Whiteness: Reconceptualizing Ethnic Difference in the Short Fiction of Carson McCullers." *Southern Literary Journal* 34.1 (Fall 2001): 44–55.

Yaeger, Patricia. "The Poetics of Birth." *Discourses of Sexuality: From Aristotle to AIDS.* Ed. Domna Stanton. Ann Arbor: U of Michigan P, 1992.

———. *Dirt and Desire: Reconstructing Southern Women's Writing, 1930–1990.* Chicago & London: U of Chicago P, 2000.

Young, Iris Marion. *Throwing Like a Girl and Other Essays in Feminist Philosophy and Social Theory.* Bloomington: Indiana UP, 1990.

———. "Throwing Like a Girl." *Body and Flesh: A Philosophical Reader.* Ed. Donn Welton. Oxford: Blackwell Publishers, 1998.

———. "Pregnant Embodiment." *Body and Flesh: A Philosophical Reader.* Ed. Donn Welton. Oxford: Blackwell Publishers, 1998.

Youngblood, Sara. "Structure and Imagery in *Pale Horse, Pale Rider.*" *Critical Essays on Katherine Anne Porter.* Ed. Darlene Harbour Unrue. New York: G. K. Hall & Co., 1997.

Chronology

1917	Lula Carson Smith born on February 19 in Columbus, Georgia, the first child of Lamar Smith and Marguerite Waters Smith.
1919	Brother Lamar Smith Jr. born on May 13.
1922	Sister Margarita Gachet Smith born August 2.
1930	Drops the use of "Lula" in her name.
1932	As a senior in high school, suffers from rheumatic fever, which is thought to have contributed to her crippling strokes later in life.
1933	Graduates from Columbus High School. Writes plays and first short story, "Sucker."
1934	Travels to New York City, where she enrolls in creative writing courses at Columbia University.
1935	Meets Reeves McCullers through mutual friend. Studies writing at New York University.
1936	First published story, "Wunderkind," appears in *Story* magazine. Seriously ill, lives at home through the winter; starts work on "The Mute," which becomes *The Heart Is a Lonely Hunter*.
1937	On September 20 marries Reeves McCullers. Moves into Reeves's apartment in Charlotte, North Carolina, and continues work on her novel.

1940   *The Heart Is a Lonely Hunter* is published. *Reflections in a Golden Eye* is published in two parts in October and November in *Harper's Bazaar*. Carson ill for most of winter.

1941   *Reflections in a Golden Eye* published in book form. In February, stricken with first cerebral stroke. Initiates divorce proceedings against Reeves. First published poem, "The Twisted Trinity," appears in *Decision*. Suffers second major illness of the year with pleurisy, strep throat, and double pneumonia.

1942   Notified of award of Guggenheim Fellowship. "A Tree, a Rock, a Cloud" published in *Harper's* and selected for the annual *O. Henry Memorial Prize Stories* anthology.

1943   *The Ballad of the Sad Café* published in *Harper's Bazaar*. Awarded $1,000 from the American Academy of Arts and Letters and the National Institute of Arts and Letters.

1944   Suffers a severe nervous attack. Father dies in August of a heart attack. Moves with mother and sister, Rita, to Nyack, New York.

1945   On March 19, remarries Reeves in New City, New York.

1946   Reeves granted physical disability discharge from the army. *The Member of the Wedding* published. Awarded second Guggenheim Fellowship. Visits Tennessee Williams on Nantucket Island and begins rewriting *The Member of the Wedding* as a play. In autumn, leaves for Europe with her husband; they plan to live in Paris.

1947   Suffers two serious strokes and is paralyzed on left side. In December, flown home because of paralysis; her husband, who suffers from delirium tremens, accompanies her.

1948   In March, attempts suicide and is hospitalized in Manhattan.

1950   *The Member of the Wedding* opens on Broadway. It wins the New York Drama Critics' Circle Award for best play of the season as well as other awards.

1951   Sells screen rights to *The Member of the Wedding*. Collected works are published as *The Ballad of the Sad Café and Other Works*.

1952   *The Ballad of the Sad Café and Collected Short Stories* published. Inducted into the National Institute of Arts and Letters. With Reeves, buys home outside Paris.

1953	Carson and Reeves experience severe marital problems. Reeves tries to convince her to commit a double suicide. In November, Reeves kills himself in a Paris hotel.
1955	Travels with Tennessee Williams to Key West in April to work on dramatizing three manuscripts. On June 10, mother dies unexpectedly and Carson is utterly devastated.
1957	*The Square Root of Wonderful* opens on Broadway but closes after only forty-five performances.
1958	Carson suffers acute depression over play's premature closing.
1959–62	Undergoes several operations on arm, hand, and/or wrist, as well as surgery for breast cancer. In 1961 *Clock Without Hands* published. By 1962, spends most of her time in a wheelchair.
1963	"Sucker," first short story written in 1933, published. Edward Albee's adaptation of *The Ballad of the Sad Café* opens on Broadway.
1964	In the spring, breaks right hip and shatters left elbow. Collection of children's verses, *Sweet as a Pickle, Clean as a Pig*, is published.
1966	Works on autobiography.
1967	On August 15, suffers final stroke and is comatose for forty-seven days. Dies on September 29.
1968	Film version of *The Heart Is a Lonely Hunter* released.
1971	Margarita G. Smith, Carson's sister, edits *The Mortgaged Heart*, a collection of Carson's short stories, poems, and essays.
1999	Unfinished autobiography, *Illumination and Night Glare*, edited by Carlos L. Dews, published.

Contributors

HAROLD BLOOM is Sterling Professor of the Humanities at Yale University. He is the author of 30 books, including *Shelley's Mythmaking*, *The Visionary Company*, *Blake's Apocalypse*, *Yeats*, *A Map of Misreading*, *Kabbalah and Criticism*, *Agon: Toward a Theory of Revisionism*, *The American Religion*, *The Western Canon*, and *Omens of Millennium: The Gnosis of Angels, Dreams, and Resurrection*. *The Anxiety of Influence* sets forth Professor Bloom's provocative theory of the literary relationships between the great writers and their predecessors. His most recent books include *Shakespeare: The Invention of the Human*, a 1998 National Book Award finalist, *How to Read and Why*, *Genius: A Mosaic of One Hundred Exemplary Creative Minds*, *Hamlet: Poem Unlimited*, *Where Shall Wisdom Be Found?*, and *Jesus and Yahweh: The Names Divine*. In 1999, Professor Bloom received the prestigious American Academy of Arts and Letters Gold Medal for Criticism. He has also received the International Prize of Catalonia, the Alfonso Reyes Prize of Mexico, and the Hans Christian Andersen Bicentennial Prize of Denmark.

TONY J. STAFFORD is a professor of English at the University of Texas at El Paso. He has published many essays and also is a playwright who has had his work produced in numerous theaters across the country.

RACHEL ADAMS is an associate professor of English and comparative literature at Columbia University. She is the author of *Sideshow U.S.A.: Freaks and the American Cultural Imagination* and coeditor of *The Masculinity Studies Reader*.

CYNTHIA WU is an assistant professor of English at Agnes Scott College.

SARAH GLEESON-WHITE is an independent scholar living in Sydney, Australia. She attended the University of New South Wales and is the author of *Strange Bodies: Gender and Identity in the Novels of Carson McCullers*.

DOREEN FOWLER is a professor at the University of Kansas. She is the author of *Faulkner: The Return of the Repressed* and coeditor of numerous collections of essays on Faulkner.

BETTY E. McKINNIE is an assistant professor in the language and literature division at Gulf Coast Community College.

CARLOS L. DEWS teaches at John Cabot University in Rome, Italy. He is the editor of *Complete Novels*, an edition of McCullers's work, and he is the founding president of the Carson McCullers Society.

JEFF ABERNATHY is professor, vice president, and dean of the college at Augustana College in Rhode Island. He is the author of *To Hell and Back: Race and Betrayal in the Southern Novel*.

JENNIFER MURRAY is an associate professor in North American literature at the University of Franche-Comté in Besançon, France. She has written on Tennessee Williams, Flannery O'Connor, and Margaret Atwood.

NAOMI MORGENSTERN is an associate professor in the English department at the University of Toronto. She has published essays on a range of twentieth-century writers and theorists.

ELLEN MATLOK-ZIEMANN is a student counselor and teacher at Uppsala University in Uppsala, Sweden. Her research interests include Southern literature, popular fiction, feminist theory and philosophy, and science and the history of science.

Bibliography

Albee, Edward. *Stretching My Mind*. New York: Carroll & Graf Publishers: distributed by Publishers Group West, 2005.

Bombaci, Nancy. *Freaks in Late Modernist American Culture: Nathanael West, Djuna Barnes, Tod Browning, and Carson McCullers*. New York, N.Y.: Peter Lang, 2006.

Bloom, Harold, ed. *Carson McCullers' The Ballad of the Sad Café*. Philadelphia: Chelsea House Publishers, 2005.

———. *Carson McCullers' The Member of the Wedding*. Philadelphia: Chelsea House Publishers, 2005.

Bradshaw, Charles. "Language and Responsibility: The Failure of Discourse in Carson McCullers's *The Heart Is a Lonely Hunter*." *Southern Quarterly* 37, no. 2 (Winter 1999): pp. 118–26.

Chamlee, Kenneth. "Cafés and Community in Three Carson McCullers Novels." *Studies in Amerian Fiction*. 18 (1990): pp. 233–40.

Clark, Beverly Lyon, and Melvin Friedman, ed. *Critical Essays on Carson McCullers*. London; New York: Prentice-Hall International, 1996.

Crocker, Halie. "Carson McCullers since 1980: A Bibliography." *Bulletin of Bibliography* 57, no. 3 (September 2000): pp. 153–7.

Earthman, Elise Ann. "Critiquing 'the We of Me': Gender Roles in Carson McCullers' *The Member of the Wedding* (1946)." In *Women in Literature: Reading through the Lens of Gender*, edited by Jerilyn Fisher and Ellen S. Silber. Westport, Conn.; London: Greenwood Press, 2003.

Fahy, Thomas. *Freak Shows and the Modern American Imagination: Constructing the Damaged Body from Willa Cather to Truman Capote*. New York, N.Y.: Palgrave Macmillan, 2006.

Fallon, April D. "The Grotesque as Feminist Revision of the 'Southern Lady' in Carson McCullers's and Flannery O'Connor's Fiction." *Journal of Kentucky Studies* 23 (September 2006): pp. 113–21.

Fine, Laura. "Gender Conflicts and Their 'Dark' Projections in Coming of Age White Female Southern Novels." *Southern Quarterly* 36, no. 4 (Summer 1998): pp. 121–9.

Gervin, Mary. "Illuminations and Night Glare: Carson McCuller's Sad Songs of the South." In *Conflict in Southern Writing*, edited by Ben P. Robertson. Troy, Ala.: Association for Textual Study and Production, with Troy University, 2006.

Gleeson-White, Sarah. *Strange Bodies: Gender and Identity in the Novels of Carson McCullers*. Tuscaloosa, Ala.; London: University of Alabama Press, 2003.

Hannon, Charles. "*The Ballad of the Sad Cafe* and Other Stories of Women's Wartime Labor." In *Bodies of Writing, Bodies in Performance*, edited by Thomas Foster, pp. 97–122. New York: New York University Press, 1996.

James, Judith Giblin. *Wunderkind: The Reputation of Carson McCullers, 1940–1990*. Columbia, S.C.: Camden House, 1995.

———. "Carson McCullers, Lillian Smith, and the Politics of Broadway." In *Southern Women Playwrights: New Essays in Literary History and Criticism*, edited by Robert L. McDonald and Linda Rohrer Paige, pp. 42–60. Tuscaloosa, Ala.; London: University of Alabama Press, 2002.

Jenkins, McKay. *The South in Black and White: Race, Sex, and Literature in the 1940s*. Chapel Hill: University of North Carolina Press, 1999.

Madden, David. *Touching the Web of Southern Novelists*. Knoxville: University of Tennessee Press, 2006.

Merva, Michael. "An Illusion of Understanding: Listeners and Tellers in Sherwood Anderson's *Winesburg, Ohio* and Carson McCullers' *The Heart Is a Lonely Hunter*." *Midwestern Miscellany* 33 (Fall 2005): pp. 36–47.

Mukherjee, Srimati. "The Impoverishment of the Female Hero in 'The Ballad of the Sad Café.'" *Proceedings of the Philological Association of Louisiana* (1992): pp. 105–9.

Oates, Joyce Carol. *Uncensored: Views & (Re)views*. New York: Ecco, 2005.

Palmer, Louis H., III. *Carson McCullers'* The Member of the Wedding. In *American Writers: Classics*, volume II, pp. 199–213. New York, N.Y.: Scribner's, 2004.

Portada, Arleen. "Sex-Role Rebellion and the Failure of Marriage in the Fiction of Carson McCullers." *Pembroke Magazine* 20 (1988): pp. 63–71.

Poston, David. "The Myth of the Explosion: Inverted Archetypes in the Fiction of Carson McCullers." *Mount Olive Review* 7 (Winter–Spring 1993–1994): pp. 13–22.

Richards, Gary. *Lovers and Beloveds: Sexual Otherness in Southern Fiction, 1936–1961*. Baton Rouge: Louisiana State University Press, 2005.

Slabey, Robert M. "Carson McCullers' Allegory of Love." *Xavier Review* 13, no. 2 (Fall 1993): pp. 47–59.

Walker, Sue. *It's Good Weather for Fudge: Conversing with Carson McCullers*. Montgomery, Ala.: NewSouth Books, 2003.

Westling, Louise. "Carson McCullers's Tomboys." *Southern Humanities Review* 14 (1982): pp. 339–50.

———. *Sacred Groves and Ravaged Gardens: The Fiction of Eudora Welty, Carson McCullers, and Flannery O'Connor*. Athens: University of Georgia Press, 1985.

Whatling, Clare. "Reading Miss Amelia: Critical Strategies in the Construction of Sex, Gender, Sexuality, the Gothic and the Grotesque." In *Modernist Sexualities*, edited by Hugh Stevens and Caroline Howlett, pp. 239–50. Manchester; New York: Manchester University Press; New York: distributed exclusively in the USA by St. Martin's Press, 2000.

Whitt, Jan, ed. Reflections in a *Critical Eye: Essays on Carson McCullers*. Lanham, Md.: University Press of America, 2008.

Wu, Cynthia. "Expanding Southern Whiteness: Reconceptualizing Ethnic Difference in the Short Fiction of Carson McCullers." *Southern Literary Journal* 34, no. 1 (Fall 2001): pp. 44–55.

Acknowledgments

Tony J. Stafford, "'Gray Eyes Is Glass': Image and Theme in *The Member of the Wedding.*" From *American Drama* (Fall 1993): pp. 54–66. © 1993 by American Drama Institute. Reprinted by permission.

Rachel Adams, "A Mixture of the Delicious and Freak: A Queer Fiction of Carson McCullers" in *American Literature*, vol. 71, no. 3, pp. 551–583. Copyright, 1999, Duke University Press. All rights reserved. Used by permission of the publisher.

Cynthia Wu, "Expanding Southern Whiteness: Reconceptualizing Ethnic Difference in the Short Fiction of Carson McCullers." From *The Southern Literary Journal* 34, no. 1 (Fall 2001): pp. 44–55. © 2001 by the department of English of the University of North Carolina at Chapel Hill. Reprinted by permission.

Sarah Gleeson-White, "Revisiting the Southern Grotesque: Mikhail Bakhtin and the Case of Carson McCullers." From *The Southern Literary Journal* 33, no. 2 (Spring 2001): pp. 108–23. © 2001 by the department of English of the University of North Carolina at Chapel Hill. Reprinted by permission.

Doreen Fowler, "Carson McCullers's Primal Scenes: *The Ballad of the Sad Café.*" From *Critique* 43, no. 3 (Spring 2002): pp. 260–70. Reprinted with permission of the Helen Dwight Reid Educational Foundation. Published by Heldref Communications, 1319 Eighteenth St., NW, Washington, DC 20036-1802. Copyright © 2002.

Betty E. McKinnie and Carlos L. Dews, *Southern Women Playwrights.* Copyright 2002 by University of Alabama Press. Reproduced with permission of University of Alabama Press in the format other book via Copyright Clearance Center.

Jeff Abernathy, "Divided Hearts: Carson McCullers and Harper Lee Explore Racial Uncertainty." From *To Hell and Back: Race and Betrayal in the Southern Novel*, pp. 84–106. © 2003 by the University of Georgia Press. Reprinted by permission.

Jennifer Murray, "Approaching Community in Carson McCullers's *The Heart Is a Lonely Hunter.*" From *The Southern Quarterly*, vol. 42, no. 4 (Summer 2004): pp. 107–114. © 2004 by the University of Southern Mississippi. Reproduced by permission.

Naomi Morgenstern, "The Afterlife of Coverture: Contract and Gift in 'The Ballad of the Sad Café'" in *differences*, vol. 16, no. 1, pp. 103–125. Copyright, 2005, Brown University and *differences: A Journal of Feminist Cultural Studies.* All rights reserved. Used by permission of the publisher.

Ellen Matlok-Ziemann, "Ambiguity—the Ideal Way of Having the World." From *Tomboys, Belles, and Other Ladies: The Female Body-Subject in Selected Works by Katherine Anne Porter and Carson McCullers*, pp. 138–57. © 2005 by Ellen Matlok-Ziemann. Reprinted by permission.

Every effort has been made to contact the owners of copyrighted material and secure copyright permission. Articles appearing in this volume generally appear much as they did in their original publication with few or no editorial changes. In some cases, foreign language text has been removed from the original essay. Those interested in locating the original source will find the information cited above.

Index